The Medieval Foundation of England

THE
Medieval Foundation
OF
ENGLAND

by

ARTHUR BRYANT

COLLIER BOOKS
NEW YORK

Library of Congress Catalog Card Number: 67-12856

FIRST COLLIER BOOKS EDITION 1968

The Medieval Foundation of England was originally
published in a hardcover edition by Doubleday &
Company, Inc. and is reprinted by arrangement.

The Macmillan Company, New York

Printed in the United States of America

To
LORD GODDARD
formerly
Lord Chief Justice
of England

CONTENTS

FREEDOM'S ISLAND

THE HISTORY OF England began eight thousand years ago
when the sea broke through the isthmus joining an Atlantic
peninsula to the world's largest land-mass. Because of the
security given by that moat of stormy tidal water her people,
more fortunate than others seeking the same goal, were able
little by little to develop a polity in which the sanctity of the
individual counted for more than that of authority, and in
which power, instead of being centralised in a few hands, became distributed in many. Yet, immense though its consequences, England's immunity from invasion is comparatively
recent. Though an island geographically for eight thousand
years, she has been one strategically for less than a thousand.
No island was at first so easy to invade; none more tempting
to invaders. Iberian and Neolithic men, Bronze Age pastoral
warriors, Celts, Romans, Jutes, Angles and Saxons, Danes,
Norwegians and Normans, all in turn descended on her. Her
coastline of four thousand miles was indefensible by a small
population. It could only be defended by sea. And since her
southern and eastern lowlands were easiest to conquer and
cultivate, each invader tended to settle there, driving earlier
comers into the mountains, bogs and mists of the west, where
—since these offered little to tempt conquerors—they survived.

The colonisers of Britain were confronted by a wet, windswept northern island. Even when they had won the land
they had to win a tougher and longer battle against nature.
They had to fell dense forests, covering at first the entire
lowlands, clear and drain swampy river valleys and break up
the thick cold clays with implements the making of which
called for all their skill and ingenuity. Yet, though it offered
them much to master, the climate was never too harsh to

endure. It steeled, but did not ossify, stamina and character. Gusty and invigorating, it was tempered by a warm ocean stream from the south-west that spared the island continental winters. The soil, infinitely varied, was nearly all fertile. It bred vigorous, hardy and adaptable plants, beasts and men.

The survival of racial minorities, defying yet ultimately intermarrying with the predominant majority, together with the island climate and situation shaped English history. Long skull and broad mingled, short build and tall, dark pigmentation and blonde; so did the instincts and memories of a score of races. Such intermixture in so small an island helped to make its people many-sided and versatile. Left to themselves the Anglo-Saxons of a thousand years ago—florid, large-limbed, blue-eyed, phlegmatic—might have settled down into a sluggish complacency. But they were harried by the Danes and Norsemen, and later conquered by the Normans. In face of these powerful minorities they had to struggle for centuries to retain their customs, institutions, and language. And beyond their well-ploughed shires, and in the hills, marshes and woodlands in their midst, lurked the pre-Saxon inhabitants of the island—fierce red-haired Celts and little dark Neolithic and Bronze Age peoples with rugged irregular features, loose mouths and deep-set eyes. They, too, constituted a perpetual callenge to the dominant majority, their Highland and Cymric raids and the alluring, alien ways of their young men and maidens bringing deeper and more mysterious strains into the blood of the honest, ox-like Saxons. The island was full of unexpected and mysterious influences— Wendish customs among the sandy Surrey gravels beside the Thames at Wandsworth, Scandinavian usages in the Chilterns, ancient pre-Roman and even pre-Celtic settlements in hollows on the lonely Wiltshire and Dorset downs. And along the Marches of the Celtic west and north ran the incessant, challenging warfare of the races:

> "When Severn down to Buildwas ran
> Coloured with the death of man,
> Couched upon her brother's grave
> The Saxon got me on the slave . . .

> "In my heart it has not died,
> The war that sleeps on Severn side;
> They cease not fighting, east and west,
> On the marches of my breast."

It is this perhaps that has accounted for the intermixture in the British blood of the matter-of-fact with the poetic; of love of home with the itch to adventure; of business aptitude with fantasy, speculation and idealism. English literature is full of examples of this conflict in the national make-up; of books like *Alice in Wonderland* written by a professor of mathematics, or *Songs of a Shropshire Lad* by a clerk in the Patent Office who became a master of Latin philology. "Lord", prayed the commander of the royalist foot at Edgehill, "Thou knowest how busy I shall be this day; if I forget Thee, do not Thou forget me. March on, boys!" So too Cromwell, on the other side, bade his men trust in God and keep their powder dry. The British—and more particularly the English in whom the mingling of the races has been most marked—have often been charged with hypocrisy, with serving both God and Mammon, with trying to eat their cake and have it. Since they have so many sides to their nature, there has been truth in the charge; yet, in a world in which spirit and matter are inextricably mingled, it has not served them badly. Their greatest poet wrote that men were such stuff as dreams are made on, yet contrived by sound business methods to make a competence in real property.

This clash of racial characteristics and cultures may have accounted, too, for the extraordinary range of British genius: in politics, agriculture and commerce, in literature and the arts, in craftsmanship, war, adventure and colonisation. So much diversity among neighbours was a constant stimulus and education. "No nation," wrote Emerson, "was ever so rich in able men." Shakespeare and Milton, Elizabeth and Cromwell, Chatham and Churchill, Drake, Nelson and Wellington, Wren and Purcell, Newton and Darwin, the inventor of the steam-engine, and the discoverers of the anaesthetic, electricity and the atom, were a remarkable harvest for one small island. And Washington, Jefferson, Lee and Lincoln were of the same argumentative, versatile stock.

Yet England was fortunate that the invasions which gave her so mixed an ancestry were separated by long periods. This enabled each new influence to be digested and saved the island from anarchy. The sea-barrier, even before the islanders learnt to hold it, proved a better protection than a land frontier. And after the Norman Conquest the growing use by her kings of the sea for defence gave her almost complete freedom from armed invasion. The only invaders who settled in Britain thereafter were refugees flying to her shores from persecution: Flemings in the fourteenth and sixteenth centuries, Huguenots in the seventeenth century, Jews in the eighteenth, nineteenth and twentieth centuries. The racial challenge became a purely internal one: of Norman, Saxon and Celt, Englishman, Scotsman, Welshman and Irishman, contending and competing with one another.

This, and the strong rule of her early kings—Norman, Plantagenet and Tudor—gave the country, for all its diversity, an inherent unity. Beneath immense differences of speech, outlook and custom there grew up, under protection of the Common Law within and the patrolled seas without, first an English, and later a British, identity. This cohesion existed side by side with the most strongly-held and freely expressed differences of opinion. But it never failed to unite the islanders when any major threat arose from outside.

Even more striking than England's unity has been the freedom of individual choice on which it has been based. Not being threatened across a land frontier, her people had no need to entrust their rulers with standing military forces or despotic rights over private liberties. Authority normally was exercised only after those subject to it had an opportunity to make their views known. From the Saxon Witanagemot to the twentieth century parliament, from the village hustings and manor court to the trade union lodge and parish council, there was nearly always some working machinery by which those in authority could test the opinion of those over whom authority had to be exercised. Government has been conducted subject to the right of the governed to criticise and, within lawful limits, to oppose. "His Majesty's Opposition" is the most characteristic, and certainly the most original, of English contributions to politics; today the leader of the Opposition is even paid by the State. However inefficient in the short run, such a system proved efficient in the long, because, by delegating responsibility, it trained men for it.

For, like the Americans after them, the English regarded the person—even if at first only the privileged person—as more important than any abstract ideal. The State, they felt, existed more for the individual than the individual for the State. Their history was a struggle for the freedom of individuals. It was fought for at every stage of their developing consciousness, from the barons' stand for Magna Carta to the Tolpuddle martyrs paying with transportation for the rural worker's right to combine against his employer.

England's rulers often contended against this national distaste for authority. King John tried to repress his barons, Mary Tudor the protestants, King Charles his unruly parliaments. The eighteenth century landowners sought to extinguish the independent cultivators of the common-field village and were themselves overthrown by the yeomen who turned to industry. And the nineteenth century manufacturers tried to repress the trade unions of their rough, liberty-loving factory-hands. Dr. Johnson expressed the eternal English answer to such attempts. "From this neglect of subordination I do not deny that some inconveniences may from time to time proceed. . . . But good and evil will grow up in this world together; and they who complain, in peace, of the insolence of the populace, must remember that their insolence in peace is bravery in war."

Loving private liberty, yet finding that it could not exist without public order, the English devoted themselves to making the two compatible. Freedom within a framework of discipline became their ideal. They achieved it through the sovereignty of law. "All our struggles for liberty," wrote Disraeli, "smack of law." And by law the English meant an enforceable compact between themselves and their rulers, deriving not from unilaterally imposed force but from assent freely given. Both they and their American descendants constituted such law, rather than the Executive, their ultimate sovereign.

This respect for law gradually made the English people, who might otherwise have been one of the most difficult to govern, one of the easiest: easy, that is, so long as they were governed lawfully. It became habitual to them to obey the law and see it enforced. Their inter-racial experience in a small island left them with a profound distrust of violence. "Force is not a remedy," declared John Bright: "all force," wrote the great Lord Halifax, "is a kind of foul play." From this sprang the curious tolerance of a fighting people with strong convictions for minority opinions, nonconformity and eccentricity. No other community has ever so richly rewarded its critics or been so indulgent to those it terms conscientious objectors.

Compromise, give-and-take, live-and-let-live thus became a national habit. The freedom of the Press was an English invention; so was the secret ballot which enabled a man to record an unpopular vote without danger to himself. The English, as self-opinionated as any people, mastered the lesson that they could only possess liberty by allowing it to others, enjoy the propagation of their own views by listening patiently to their neighbours'. "Opinion in good men," wrote one of their poets, "is but knowledge in the making." "I beseech you, in the bowels of Christ," Cromwell implored the religious dogmatists "think it possible you may be mistaken!"

This hard-learnt toleration, and all the tolerated eccentricity that sprang from it, have rested in the last resort on the Christian belief in the sanctity of the individual. It stemmed from the creed of personal responsibility to which, first the Celts of Wales, Ireland and Scotland, and then the Anglo-Saxons of England, were won by the great missionaries of the fifth, sixth and seventh centuries. At its core lay the thesis that every man, being free to choose between good and evil, was a soul of equal value in the eyes of God. It was this that gave rise to an Englishman's saying in the English revolution of the seventeenth century that "the poorest he in England hath a life to live as the greatest he."

From Sidney passing the cup to the dying soldier to Oates walking into the blizzard to save his friends, from Coeur-de-Lion forgiving the archer who shot him to the men of the Forty-third standing motionless on the deck of the sinking "Birkenhead" while the women and children were lowered to the boats, the common denominator of the nation's idealism has remained constant. It was expressed in the fourteenth century *Piers Plowman,* in the seventeenth century *Pilgrim's Progress* and in the nineteenth century *Christmas Carol.* Langland, Bunyan and Dickens spoke with the same voice. Whenever England has been false to that voice she has been false to herself. The English, Disraeli said, have not committed fewer blunders than others, but, being free to criticise their rulers according to individual conscience, have shown themselves as a people more sensible of their errors. In the end it has usually been the English themselves who have made amends for their injuries to others and reformed the abuses they had perpetrated. "I choose the people under whom we suffered forty years ago," declared General Smuts in 1940, "but who, when we were at their mercy, treated us as a Christian people!"

"By the sacredness of individuals," wrote Emerson, "the

English have in seven hundred years evolved the principles of freedom." In these two volumes—in which, set in a wider framework, I have embodied many passages descriptive of English social life from my writings of the past forty years—I have tried to show how a group of warring tribal communities became a nation under the tutelage of the medieval Church, and then how, after repudiating and casting off the latter's leading strings, it grew into the inventive and expanding society that was to revolutionise first its own life and then that of the world. For neither the French and American revolutions of a century ago nor the Russian, Asian and African revolutions of our own time have made such an impact on the everday existence of mankind as the English industrial revolution. The former were political revolutions, resulting in changes of ruler and governing institutions; having through trial and error in earlier political revolutions evolved a system that allowed the maximum freedom of choice and opportunity to the individual, the English wrought a bloodless revolution that transformed first their own economy and then, in ever increasing measure, everyone else's. Whether the world is a happier place for that transformation of a feudal and peasant society into an industrial and urbanised one is a matter of opinion; what is certain is that it is that it has been, and is still being, changed out of all recognition.

My book is not a political, constitutional or economic history of England—it is social history. Yet it is not so much a history of the objects of everyday life—of houses, clothes, transport, crafts and industries—as of the changing social life, habit and beliefs of an evolving people. It attempts to show how the English lived and developed in two contrasting periods of time; the one a formative one in which their social and political institutions were made, the other one of material achievement in which those institutions were tested.

Such a broad landscape of a people's social life can only cover a minute fraction of all the diverse and changing phenomena of their existence. I am very conscious how incomplete and overgeneralised my picture necessarily is. The surroundings, habits and ways of thought of the early Victorians were very different, for instance, from those of their grandchildren at the end of the old queen's reign; those of Henry III's subjects to those of Edward IV and Henry VII. Yet, though local variations were then greater, the tempo of change was far slower. Life in a country village has been transformed almost out of recognition since I was born at the end of the last century; it was in many ways much the same in the year 1200 as in 1500, or even 1700.

Within these limitations I have sought to show what sort of a people the English were and how they came to be what they are; to depict an evolving society from the time when England had still to become a nation to the day when, already highly urbanised, she stood on the threshold of the social revolution through which she is still passing.

The Medieval Foundation of England

CHAPTER I

RUDE SETTLERS

It was not those who inhabited Britain before she became an island—aborigines sleeping like beasts in caves and pits among the rocks of the Cheddar Gorge or Gower peninsula —who were to set the course of her history. It was those who, migrating west from Asia, reached the Atlantic and, learning to navigate its waves and tides, put out in frail coracles to seek a home in a green, misty northern isle. The ancestors of the British people were seamen and colonists, pioneer bearers of new beliefs and techniques. The earliest of all were traders in tin and copper from the Mediterranean, adventuring into the Atlantic through the Pillars of Hercules —today the Straits of Gibraltar—and tribal families wandering up the eastern coast of Spain and the south-western plains of France in search of fresh soil and hunting grounds. Some, striking across the Soundings, made landfalls in Cornwall, Pembrokeshire, Anglesey, Ireland and the islands to the west of Scotland. Others, crossing Europe by a more northerly route, entered Britain across the Dover strait. Such pioneers brought with them a knowledge of agriculture; of grain growing and domestic animals, of the hoe, spade and grindingstone; of weaving clothes and fashioning pots of clay. They brought, too, another art: of making boats and navigating.

The settlements of these Iberian and Mediterranean colonisers—little, dark men grouped around Britain's western seas —were at first few and far between. Their primitive mattocks and hoes allowed them to break only the lightest soils: those on the hilltops out of reach of the all-pervading forest, on the drier gravel-terraces above the rivers, and on rocky shores and islands along the coast. Yet during the first five hundred years of their occupation—a period as long as that which divides us from the Wars of the Roses—the appearance of the country began to change. Settlements of beehive-shaped huts, covered with branches and surrounded by little fields, hewn or burnt out of the forests, appeared on higher ground; earthwork entrenchments were dug along the chalk and limestone hills to protect the seasonal round-up of flocks and cattle; tangled downland bushes and scrub were nibbled away by generations of sheep, goats and swine. And in chalk galleries beneath the ground—like those of Grimes' Graves at Brandon—men quarried with antler-picks for flint to grind into axes and spear-heads. The foundations of settled life, tillage and pasturage were being laid.

Great stones or "dolmens" and mysterious hollow mounds and barrows with tunnelled chambers appeared, too, on the western coasts and the high, inhabited uplands: tribal tombs, where the spirits of the dead were believed to await, like seeds, a day of resurrection and rebirth. For these primitive farmers, having raised themselves above animal existence and learnt to contemplate past and future, were much concerned with the mystery of life and death. Like the river valley-folk of the East, they worshipped the dead and the powers of fertility which recreated life in each generation and spring. To propitiate them and secure their help for the tribe, their priests or magic men offered up human and animal sacrifices in sacred places. And when their leaders died, hopeful of rebirth they were buried with their belongings around them.

The first invaders were followed by others. There was nothing to stop them but the waves and tides. Some continued to come from the south in search of Ireland's gold and of the tin and copper which the wandering smiths of that land and Cornwall were learning to smelt into a hard and durable alloy called bronze. Others came from the east across the shallow straits and North Sea. Among them were men of a fairer, stronger race, moving from eastern Europe through dense forests and the plains of the Low Countries. These Beaker Folk, as archæologists call them from their buried drinking-vessels, were nomads from the steppes of western Asia who had learnt a new technique of living—breeding and pasturing flocks which they drove from one grazing-ground to another. They had mastered, too, another technique, that of war, which they waged with bows and arrows and sharp axes, first of polished stone and later of bronze. These lordly shepherds had some affinity with the nomadic warrior peoples who overran the ancient city civilisations of the Middle East: the Semitic tribes who founded Babylon, and the Shepherd kings who ruled Egypt in the days of Joseph and his brethren. Toughened by their wandering and possessing stronger weapons through their bronzesmiths' skill in metalwork, they were able to impose their will on their lighter-armed, smaller predecessors. They did not annihilate them—for there was still plenty of room for all even in a little island covered by forest and marsh. But they made them work for them. And they bred from their womenfolk. After a time intermarriage brought a blending of the types; in their burial grounds the bones of the races are mingled.

These newcomers were also concerned with the causes of life and with what happened after death. But, like their fellow pastoralists in the East, they worshipped, not the patient cultivator's earth-mother, but the sun which, as they watched their flocks on the heights, they conceived to be the source of life. At the axis of their radiating sheep-tracks along the bare chalkdowns of the south-west, they and their slaves laboriously dragged and erected huge stones in mysterious clusters, where they sacrificed men and beasts to their flaming god. The stone circles at Avebury and Stonehenge are among the greatest monuments of early man; they seemed to have enshrined the religious beliefs and ritual both of the new Beaker and old Iberian folk.

The men who brought these vast rocks—some like the blue Pembrokeshire stones of Stonehenge from hundreds of miles away—and placed them in elaborate patterns based on the movements of the sun and stars must have learnt much, including the practice of subordination to authority. They created something which has lasted for more than thirty centuries and may still stand on the Wiltshire uplands when we and our works are forgotten.

For more than a thousand years the men of the Bronze Age dominated southern Britain. The earthen ditch in the chalk or oolite, the lonely dewpond on the height, the hill-turf nibbled close and enriched by countless generations of sheep are their legacy. Theirs was a society built on the flocks that gave them food and raiment. Their priests tended the sun-temples, their craftsmen made vessels and weapons of bronze from the tin and copper mines of the south-west, their princes wore splendid helmets and rings and bracelets of gold brought by Irish smiths from Wicklow streams. Their traders, travelling

the green hillroads—Icknield Way, Whiteway, Ridgeway—
that linked their priestly capital on Salisbury Plain with the
uplands of the east and south-west carried from earthwork
fort to fort the bronze weapons, tools and ornaments that
were their wealth. Others, more daring, trafficked tin and copper across the Channel or with Carthaginian merchants from
North Africa. Irish gold objects of this period have been
found as far away as Denmark and the Mediterranean and
Aegean cities, where this remote, half-fabulous country at the
world's end was known as the Tin Islands.

The Bronze Age men had their hour, giving place in the full-
ness of time to others. New races were on the march, moving
westwards from the great heartland of the human family on
the Asian plains. It is doubtful if at any time during the two
thousand years that followed the first Neolithic colonisation
of Britain such infiltration ever ceased. There was no central
government and, save in a few settled places along the coast,
no-one to oppose a landing. The numbers involved in each
invasion must have been very small, for boats were few and
minute.

Most of the invaders brought to the island something new,
in husbandry, craftsmanship or ways of living. The most important of all was a language which had originated in
western Asia and spread, with the movements of the nomadic
peoples who spoke it, into India, Persia, the Aegean, Italy
and most parts of western Europe. From the basic sounds of
this so-called Aryan speech—"outlines . . . drawn only in
sound, in the air, as elusive almost as the call of birds" [1]—
are derived certain words, used with variations by successive
invaders, which still constitute the foundation of our language
and are to be found, in not dissimilar forms, in other countries
colonised by tribes of Aryan stock. Among these are *father,
mother, daughter, sister, brother, son* and *widow*, the first ten
numerals, and some of the more important parts of the body,
like *knee, foot* and *tooth*. So are *night, wind* and *star*, and the
names of domestic animals, *cow, ox, steer,* with their plurality,
herd, hound, goat, sow and *goose, ewe* and *wether* and their
product, *wool*. The words *wheel, axle* and *yoke* show the
nomadic character of these Aryan ancestors; our modern
wain or *waggon* is derived from another of their basic sounds.

[1] Jacquetta Hawkes, *A Land,* 174.

Other words, whose derivations are not to be found in the speech of the Asiatic descendants of the race but are known to its European descendants—*beech, elm* and *hazel, throstle, finch* and *starling*—must have been added in the centuries when the latter were dwelling, in the course of their westward march, among the forests of central Europe. Similar words were added, too, before the western branch split into Greek, Latin, Celt and Teuton, that reveal the substitution of agricultural for nomadic life—*corn* and *ear, furrow, bean* and *meal*.

It was between three thousand and two thousand-five-hundred years ago—between 1000 B.C. and 500 B.C.—that an Aryan-speaking race, the Celts or Gaels, first appeared in Britain. They were a tall, blue-eyed, flame-haired folk who had crossed Europe from the east and settled in the country which is now called France and which took their name of Gaul. For as long a time as that which divides us from the Crusades Celts were moving into Britain and Ireland, first in small bands and families and later in tribal armies, until they had become the dominant racial strain in both islands. The earlier peoples survived, but were mostly driven into the western moors and hills. They figure in Celtic legends as the faeries or little people—the *Tyiwyth leg*—elusive, mysterious and dangerous, who sometimes stole their neighbours' children or provided a bride, dark, shy and inscrutable, for some giant, clumsy, good-humoured Celtic farmer. In such tales a recurrent feature is their dread of iron—the metal whose use the Celtic smiths introduced from the steppes and which, forged into swords and chariots, gave the latter's warriors their long ascendancy. Smelted in charcoal furnaces in the demon-haunted and till now uninhabited lowland forests, it was made also into rotary-lathes to make wheels, and into ploughs which, drawn by oxen, could break virgin soil too stiff for the hand hoes and small wooden ploughs of the past. This brought about a gradual increase in population which, it is estimated, rose during the Celtic occupation to around a quarter of a million—say about a two-hundredth part of its present size. These iron-users were probably the first of Britain's invaders to create permanent fields and villages, mostly on the greensands and light clays of the south-east and south-west. At their zenith they may have occupied a sixth of the country. The rest of it, including the thick forest clays of the Midlands, remained uninhabited.

The island still had no unity; it had not even a name. To visualise it we must think of it as divided into loosely defined and warring tribal areas, rather like South Africa in the days of the Zulu and Kaffir wars. In the south-east were the latest comers, the warlike Belgae, whose territory stretched as far west as Salisbury Plain and the Dorset coast, with their fine blacksmiths and iron chariots and plough-coulters. Their name survives only on the far side of the Channel in the country from which they came, though one of their tribes, the Cantii, gave theirs to Kent and Canterbury. Another tribe, whose name has endured on the continent, were the Parisii—a war-like people from the Seine and Marne valleys, who, landing in the Humber, conquered the plain between what is now Yorkshire and Lincolnshire. Others, like the Brigantes of the Pennine dales and the Iceni of Norfolk, dispersed by later invasions have left little memorial of their sojourn. But in the south-west, where Celtic and pre-Celtic stock has always been predominant, the Dumnonii and the Durotriges have transmitted their names to the Devonians and men of Dorset. And for no very clear reason one group of invaders—the Prythons or Brythons—later gave their name to the whole island.

The hereditary chieftains of these tribes seem to have had a love of beautiful things. They employed craftsmen whose graceful designs surpassed anything yet seen in the barbaric West. When they died their treasures were buried with them —bronze armour and helmets, embossed shields decorated with vivid enamels, like the one found in the Thames at Battersea, golden torques, bracelets and brooches with which to fasten their tartan plaids; amber cups and hand-mirrors engraved with exquisite circular designs like the Birdlip mirror in the Gloucester Museum. Vanity was a characteristic of the Celts; a Greek traveller of the time describes them as smear-ing their fair hair with chalk-wash to make it still brighter and then drawing it tightly back from the foreheads till they looked like hobgoblins. "Their nobles let their moustaches grow so long that they hide their mouths and, when they eat, get entangled in their food. . . . They use amazing colours, brightly dyed shirts with flowing patterns, and trousers called breeches. . . . Their appearance is amazing, with voices deep sounding and very harsh." They were boastful, threatening and braggarts, he added, but their intellects were keen, and they were quick to acquire knowledge. "When they have killed their foes, they cut off their heads. . . . They nail them up on their walls as trophies and preserve those of their chief enemies in boxes."

These head-hunting tribesmen cannot have been comfortable neighbours. At Salmonsby in Gloucestershire they were still eating their womenfolk about two thousand years ago. Their religion reeked of blood, and travellers from the civilised South, whose own ideas about sacrifice were far from squeamish, brought back horrifying tales of ritual massacres in dark sacred groves by their magicians or druids. And they were incorrigible fighters. They crowned Britain's hilltops, not with burial-barrows and sun-temples, but with vast earthwork castles with concentric ditches and ramparts, like Mai Dun or Maiden Castle in Dorset, Chanctonbury Ring in Sussex, Almondbury in Yorkshire and the great Dun of Downpatrick in Ireland. In the ancient Celtic ballads of Ireland, Wales and the Scottish Highlands—the parts of Britain least affected by later invasions—pride of battle takes precedence of every other emotion. For centuries these fierce, passionate, braggart, though sometimes touchingly noble, tribesmen constantly raided one another's lands for heads, slaves and cattle, but observed the rules and rites of their savage code of honour. The wars of the early Greeks, fought in the Aegean sunlight and sung by Homer, were matched by wars fought under the misty skies and dripping hills of western Britain by men of the same remote ancestry. In Celtic Ireland, as well as in Wales and the Scottish Highlands, this "heroic" age continued long after it had ceased in Greece and the British lowlands. The flashing swords and flails of the Fianna, and Finn Mac Cool and Gull Mac Morna setting targe to targe, were the counterparts of "godlike Achilles and his squire Automedon and Alkimas in battle upgrown." And the story of how Grainne, daughter of King Cormac, eloped with Diarmuid, echoes the tale of Helen of Troy.

By now a conqueror of a different kind was approaching Britain. With their breast-plated, helmeted, disciplined infantry and their fleets of triple-banked oar-propelled warships, the Romans were the greatest conquerors the world had known. They were a people of high courage and patriotism with an instinctive feeling for order, led by aristocrats of a strong practical bent. Just over two thousand years ago, having overrun Italy and most of the countries fringing the western

Mediterranean, they crossed the Alps and invaded Gaul. In three years their great general, Julius Caesar, conquering by dividing, subdued the warlike Celtic tribes of that land and carried the Roman rule to the Channel. Behind his legions came the metalled military roads, the stone walled cities, the laws and administration which the Romans took with them wherever they went.

Though Caesar made two brief punitive and exploratory expeditions to Britain, for nearly another century it remained outside the great union of races welded together by Roman discipline and good sense—a misty, unexplored forest land of squabbling tribesmen on the world's fringe. But in A.D. 43, the interference with trade caused by tribal war provoked the Roman imperial authorities into a full-scale invasion, followed by annexation. Thereafter for three and a half centuries the southern half of Britain, comprising virtually the whole of what today is England, was a Roman province. It was Rome's policy to tame the native tribal chieftans by making them citizens; the city was the instrument by which, having conquered barbarians, she shaped them to her ends. They were encouraged to transform the old tribal camps and cattle-kraals into towns on the universal Roman model; to vie with one another in raising temples, colonnades, pillars and arches, and to build themselves houses and gardens where, garbed like Roman patricians, they could live out their lives in luxury under the eyes of authority. Their sons were educated in Roman schools and taught Latin, and their tribal warriors conscripted into the legions or auxiliary regiments and turned into Roman soldiers.

Behind the legions rose the cities on which Roman civilisation depended: rustic miniatures of Rome, even in this remote frontier land, with neat chess-board-pattern streets, forums and temples, porticoed town-halls and amphitheatres, public baths, aqueducts and drains. The capital of the Catuvellauni became *Verulamium*, or in modern English St. Albans; that of the Atrebates of the Thames valley *Calleva Atrebatum* or Silchester; that of the Iceni *Venta Icenorum* or Caistor-next-Norwich; that of the Dumnonii *Isca Dumnoniorum* or Exeter. Even the wild Silures of Wales built *Venta Silures* or Caerwent and boasted of the little garrison-town of Caerleon with its golden roofs and towers. In these minute but elegant tribal capitals traders built shops, and tribesmen brought their crops and cattle to market and assembled at sacred seasons to sacrifice to their local gods. Yet though Rome, true to her universal policy, encouraged the worship of the older native deities, she subordinated it, as she had done that of her own gods, to that of the all-embracing State. For its head, the Emperor, sacrifice and tribute were asked of all. It was to express and enforce that authority that the cities arose. More even than markets and dwelling places, they were temples to Caesar and the imperial bureaucracy.

At the height of the Roman occupation there were more than fifty cities in southern Britain. Most of them were very small by continental standards, with between two and five thousand inhabitants. The largest, *Londinium*, the hub of the country's road and trading system, may have had four or five times as many.[1] Though all these cities later perished, at Bath or *Aquae Solis*, the fashionable watering-place in the southern Cotswolds, the old Roman bath and its tutelary god can still be seen, much as they were when the rich provincials of eighteen centuries ago flocked there for health and amusement. Beyond the tribal capitals and close to the untamed northern and western moors lay the garrison cities of York, Chester, Uriconium and Caerleon, and in their rear Lincoln, Colchester and Gloucester—the *coloniae* where soldiers' families were settled on retirement with land and houses to breed more soldiers. There were also the Channel ports of Richborough, Porchester, and Chichester, and naval Dover with its lighthouse or *pharos*, guarding the island's communications with the Mediterranean empire of which it was the farthest province.

Linking the towns and camps ran straight Roman roads, paved and cambered on stone causeways, with milestones marking the distances to the imperial capital on the Tiber. Along them passed, not only the marching legionaries who were the guardians of all this order and prosperity, but the native corn, minerals, slaves and hunting-dogs which were exchanged for jewels, statues, wine and oil in jars, perfumes, marbles, mosaics, glass and pottery from the continent. Britain in those years was called the granary of the north. Though the oak forests of the Midland clays still remained untouched and uninhabited, her population, as a result of agricultural improvements, seems to have risen to more than half a mil-

[1] It covered about 350 acres along the north bank of the Thames. The site of its basilica or town hall is now occupied by Leadenhall Market.

lion. The chief grain exporters were the Celto-Roman land-owners, living in *villas* or country-houses on sheltered sunny slopes in the southern half of the island. Here, amid mosaics and tessellated pavements, glazed windows, baths and central heating, statues and terraces, they aped the life of the Mediterranean and tried to ignore the northern mists and forests around them. Drawing their culture from a wider civilisation, these aristocrats, with their stately Roman manners and Latin speech, introduced into Britain the poultry and geese of her farmyards, the pheasants of her woods, the pears, cherries, figs and mulberries that, planted in their gardens, survived when their gardens and civilisation were no more. They worked their great farms with slave labour which they housed in barracks at their gates.

But there was a flaw in the Roman political system. Everything was centralised in the State's officials yet the succession to the supreme office of all was uncertain. Again and again the Emperor's death was followed by a scramble for power. Sometimes he was assassinated by rivals or his own Praetorian guards, who became the arbiters of the Empire. The Roman world worshipped a ruler who was the guarantor of its peace, and that ruler turned out as often as not a parade-ground bully or a crude political intriguer who stopped at nothing to achieve his ambition.

By treating its possessors as divine Rome deified despotic power. Those in authority were not responsible to the moral feeling and wishes of those they governed; their sway, while it lasted, was uncontrolled. An all-pervading bureaucracy, increasingly wasteful and petty-minded, represented omnipotence at every level. The cost of that immense army of officials plunged society into ever deeper debt and taxation, and, a millstone round the neck of production and trade, destroyed all private independence and sense of initiative. Little by little it reduced the population of every city in the Empire to a mob.

Rome had grown out of greatness of individual character. It became a community in which individual character counted for nothing compared with an abstraction which proved, in the hour of testing, capable of nothing. By sacrificing the individual to the State the rulers of the Roman world undermined the real virtues which sustained it. They turned active and self-respecting citizens into inert and selfish ones. They discouraged the capitalist from thrift and foresight, the trader from enterprise, the craftsman from his hereditary skill, the husbandman from pride in the soil, the mother from maternity, and the soldier from courage and self-sacrifice. They made the moral shell that protected society so soft that it could protect it no longer. A creeping inertia paralysed everyone and everything. Even before the barbarians broke in, the elegant cities had begun to crumble, trade to die for want of purchasers, learning, art and even bureaucratic efficiency to disappear for lack of men of ability. The middle-class was exterminated. Civilisation slowly gave place to barbarism at the empire's heart.

By the end of the fourth century after Christ the Roman empire was disintegrating, both from internal dissension and inertia and from the attacks of barbaric tribes from outside. Already it had broken into two, one half governed from a Greek city on the Bosphorus named Consta ti on'e, the other —itself split between the rival garrisons of Italy, Gaul, Spain and Britain—nominally subject to Rome. On the last night of A.D. 406, a vast horde of Teutons from the German forests poured across the frozen Rhine into Gaul. Soon every city north of the Alps was in flames. The last legions in Britain were recalled to defend Italy. In 410 a Visigoth host sacked the imperial city itself.

Thus fifteen hundred years ago the British people were cut off from the civilisation to which they had belonged for nearly four centuries. Their appeals for help were unanswered and they were left to defend themselves. At first, freed from the restrictions of an over-centralised bureaucracy, they seem to have organised themselves under local generals or tribal princes, particularly in the north-west, where the old Celtic organisation had survived and resistance to the Picts had kept men hardy and self-reliant. The province's only land-frontier was short, and the barbarians of Caledonia, though fierce, were few in number, with no new races on the march behind them. For perhaps fifty years British-Roman civilisation, though fast disintegrating, appears to have survived.

Yet the threat of barbarism came not only from the land. The fishermen and whalers of the desolate marshes along the eastern shores of the North Sea—the "Saxons" or men of the long knives, as the British called them—had also felt the pressure of Asiatic hordes moving westward through the forests behind them. Even before Rome fell, spurred on by hunger and hope of loot, they had taken to their boats to prey on the rich Roman island beyond the sunset. From Frisia and the mouths of the Rhine, Ems and Weser, from Schleswig and Angle in what is now Holstein and Denmark, they poured up the estuaries and rivers of southern Britain to plunder and slay. The island became a magnet for the boldest of all the barbarians—the men of the sea. On the continent the cities which had been the glory of Roman civilisation escaped complete destruction, for the barbarian chieftains, fancying themselves heirs of the emperors before whom they had so long trembled, made them their own. But in Britain the invaders came from remote shores and mud-flats where the fame of Rome had scarcely penetrated. They despised, not only the effete, luxurious owners of the wealth they seized, but the wealth itself. They took the land, the crops and flocks, the slaves and treasures of gold and silver, but destroyed or shunned the cities—the *chesters*, as they called them—leaving only their charred, lonely, ghost-haunted ruins. For they were countrymen who hated towns and regarded their refinements as vices.

During this confused and savage age, which only the most exquisite scholarship has been able to rescue from oblivion, the island, with its dense forests and undrained valleys, was inhabited by three separate peoples. There were the Teuton invaders, with their boarcrested helmets, woollen cloaks and long ash-shafted spears, moving up the rivers in their shallow war boats or tramping the disused Roman roads—rechristened now with Saxon names like Watling Street and Fosse Way—in search of plunder and land. Behind them came their sturdy women-folk and children, brought across stormy seas in open boats from the Saxon and Angle settlements in Europe. Opposed to them, fighting also in small divided bands and driven ever farther into the west—into what today are Devon, Cornwall, Wales, the Lake District, and the south-western corner of Scotland then called Strathclyde—were the descendants of the British or Celtic-Roman provincials. But though their petty tyrants or princes, for ever squabbling with one another, might still wear Roman armour and flowing togas—or plaids, as they later became called—and boast high-sounding Latin names, the few towns left had become little more than squatters' settlements bereft of trade and the arts of civilised living, and their inhabitants almost as savage as the barbarians who had driven them from their former homes. And left behind by the receding British tide in squalid, remote villages as the victors' slaves, were the primitive, pre-Celtic peasants who continued to live much as before. They survived in the impenetrable scrub of the Chiltern hills, on the Pennine and northern moors, in the marshy islands of the Fens—now reverting to inland sea with the decay of the Roman dykes—and in the ancient chalk uplands of the south-west. They were not exterminated but surrounded and absorbed. And their womenfolk, and those of the Celts, bore children to the conquerors.

Nor, for all the bloody battles and massacres of that terrible time, did the British tribes of the West perish. They merely ceased to be civilised and Roman, and became pastoral and Welsh. Like their remote ancestors of the Age of Bronze, they reverted to the hills and sheep. For a time, rendered desperate by suffering and schooled by hardship, they fought back so fiercely that the Saxon advance was halted. And they were sustained, like many others in that calamitous age of falling civilisation, by a Faith called Christianity which had spread across the empire during its decline and which, hailing from the East, taught men that happiness could be achieved only by sacrifice. Under two successive leaders with Roman names, Ambrosius Aurelianus and Arturius or "King" Arthur— heroes of whom little is known save the legends handed down by unlettered folk and later enshrined by poets—they won a series of battles culminating in the victory of Arthur and his cavalry at Mount Badon which ensured the survival in Britain of the Celtic tribes and the Christian Faith. The Celtic names of streams, rivers and hills, which, outlasting the Teuton flood, mark our maps, and the scattered farms and hamlets of the West Country are, as much as the Arthurian tales, a memorial to this heroic king and the breathing-space he gained for his people. For fifty more years the invaders were confined to the eastern half of the island, the two races— speaking different tongues and holding different beliefs—facing one another in an uneasy, bitter truce across an uncertain frontier.

But in the middle of the sixth century the Saxons and Angles, first in the south and then in the north, resumed their advance. By the end of it the Britons of the south-west, driven into the Devonian-Cornish peninsula, were cut off from their Celtic kinsfolk of the little, quarrelling principalities of Wales—Gwent, Dyfor, Powys, Gwynnedd. In the north the creation of an English kingdom called Northumbria, stretching from coast to coast across the Pennine moors, soon afterwards separated the Welsh from their fellow Celts of the Cumbrian mountains and Strathclyde. In 603 the Northumbrian king defeated the Britons of Strathclyde and their northern Christian neighbours, the Scots of Dalriada or Argyllshire, in a great battle in Liddesdale. "From that day," a Saxon boasted, "no king of the Scots dared to meet the English nation in battle." From the North Sea to the Severn and Dee, from the Channel to the Forth, the conquest of Britain was complete. Except for the rocky, rainswept west, it was Britain no longer. It had become England.

What manner of people were these Anglo-Saxons? They were great seamen, fighters and colonisers. Coming from desolate coasts and windswept mud-flats, gale and storm were in their blood. "The blast of the tempest," sang one of their poets, "aids our oars, the bellowing of the heaven, the howling of the thunder hurt us not; the hurricane is our servant and drives us where we wish to go." They crossed the seas in undecked, mastless, clinkerbuilt boats—"foam-cresters"— seventy or eighty feet long and scarcely a dozen wide, with a paddle in the stern for steering and fourteen or sixteen oars a side. If they were without mercy to their foes, they looked for none at the hands of a Nature very different from that of the sunny Mediterranean of Roman civilisation. They viewed even shipwreck as a form of practice. Theirs was a world in which there was no place for the weak or craven. One thinks of them, in those days before they found a permanent home, as wild geese, tense on their solitary flight over the waste of waters as they followed the whale, the herring and the seal.

They loved fighting. Their poetry, chanted in the mead-halls of their chieftains as they sat feasting at the long benches, is full of the clash of "the hammered blades", "the serried bucklers", "the shields of linden wood", of "arrows sleeting like hail". They loved the symbols of death and carnage: the raven who followed the host with his beak dripping blood, the hungry hawks hovering over the battlefield, the funeral pyre hung with shields and helmets—"the beacon of the man mighty in battle"—round which the companions of the fallen sang the joys of war and the warrior's virtues.

Yet they had another side. Though to the defeated Britons, to whose homes they had brought fire and sword, they seemed only cruel, boorish savages, they were great farmers: by far the best the island had known. Their first settlements were on the lighter soils, but presently, with their iron axes and deep four or eight-ox ploughs, they embarked on the titanic task of clearing the forests and heavier clay soils of the eastern midlands: rich land that Neolithic and Bronze Age men, Celts and Romans alike had left untouched. For, barbarians though they were, they were more patient, industrious and methodical than any of the peoples they had conquered. And, on the lowest and working social level, they had more genius for co-operation. They worked together, just as they had rowed and fought together. Wherever they settled they waged their battle against nature shoulder to shoulder. They shared the same ploughs, helped to cultivate one another's land and followed common rules of tillage and forestry. In this way they were able to make far steadier progress against the cold, stubborn clay and oaken wilderness around them than any of their predecessors. In their homesteads or "tuns" of thatched, tent-shaped huts, sited by streams in the forest clearings, and in their closely-knit communities whose names—Barkings of Barking, Hastings of Hastings, Gellingas of Ealing—still mark our maps, these sturdy colonists, with their fine smiths, carpenters and wrights, cleared virgin ground to support growing numbers of their folk. In doing so they created in the course of time the English countryside, turning marshy valley bottoms into water-meadows, terracing fields on the slopes and eating ever farther into the forests. As each village became established, the younger and bolder spirits, for whom the cleared land was insufficient, "swarmed off" to found, still deeper in the woods, new settlements which they distinguished from the old by the addition of prefixes like Upper and Lower, East, West, South and North, and suffixes like Bottom and End, Bere and Den—pig-pasture—Ley and Hurst.

For these people loved the soil and the tending of it and its beasts. They loved it as much as their fathers had loved fighting and the sea. They left their memorial, not like the Romans in stone or the Bronze Age men in burial-grounds, but in the imperishable shape of the earth they tilled; it is writ large across our shires, with their villages, meadows, farms and ploughlands. And in the work of their artists that has come down to us, in their carvings in wood and stone of leaves, trees and animals, we can see their deep feeling for nature. "His coat", runs the old song, "is of Saxon green", and it is of a green-clad folk in a green land that we must think of them, swinging their axes and driving their ploughs through mysterious forest and dark earth to make the land we love.

Their main settlements were at first near the coast—the East Saxons of what became Essex, their big-nosed Jutish neighbours across the Thames in Kent and the Isle of Wight; the flaxen-haired, blue-eyed, heavy-limbed South Saxons of Sussex; the West Saxons who, coming from the Wash or up the Thames, settled on Salisbury Plain or, in smaller numbers, landed near Southampton Water and followed the Avon to the Plain; the Angles of East Anglia—the North-folk and South-folk—and their kinsmen who, pushing up the Midland rivers, established the tribal communities that by the beginning of the seventh century had merged to form the kingdom of Mercia. Farther north other Angles, overrunning and inter-marrying with the British tribes of Deira and Bernicia between Humber and Forth, founded the still greater kingdom of Northumbria in what today is northern England and south-eastern Scotland. All brought from their diverse starting-points in Europe different customs and ways of life, which they continued to follow in their new homes. And all were separated from one another by trackless expanses of oak forest, thorn, scrub and swamp, like the dense Epping and Chiltern woods that hemmed in London from the north, the eighty-mile wide Andredsweald between the North and South Downs, Selwood in the west, the Midland forests of Bernwood, Arden and Wyre, Cannock Chase, Sherwood and Hatfield.

The population of these pioneer communities in the backwoods was at first very small. In the whole of Mercia—an area today comprising a dozen crowded counties—there were only 12,000 households a century and a half after the first invasion. Their form of government, though aristocratic, was far simpler and freer than that of Rome. There were no officials, no central administration, and every village community kept its own peace and justice. No-one could write or keep records, and the only checks on a man's conduct were the customary vengeance of his kin and neighbours, or of his lord or the more distant king for breaches of their simple laws.

The pioneer farmer, or ceorl as he was called, was the core both of the local community and of the petty kingdom or "kindred" to which he belonged. He was a freeman, responsible only to his neighbours and to his fighting leader—king or lord: a man, to use the old English phrase, "moot-worthy, fold-worthy and fyrd-worthy", worthy, that is, of a place in the justice-court, the sheep-fold and the tribal fyrd or militia that turned out at the king's summons in time of war. He was wont to speak his mind out freely in the court of the village or tun, for among this simple people the man who spoke truth fearlessly was as honoured as the man who fought bravely. Though ready to enslave others, the English were great lovers of their own freedom. Their homes, rude and rough though they were, were their castles.

The tribal king was chosen for life by the kinsfolk and chief warriors from the descendants of the hero who had led the warband or folk during the invasion. He lived in a little earthwork palisaded fortress called a burgh with his thanes or gesiths—war-companions—and their servants and slaves. Such kings, some of them ruling kingdoms smaller than a modern county, were little richer than their subjects. They might wear a few ornaments and jewels in their rough, home-spun clothes and own gold or silver-mounted cups, armour of chain-mail and finely made swords, daggers and shields, like those found in the seventh century royal ship buried in the sands of Sutton Hoo in East Anglia. Yet a king's or lord's hall was merely a gabled log-barn, with stag-horns and rude arms on its unplastered walls, a sunk open hearth on the centre of a rush-strewn earthen floor, and a hole in the roof to let out the smoke. Here on great occasions he and his companions would gorge themselves on meat and hot spiced ale and mead—a fermented spirit of honey and herbs—and, while the harp passed from hand to hand and the minstrels sang their sagas, shout with drunken joy at the remembrance of their forefathers' heroic deeds and battles.

For the gods of these simple forest folk—seamen and warriors turned farmers—were the spirits of Battle, Storm and Nature common to all the Nordic peoples. They honoured only the brave and warlike. It was because of this that, despite their love of independence, they gave such loyalty to their kings and lords, heirs of the warriors who had led them to conquest and who, perhaps, boasted descent from Woden, god of victory and plunder, or Thunor, god of the mountain-thunder, deities whose names, like those of Tiw and Freya, spirits of war and fertility, survive in the days of our week.[1] The greater the king's prowess, the larger his following of thanes and companions. They felt for him as dogs for their hunting masters: "happy days," sang one, "when I laid head and hands on my lord's knee." From him they received the meat, bread and salt, the ale and mead on which they feasted in the winter, the bracelets and buckles of gold and silver, the gems and embroidery with which they loved to adorn their shaggy persons, the crested helmets, ringed mail and runed swords, said to be made by Wayland the smith-giant, which they used in battle.

Such men, though they might slaughter man, woman and child in anger or to placate their cruel gods, were not without rough virtues. They were brave, loyal and true to their kin and leaders; there was no shame in their eyes like that of the man who turned his back in fight or betrayed lord or comrade. Those who had eaten a man's salt must die by his side. "Never shall the steadfast men round Stourmere", cried the Essex thane as his eorl fell, "reproach me that I journey lordless home."

In this lay the nobility of these far-off ancestors of ours. There was no weak comfort in their harsh creed. They believed that the end of all was death: that no triumph or happiness, however great, could last. "Now," sang their bards, "is the flower of thy strength lasting awhile, yet soon sickness or the sword, fire or flood, the arrow's flight or blinding age shall take away thy might." They saw in the mystery of life a riddle beyond man's explaining. "Where," they asked, "is the steed? were the rider? were the giver of treasure? The bulwarks are dismantled, the banqueting-hall in ruins, the lords lie bereft of joy, and all their proud chivalry is fallen by the wall!" It was not in man's power to control his lot; his virtue lay in his capacity for suffering and endurance. Even the gods, feasting in their paradise of Waelhaell or Valhalla, must fall in the end to the hateful hags, Hel and Weird—the Fates to whose inexorable decree all things

---

[1] Also in the names of towns and villages like Wednesbury (Woden's burgh or borough) and Tewesley (Tiw's lea).

bowed. There was no escape, no mercy or tenderness on icy earth or in storm-riven sky.

In the eyes of this brave people there was only one rule: to accept without flinching whatever the Fates had in store. The craven whined; the valiant kept his grief locked in his heart. The worse fortune treated him, the truer he must be to creed and comrade; the craven and traitor could gain only shame by their baseness. It was a rough, masculine creed, without much subtlety or refinement. It judged men, not by what they said or thought, but by their deeds. Yet it bred a sense of duty and responsibility without which no nation can be great or endure. It taught the rank and file to be loyal, and their leaders to sacrifice themselves for the led. "I have bought with my death a hoard of treasures", cried Beowulf after his fight with the dragon, "I give thanks that before my dying day I have won it for my people". So long afterwards on the battlefield of Maldon the outnumbered English fought on without hope of victory:

"Thought shall be the harder, heart the keener,
Mood shall be the more as our might lessens."

In the hour of adversity and danger they closed their ranks and were true to one another.

CHAPTER II

THE CROSS AND THE SWORD

"I saw them march from Dover, long ago,
With a silver cross before them, singing low,
Monks of Rome from their home where the
blue sea breaks in foam,
Augustine with his feet of snow."

FLECKER

MORE THAN TWO HUNDRED years after the last legions left Britain, and soon after the completion of the English conquest, a tall dark stranger stood before the king and chieftains of Northumbria. His name was Paulinus, and, like the men who had once governed Britain, he was a Roman. But he bore no arms and stood there at the mercy of the rough warriors around him.

He had come to Northumbria—the wild northern kingdom that stretched from the Forth to the Humber—with a Kentish bride for its king. Thirty years earlier, in A.D. 597, the Jutish ruler of Kent, the most civilised of the English tribal kingdoms, had invited to his capital a band of Roman monks to minister to his queen, a Christian princess from Gaul. It proved the most important of all the invasions of England and the most peaceful. Marching across the downs from Dover with a silver cross and banners under their leader Augustine, they had been received by King Ethelbert sitting at his tent door lest they should cast spells on him. He listened to what they had to say, gave them a ruined Roman church in his capital, Canterbury and resolved to embrace their creed. After he was baptised thousands of his thanes and warriors followed his example.

The Northumbrians were no friends to Christianity—the

mysterious eastern religion that, officially adopted by the Roman Empire in the days of its decline, had survived the latter's collapse on the continent and, though rooted out of southern Britain, had lingered on in the mountains and islands of the Celtic west. Fourteen years before, they had slaughtered hundreds of its priests after a great victory over the Britons of North Wales. The very word, *church,* that they used for its houses of worship was associated in their minds with plunder.[1] They listened, therefore, to the eloquent Italian with suspicion. Yet what he told caused them to do so in silence. For it was a tale of heroism and devotion. Its purport was that behind the forces of fate was a God who had made men in his own image and, loving them, had given them freedom to choose between good and evil. He had made them, not helpless actors, but partners in the drama of creation. And because men had misused that freedom and God still loved them, He had sent His son as leader and saviour to show them, by revealing His nature, how to live and, by sharing theirs and dying on the Cross, how to overcome sin and death.

Paulinus's tale cannot have seemed wholly strange to his hearers. He had spoken of a leader who had been brave and true, who offered his followers a freeman's choice between good and evil and a hero's reward for those who were faithful. But in two respects his message was revolutionary. For the virtues Jesus had shown were not merely those the English honoured, but others they had never regarded as virtues at all. Love not hate, gentleness not force, mercy not vengeance had been the armour of this great captain. The Northumbrians' own valour in battle was small compared to the cold courage of facing death with only these meek virtues. And, as proof of it, here was this solitary stranger standing unarmed in their midst.

Most startling of all, Paulinus's message offered the English hope beyond the grave. Here was the reply to a problem deep in the human heart which their priests had never answered. When he ended, an old counsellor spoke. "The life of man, O king," he said, "is like a sparrow's flight through a bright hall when one sits at meat in winter with the fire alight on the hearth, and the icy rain-storm without. The

[1] Derived, through the German mercenaries serving in the Eastern provinces of the Empire, from the Greek word, *kuriakon*—the Lord's house. L. P. Smith, *The English Language,* 98.

sparrow flies in at one door and stays for a moment in the light and heat, and then, flying out of the other, vanishes into the wintry darkness. So stays for a moment the life of man, but what it is before and what after, we know not. If this new teaching can tell us, let us follow it!"

As the Northumbrians crowded round the man who brought them these tidings, their own high priest was the first to cast his spear at the idols their fathers had worshipped. Afterwards they were baptised in thousands, pressing into the Yorkshire streams to receive from Paulinus's hands the cross of water which enrolled a man as Christ's follower and offered him deliverance from the grave. For Christianity had been presented to them as a correction, rather than a denial, of their own heathen beliefs. They were used to thinking of gods as controlling their fate, though gods of terror. They were now told there was one God—of justice, peace and love. They were used to offering sacrifices to appease the wrath of Heaven; they were told of a new form of sacrifice, self-sacrifice. They believed in magic, and learnt of a heavenly king who was born in a manger, gave his life for man on the "healer's tree", and rose from the grave to sit on God's right hand. They were wont to celebrate the seed sown in winter darkness and the renewal of life in the spring; they were given a midwinter feast to celebrate Christ's birth and a spring one for his resurrection. Their fertility festival to Eastra, a Teuton goddess, purged of its grossness became Easter; their Yuletide junketings around the December logfires the Christ Mass or Christmas.

Such a conversion was necessarily incomplete. It made heathens Christian, yet it also made Christianity a little heathen. And it suffered from the disadvantage—the reverse of its bloodless character—that it was a conversion from the top. It rested too much on the Germanic principle of lordship. It depended on the changing policies of a Court rather than on the hearts of a people.

Yet it was not only from Rome that the Faith was brought to England. Two centuries earlier, when the Saxons had first overrun the lowlands, the Roman-Celts among the mountains and moors of Strathclyde, Wales and Cornwall had fallen back on the one creed of a dissolving civilisation that gave them courage and hope to endure. And though, in their harsh life of struggle and poverty, they grew almost as barbarous and illiterate and quite as fierce, as their foes, the

light of Christ's teaching still shone through the war-clouds
that overhung their rugged lands. Chapels of wood and wattle with beehive vaulting, and monasteries with tiny enclosed
grass lawns or "llans", appeared in Welsh valleys, and gran-
ite wheel-head crosses flowered beside the Atlantic among
the Cornish rocks. All round the western seas, from Brittany
to the Isle of Man and Clyde, the names of Celtic saints are
still commemorated where once, in tiny cells and oratories,
they lived their lives of faith and self-denial—Ninian who
converted the Picts of Galloway; Dyfrig, Illtyd, Govan, Teilo,
Padarn and David, the apostles of Wales; Samson of Dol
who crossed the seas from stony Caldey to preach to the
Bretons; Morwenna, Cleder, Endellion and a score of others
Who made the name of Christ loved by the lonely fishermen
and herdsmen of Cornwall.

The distinguishing trait of these early evangelists was their
selflessness in the love of God and their sublime faith that
there was nothing they could not dare in their Master's
name. St. Patrick's mission to the heathen Irish in the fifth
century is one of the great stories of mankind. By convert-
ing them he made Ireland, in the dark centuries after Rome's
fall, a Christian haven in a world of storm. The most famous
of his disciples was the evangelist, Columba, who founded a
monastery church on the island of Iona off the coast of Dalriada. Up and down the northern moors where even the
Roman legionaries had never penetrated, Columbia's monks
made their way, preaching, healing and winning men's hearts.
One of them, St. Aidan, became the Celtic apostle of northern England, planting the Christian ideal among the Northumbrian tribesmen. The contribution of the Celtic evangelists to England's conversion lay not in doctrine but in example. It was this that won the simple English to Christ. For
if the preachers' arguments were sometimes a travesty of
their Master's, their lives were touchingly like his. Like him
they took no thought for the morrow, of what they should
eat or wear; they put their faith in his spirit and, giving
themselves to his selfless gospel, lived it. With those among
whom they went, purseless and on foot, they left an image
of the Good Shepherd giving his life for his sheep that was
to run like a silver thread through the English tradition.

So it came about that in the seventh century England became a Christian land. From Canterbury Roman monks carried their missions into Wessex—the kingdom of the West

Saxons—making Christians of the warrior farmers who had driven the Britons beyond Exe and Severn. From Northumbria the disciples of Aidan took their message of faith and goodness to the peoples of Mercia. Though they only partly comprehended its revolutionary creed of love, humility and self-sacrifice, it came to them as a wonderful revelation. It took the darkness out of their sad, fatalistic beliefs and offered them hope and purpose.

In the century that followed, the national genius flowered for the first time. During it the earliest English churches were built, like Brixworth in Northamptonshire and Escombe by the Wear, and the tall, beautiful, sculptured Celtic crosses, with their runic inscriptions and Gospel figures of men and beasts, before which the Angles of the north worshipped in the open air. It was the age in which the first English books and manuscripts, with their exquisitely interlaced illuminations of birds and dogs, were copied and painted by monks in their cells; in which the stately Wilfred taught Northumbrian choirs to sing double chants, and Aldhelm, a prince of the West Saxons—the reputed builder of the little cruciform church at Bradford-on-Avon who became abbot of Malmesbury and first bishop of Sherborne—used to stand on Malmesbury bridge singing the songs of his native land until he had gathered a crowd of listeners, and then preach the gospel story and the wonders of God's universe. In that dawn of childlike faith when Cuthbert, the shepherd bishop of Lindisfarne, tramped his wide diocese, the moorland peasants came running to him to confess their sins and beg his intercession. The inspiration of the gentle barefoot saint can still be seen in the beautiful Lindisfarne Gospel in the British Museum, written on Holy Island "for God and St. Cuthbert," and in the great cathedral shrine that long afterwards rose on the rocks above the river at Durham to house his bones.

Perhaps the most wonderful of all the achievements of the time was that of the Venerable Bede, the greatest scholar in Christendom. From his monastery cell as Jarrow he poured out a never-ceasing stream of books: history, theology, poetry, grammar and natural science. To him England owes the practice of dating years from the birth of Christ and the first prose written in Latin by an Englishman. His vision of Hell—"where there is no voice but of weeping, no face but of the tormentors"—expresses the very soul of the dark

ages he helped to illumine. The most famous of his works was
the *Ecclesiastical History of the English Nation*—the story
of the Conversion. Lucid, just, immensely learned, it is a
monument to his age, his Faith and his country. That life of
scholarship and labour, with the tireless hand writing amid
the intervals of prayer and teaching, sometimes so frozen
that it could hardly grip the pen, is one of the proud memories of England. He left his countrymen the earliest version
of the gospel in their own tongue and a tradition, rare in
that age, of gentleness, love of truth, and scrupulous fairness.

After the first enthusiasm roused by the barefoot Celtic missionaries, the spread of Christianity among the pagan peasant
masses was very gradual. For centuries, in England as on
the continent it remained mainly a religion of the upper
classes drawing its monks, saints and bishops from the well-
born. Even for them it was often only a superior kind of
magic: a means of buying, by prayers, incantations and
pious benefactions, protection from misfortune or foes and,
still more important, from the ancient equaliser, death. It
was the promise of eternal life that drew most men to Christ's
creed. The hope of everlasting heaven and the fear of its
dreadful opposite, the eternal Nordic hell, proved a rival
to the hope of plunder and the lust for pleasure and power.
    Yet, despite the slowness of Christianity's humanising
work and the immense obstacles it had to overcome, its survival in such a rude and bloody age is one of the miracles
of history. Into a world inherently unequal, where the strong
and fortunate ruled without pity, it introduced the conception of the ultimate worthlessness of earthly distinctions in
the light of the far more dreadful distinction between heaven
and hell. By its doctrine that every man had a soul to save
during his time on earth, and its insistence that the winning
of salvation was no easier for king or lord than for beggar
or slave, it gave some meaning to the life of common men.
It offered those with no prospect—the poor toiling in the
fields, the weak and sick, the slaves and prisoners—the hope
of a spiritual and eternal kingdom open to all. For the first
time men were made to feel, however dimly, that it was
wrong to maltreat those who were in their power but who
in Christ's universal family were their brothers.
    To women, too, Christianity brought a slow but percep-
tible improvement of status. For the Church taught that, if

their bodies were weaker than men's, their souls were of equal importance and recognised their moral stature by the responsibilities with which it entrusted them. It stressed the sanctity of marriage and the home. It offered to women who, renouncing the joys of family life, dedicated themselves to Christ's universal family, a career as leaders of religious society. In these early centuries queens and princesses took vows of chastity and poverty and embraced the conventual life. It was a woman, St. Hilda—a Northumbrian princess and head of the great abbey of Streoneshalh[1]—who trained many of the earliest English bishops and set the first Christian poet in England—the poor herdsman Caedmon—to sing the wonders of creation.

Christianity, too, taught men to base their social relationships on something wider than tribe or kindred. It brought the warlike tribes and nations of England into the same communion as the other western European peoples and into closer contact with one another. At the time of the conversion there were seven English kingdoms—Northumbria, Mercia, Kent, Wessex, East Anglia, Essex and Sussex. Their princes were almost constantly at war, with their own kinsmen for their crowns and with their neighbours for new territories. There was no sense of nationhood; a man thought of himself as a Kentish man or a Northumbrian, not as an Englishman. Without communications or regular administration no king's authority could reach far. Even that of the strongest died with him.

But with the coming of Christianity kings gained an instrument of governance more potent in the long run than any army. In its quiet monasteries the Church began to teach men the forgotten arts of writing and keeping records. At Jarrow and Wearmouth, Melrose and Whitby in the north, at Glastonbury, Malmesbury and Pershore in the west, at Canterbury and Minster in the south, it trained the men who showed barbarian rulers how to govern justly. It gave them clerics or clerks to reduce their chaotic affairs to order, draft laws and reckon accounts and taxes.

For the way of life the Church preached called for a law-abiding world: one in which men made and kept promises instead of perpetually resorting to force. The king's peace was a better basis for Christian relationships than vio-

---

[1] Re-named Whitby after the Scandinavian invasions.

lence and anarchy. So long as the rulers of society were faithful Christians the Church, therefore, supported their authority. It bade men, while rendering unto God the things that were God's, render unto Caesar the things that were Caesar's. It transformed the military institution of Teutonic kingship into a sacred office. In place of the traditional raising of the chosen leader on the warrior's shield by the armed host, the Church crowned him with a sacred diadem and anointed him with holy oil, praying that God would give him the armour of justice to preserve peace and do righteousness. In return, the king—sanctified as the Lord's anointed—guarded the Church's property, made gifts of land and treasure to its monasteries and conferred high office on its clerics, the only men in his realm who could read or write.

If one could have looked down on Europe in the confused and barbaric centuries following the conversion of England, one would have seen a continent in whose western half, from the Mediterranean to Scotland, Christianity had become the principal faith of man. This vast tract of land was divided into many little principalities, whose uncertain frontiers changed constantly with the wars and family quarrels of their rulers. Yet one institution transcended tribal frontiers. In a landscape of peasants' huts and rude wooden hunting-lodges, the monasteries of the Church were everywhere the largest buildings to be seen. And winding past squalid villages and little wooden castles, through forests, fords and mountain passes, ran the grassy tracks, trodden by horsehooves and the feet of monks and pilgrims, that led to Rome, the see of the pope or "Holy Father"—the spiritual head of western Christendom.

Only in the remote Celtic islands of Ireland and western Scotland, and in the south-east, beyond the Balkan mountains, where the Greek emperors still maintained the ancient pomp of the Caesars and the Byzantine Patriarch ignored the pope's claim to be Christ's vice-regent on earth, were there Christian communities that refused to acknowledge the spiritual supremacy of Rome. Yet Christendom was only a world within a world. Europe itself was half heathen. Its eastern plains and forests and mountainous northern peninsulas were still peopled by savages who had never heard of Christ. And all along the southern and eastern shores of the Medi-

terranean—the earliest cradle of the Faith—the patriarchates
of Jerusalem, Antioch and Alexandria had been overrun by
crusading tribesmen from the Arabian deserts. At the very
time that England was being converted to Christianity the
whole Arab world had been set ablaze by a new crusading
religion. The creed of Islam or "surrender" and its devotees,
the Moslems or "self-surrenderers," united the Near East,
long subject to the Greek and Roman West, in a holy war
against Christians. A sea, long given over to peaceful trade,
had become a pirate-haunted frontier between Christendom
and Islam, swept by Arab fleets. Constantinople only escaped capture through its superb strategic position. In the
East, emulating Alexander a thousand years before, Moslem
armies passed the Oxus and reached the frontiers of India.
And early in the eighth century, while Bede was still working
in his cell at Jarrow, the Moors had crossed from Africa
into Spain and planted the Crescent on the Pyrenees. Thence
they had poured through the passes into Gaul and the land
of the Franks.

In that dreadful hour it had seemed as though western
Christendom was broken. Then in A.D. 732 the Franks under
Charles Martel—mayor of the palace and chief minister to
their titular king—saved the West at Tours. Having secured
its southern frontier this great soldier with his tall Frankish
swordsmen turned eastwards against the heathens of central
Europe. It was with his help that St. Boniface of Crediton—
a Wessex thane's son who became the first archbishop of
Mainz—converted the German Saxons and advanced Christendom's outposts to the Elbe. Later this English evangelist,
with the Pope's blessing, anointed Charles's son, Pepin,
king of the Franks in place of the last Merovingian monarch.

Pepin's son, Charlemagne, like all the men of his age, was
haunted by memories of the imperial unity of the past.
Though four centuries had elapsed since the western Empire
had fallen, every attempt to revive civilisation led men back
to Rome. Though he could scarcely read and was framed
by nature for the saddle and the battlefield, Charlemagne
had a passionate admiration for learning. This blond, barbarian giant, who slept with a slate under his pillow and
made an English scholar, Alcuin of York, his chief counsellor
and head of his palace school, conceived the tremendous
ambition of reuniting the West in a new Roman empire in
place of the remote and now oriental empire of Byzantium.

He tried, though in vain, to reconquer Spain from the Moors; the heroic death of his general, Roland, in the Roncesvalles pass inspired Frankish poetry for centuries. And he sought, with greater success, to embody in his empire all his fellow Teutons beyond the Ems and Weser. For thirty years he warred against them, repeatedly defeating them and striving to break their stubborn savagery by enforced mass baptisms.

Yet more than to the eastern forests from which his fore-bears had come, Charlemagne's spirit was drawn to the Ro-man south. He saw himself as the head of Christendom and its guardian. Like his father, Pepin, he led a Frankish army across the Alps against the Lombard conquerors of north Italy. And on Christmas Day 800, as he knelt at mass in St. Peter's Rome, his ally, the pope, crowned him with tra-ditional imperial rites as emperor of the Romans. To dream-ers it appeared as if the hand of time had been set back and the Roman Empire restored. And it was now, it seemed, a Holy Roman Empire.

In Britain, too, attempts were made to revive the Roman past. Under the inspiration of Christianity the Anglo-Saxon kings were groping towards some wider union of society than the tribal gathering and pioneer settlement. Ine, king of the West Saxons—a contemporary of Charles Martel—published a code of written law for his people and made a pilgrimage to Rome. Half a century later Offa, king of Mer-cia, established an overlordship over the whole island south of the Humber and assumed the Roman title of *Rex Anglo-rum*, king of the English. He encouraged trade with the con-tinent, made a commercial treaty with Charlemagne—with whom he corresponded on friendly terms—and minted gold coins, some of which, bearing his name, circulated as far as the Moslem caliphate of Baghdad. And at home he built an earthen dyke to keep out Welsh raiders which, running from Dee to Wye, still marks the border between England proper and Wales and Monmouthshire.

Yet neither Charlemagne's vast empire, stretching from the Ebro to the Carpathians, nor Offa's smaller English king-dom endured. Barbarian kings, however lofty their aspira-tions, could not govern large areas. They lacked roads and bridges, trained servants, regular administration and justice. They could not give their peoples the security from which patriotism and the habit of subordinating self to the public interest arise. They thought of their dominions as family possessions which they were free to treat as they pleased. Even when they ruled, like Charlemagne, with a sense of vocation, they could not transmit it to their sons who by tribal custom had the right to divide their patrimony. Charlemagne's empire quickly dissolved after his death. Under his grandchildren and their heirs it was broken up into ever smaller kingdoms.

Nor were the methods by which the rulers of that age sought to widen their realms calculated to preserve them. Their Christianity, though strongly felt, was only skin-deep. Enraged by the resistance of the Saxon tribesmen, Charlemagne massacred his prisoners in thousands; Offa, founder and patron of monasteries, put out the eyes of a Kentish rival. Such actions created, not love and loyalty, but bitter hatred. When the strong hand of their perpetrators was removed, civil war and vengeance overtook the realms they had created. On Offa's death in 796 his English empire fell to pieces. So did the kingdom of Northumbria, whose rulers had tried to unite the northern half of the island by similar means. In less than a century five of its kings were murdered or slain in battle, five more deposed and four forced to abdicate.

The recurring problem of what historians call the Dark Ages—the long blood-stained centuries after the fall of Rome—was that of preventing society from disintegrating because its stronger members could not be subjected to any law but their own passions. What was lacking was a profession of dedicated kingship, pursued by hereditary princes with the power to preserve peace, social continuity and order.

It was in England that such a king appeared and at a time of universal disaster. For two hundred years Europe had been threatened from the south by crusading Moslems. Now a new and more dreadful threat arose in the north. It came from the fiords of Norway and the Jutland flats where the Scandinavian peoples—Norwegians and Danes—were on the move. The soil they tilled could no longer sustain their rising population, nor a pastoral life satisfy their more turbulent members. They were vigorous, picturesque, flamboyant rascals, younger sons of petty fiord-jarls for whom there was no place at home, with long flaxen hair, bright burnished spears and two-handed battle-axes. They delighted in silver-bound swords and jewels, golden bracelets and scarlet cloaks with brilliant borders. And, like all their race, they had a passionate love of independence. Around them they gathered bands of bloodthirsty followers, who feasted and drank in their halls in winter, sallying forth each spring "to play the game of Freyr". Berserks and wolfcoats they called themselves; wherever they went, they boasted, the ravens followed.

Accustomed to using the sea as a highway—the only communication between their scattered settlements—they were now offered a wonderful prize. Every spring the young pirate seamen of Norway and Denmark—Vikings as they were called from the *viks* or creeks they haunted—set out in fleets of long, narrow, open-decked war-boats, with carved dragon-heads, raven banners and bright, striped sails.[1] Following the mountainous island fringe of the Atlantic southwards from Norway, they plundered in turn the Shetlands, Orkneys, Sutherland and the Hebrides. In 802—two years after Charlemagne's coronation in Rome—they sacked the monastery of Iona. Then they fell on Ireland.

During the three centuries since Patrick's mission the Irish had achieved great things. Their monasteries and monastic schools were among the best and most learned in Europe; their illuminated manuscripts, like the lovely Book of Kells— still preserved at Trinity College, Dublin—the flower of western art. In the monk, John Scotus, they produced the first philosopher of the age, while their wandering scholars and poets fashioned verses more subtle than any to be found in that barbarous time. But politically they had changed little. Their titular High King still reigned with his fellow kings over their five sovereign and equal provinces, while a host of tribal chieftains kept their petty state and raided one another for cattle and hostages. Of unity, or capacity to combine against an external foe, there was none.

Thus the raiders' impact was calamitous. No-one could make any effective resistance. With their shallow-draft boats they swept up the estuaries and rivers, sacking every monastery, farm and building, and carrying off the younger men and women as slaves. Soon they took to wintering on the coast, making permanent forts on island and promontory. The round-towers whose ruins can still be seen were built as

---

[1] The word sail derives from their *seil*.

shelters from their ravages. Ireland's "golden age" of art and learning faded into the Atlantic mists at the whip of a few thousand arrogant Norsemen who knew how to combine and use the sea as a highway.

In 835 the Danes struck in force at England. That year they landed at Sheppey at the mouth of the Thames. Thereafter every spring their dragon-prowed boats, glittering with spears and axes, crept up the east-coast rivers. Securing themselves on some marsh-encircled island, they seized the horses of the neighbouring countryside and rode out to plunder and slay. If the bewildered farmers combined against them, they formed a ring and, with their massed battle-axes swinging over the "linden-wall" of shields, hacked a way back to their ships. Able to concentrate against any point, they could nearly always surprise and outnumber their victims. When they failed, they took to their boats and descended on some other point. Wherever they went they deliberately spread terror.

"From the fury of the Norsemen", prayed the peasants, "good Lord, deliver us!" So systematic were the ravages of these fearful pirates that by the middle of the ninth century, from the Humber to the Solent, hardly a vestige remained of a Saxon church within a day's ride of the coast. The kingdom of Northumbria, with its famous monasteries and beautiful crosses, crumbled to dust. So did the Fenland abbeys—Crowland, Peterborough and Ely. In 869 Edmund, last of the East Anglian kings, was barbarously slain for refusing to renounce his faith. When three years later the ruler of Mercia fled to the continent, only one English kingdom remained.

At that moment the Danes encountered in Alfred, a young prince or atheling of the House of Wessex, one of the great men of all time. Elected to the falling throne of the last Christian kingdom in England when everyone else was in despair and Christians all round the coasts of Europe were submitting to the terrible heathen, this modest, gentle, scholarly man refused to give in. He saw the weakness of the Viking leaders—their greed and savage rivalry—and knew that, if he could win time and sustain the courage of his people, he could beat them in the end.

At one time, deserted by almost everyone, he was forced to take refuge in the lake isle of Athelney, living, "in great sorrow and unrest among the woods and marshes of the

land of Somerset". Yet in the end, on the downs at Ethandun
—today Eddington—he won one of the decisive battles of
history. In victory his full stature became apparent. Having
shown heroism in adversity, he now practised the greatest of
Christian virtues. Undiscouraged by their past treachery, he
took pity on his enemies, fed them and offered them peace.
The Danish king accepted baptism—the first of his race to
do so. "King Alfred", wrote the latter's friend and biogra-
pher, Bishop Asser, "stood godfather to him and raised him
from the holy font."

For Alfred's true greatness lay not in war but peace. He
had the wisdom to see that the sword, though powerful to
defend, could settle nothing and that only a conquest of
hearts could endure. Around him lay, after two generations
of warfare, a ruined country—its farms wasted, its monasteries and schools burnt, its people reduced to ignorance and
squalor. Its nobility and even its clergy were almost completely illiterate. Alone in that ravaged land in his passion
for education—the fruits of an early journey to Rome—
Alfred set himself to teach his people. Nearly half his revenue was devoted to educational ends: to the training of
artificers, to the support of the foreign scholars and craftsmen he brought over as teachers from every country in
Christendom; to the restoration of ruined monasteries and
convents; to the great school he established for teaching the
sons of thanes and freemen to read and write and which in
the course of the next generation created something unique
in western Europe—a literate lay nobility. He made no pre-
tence of being a scholar; he sought only to expound the
learning of others. But he personally undertook the task—
as heroic as any of his feats in battle—of translating into
the rough vernacular of his country the most useful works
of Christian and classical knowledge. By doing so—for no-
one had essayed it before—he became the father of English prose.

Because of this, his work and kingdom endured. He left no
bitterness to be avenged after his death. He died soon after
his fiftieth year—probably in 899—worn out by his life of
struggle and danger. But he left to those who came after him
a free land recovering from its wounds, and an ideal of
kingship that was not of vain-glory but Christian service.
He had created two things that somehow were to survive
disaster and conquest—a kingdom to which educated En-

glishmen could feel they belonged and a native literature to enshrine their culture and traditions. More than any other man he was the first maker of England.

Alfred's policy had created a framework in which men of different races could forget their hatreds and live together in common allegiance. He and his victorious son and grandson did not drive the Danes out of England. They did something better; they turned them into willing and useful subjects. The speech and traditions of the Danes were closely akin to those of the English, and, when they had exchanged their swords for ploughshares and settled down in their new homes, they proved an asset to the nation. They were a vigorous, clear-headed folk: more alert and decisive than their English kinsmen. Like them they were excellent farmers, colonising the North-East, East Anglia and the eastern Midlands, while Norwegians settled in the Lake District, Lancashire, the Wirral and Isle of Man. Over the whole of this vast area, covering almost the entire country north of Watling Street, the newcomers were left to administer their own laws and customs. Loving liberty, they preferred a multitude of small holdings—tofts or shielings, they called them—to large estates, and covered the map of northern and eastern England with Scandinavian placenames. Like all the men of the North, they managed their own affairs in local public assemblies, gathering in the "thing" to debate questions of law and custom with their neighbours, and leaving high policy and war to their earls or jarls and the professional fighting men who feasted in their bright-painted, dragon-carved, sword-hung halls.

Their love of finery and beautiful objects—jewels, armour, splendid clothes and silver-mounted drinking horns—made the Danes great traders. When prevented from plundering, they took to commerce as the next best thing, and proved as able with the scales as the battle-axe. They loved to travel for barter and drive a bargain; they loved, too, to build and sail ships. By doing so they brought wealth of a new kind to England. They made its first trading-towns—York, Leicester, Lincoln, Nottingham, Derby, Stamford—and helped to make London again what it had been in Roman times, a great port.

It was largely due to the Danes—for having kinsmen in every maritime country they were an internationally-minded folk—that England took again to exporting surpluses of corn, skins, wool and honey. In exchange for these, foreign merchants imported wine and fish from Rouen, timber and pitch from Scandinavia, and pepper and spices for seasoning the dishes of the great, brought at incredible risk from the East by the traders of many lands—in Arab dhows across the Indian Ocean, on camels over deserts to the ports of the Levant, and thence from Venice across a turbulent Germany to Antwerp and the Thames. Others brought elephant-ivory from Africa and walrus-ivory from Greenland. Such "far-coming men" made London something more than a squalid little wooden town at a river ford in a forest clearing. Its empty spaces among the Roman ruins began to fill again with houses, its sokes or "liberties" to trade to be bought up, and its tolls, collected by the royal port-reeve or mayor, to swell the king's treasury at Winchester. With its eight mints, its rules for testing weights and measures, its guildhall and weekly folk-moot in the cathedral precincts, it became by far the largest city in the country, with perhaps fourteen thousand inhabitants by the end of the tenth century. On its wharves from Queenhithe to Billingsgate and in its streets of stalls—the Vintry where the merchants of Rouen traded, Dowgate with its Flanders and Cologne clothiers, Eastcheap with its goldsmiths from Ghent and Ponthieu—the tongues of half Europe could be heard.

The vast majority of Englishmen lived, not by selling to strangers, but by raising food for themselves in the place where they were born. Only salt for preserving—carried from village to village by pedlars—and iron for tools and ploughshares came from a distance. Except in time of war and invasion, the cycle of life never changed: the wheat or rye sown in the autumn and the oats or barley in the spring; the grain dried in the sun and winnowed on the threshing floor; the scraggy, minute cattle grazing on the common pasture or wintering on the stubble or in the byres; the herds of swine feeding on beech-mast in the woods; the lumbermen felling timber for house and palisade, tool and spear-shaft, and winning year by year more land for the plough. The "weorcman", with his bent shoulders striding beside his team of patient oxen, was the foundation on which the Anglo-Saxon kingdom rested. "I go out at daybreak", cried the ploughman in one of the earliest accounts of English rural life, "driving the oxen to the fields, and I yoke them to the plough. . . . I have a boy driving the oxen with a goad, and he is hoarse with cold and shouting. I have to fill the oxen's bins with hay and give them water and carry out their litter." His fellow labourers, the oxherd, swineherd and shepherd, had the same tale to tell. "I drive my sheep to their pasture at dawn and stand over them with my dogs in all weathers lest wolves devour them. I lead them back to their folds and milk them twice a day; and I make butter and cheese."

Such simple country folk lived, like the peasants of the East today, in rude shacks of wattle and mud with earthen floors, a hole in the roof to let out the wood-smoke and no lighting save the open door. After working all day—for only by doing so could they exist—they went to bed at dusk, having no means of light but the fire round which they slept or an occasional rushlight dipped in fat. Their shapeless clothes were of goat-hair and unprocessed wool, their food of rough brown bread and vegetable broth, small-ale from barley, bacon, beans, milk, cabbage and onion, and honey for sweetening and mead. In the summer they had boiled or raw veal and wild fowl and game snared in the forest. In the autumn they slaughtered and salted the cattle for whom there was no more pasture, and during the winter lived hard. When the harvest failed they starved, and famine was followed—as in the East today—by pestilence.

In such a life agriculture—its unchanging, unceasing demands, the knowledge and skill handed down from father to son and learnt from a lifetime of experience—occupied men's thoughts almost entirely. Their beasts and crops were their all. And since the Viking invasions had filled the woods and hills with robbers and outlaws some protection against the lawless strong had become a vital necessity for the cultivator. So had the help of some neighbour rich enough to enable him to replace his ruined crops and plundered stock. The thane, with his helmet and chain-armour—necessities far beyond the reach of the husbandman—and his burghgate and bell-house round which the community could rally, seemed the only possible linchpin of public order and security. His function was not to till the ground and gather the harvest, but to guard the peasant's home and fields, and, in time of war, turn out at the royal command in their defence. In return his neighbours, in proportion to the size of their holdings, had to contribute to his support.

In this way the small churl or free-holding farmer gradually sank into a dependent cultivator. He became a *gebur* or boor: a man whose working capital of beasts, tools and seed had been supplied by a lord to whose descendants he and his heirs paid a tribute of services, fines and produce. He continued, after paying the lord's dues, to enjoy the right to the produce of the land he tilled. The lord in turn had to pay similar dues for his lands to his own lord, who might be either the king or, more frequently, some greater lord standing between him and his sovereign. In this way he served not only to protect the local peace, but to administer the national services. Such was the beginning of what later became known as the feudal system. In a primitive age probably no better way of ensuring law and order could have been devised.

Among the royal rights over land granted to local lords by charter was the enjoyment of the fines and profits of local justice, and the franchise—called "sac and soc"—of holding private courts of law. These usually covered the enforcement of local order, and the power—*infangthef*—to try and hang a thief caught on land. The grant to a man on the spot, whose interest it was to enforce it, of the ancient tribal right to fine those who failed to attend local courts, helped to check the tendency—one natural as the State grew larger and more remote—of the peasant, absorbed in his own affairs, to leave the enforcement of law to others. To this extent such franchises, though sometimes tyrannically used, enlisted the motive-force of self-interest to preserve the principle that every man should take part in the administration of justice.

For the most valuable of all the institutions of the old freedom-loving Nordic tribes was that of communal or folk justice. The law was something that belonged to the whole community: after the soil its most precious possession and one that every man was expected to maintain. Every "kindred" or locality was traditionally responsible for the behaviour of its members and could punish and be punished for it. Communal witness to a neighbour's character lay at the root of English law. A man was publicly judged by his equals or fellow-suitors in the local court or, for graver breaches of the king's peace like resistance to his officials or the more extreme forms of violence, in the shire and hundred courts. These had grown out of ancient tribal assemblies called folk moots, and, like them, were held on benches in

the open air: usually at some sacred spot marked by a stone
and still commemorated in names like Kingston, Stone or
Maidstone. The suitors were the freeholders of the shire
or hundred, expressing their judgment by the customary
cry of "Ja, ja" or "Nay, nay", though in practice, because
of the difficulties of travelling, only the more important usually attended.

The deciding factor was the oath. Oaths were weighed
rather than counted and depended on a man's record, status
and property. A thane's oath was more valuable than a
churl's, and a churl's than a boor's. If a sufficiency of "oath-
worthy" neighbours or "compurgators" supported an accused
man's oath of denial, he was adjudged innocent. Other things
being equal, a denial outweighed an accusation. But the
oath of a man of suspicious character, or of one who had
been convicted of perjury, could be rejected in favour of
that of the plaintiff or accuser and his compurgators. A man
who could not clear himself by compurgation had to undergo
an ordeal by hot iron or water to determine his guilt.

The most common form of punishment was the fine. This
was a survival from the primitive blood-feud, by which a
man's kindred were both allowed, and in honour bound,
either to revenge an injury on the offender's kindred or exact
compensation. The Anglo-Saxon kings, seeking to end such
vendettas, which often continued for generations, encouraged
composition and, later, though with difficulty, made it com-
pulsory. And in their occasional laws they laid down tariffs
of charges for expiating particular crimes. Those committed
against men of property were more heavily mulcted than
those against humbler persons. Thus the wergild or man-
price for the murder of a "Welshman" or stranger was less
than that of an Englishman; of a Wessex churl only a sixth
of that for a nobleman, whose wergild was twelve hundred
shillings—the price of about five hundred oxen. The scale
varied from one part of the country to another; churls were
more highly valued in Kent than in Mercia or Wessex.

It was a rough and ready system. Under a strong king
justice was regularly enforced; under a weak one it degen-
erated into anarchy. Its incidence was often brutal; the basis
of Anglo-Saxon law before the Conversion had been an eye
for an eye and a tooth for a tooth. Many of its punishments
were those of barbarous savages. That for arson was burning,

for slander cutting out the tongue, for striking bad money the nailing of the coiner's hand to the door of his mint.

But for the Church and its creed of mercy, English law might always have remained savage and cruel. But because the Church taught that every man possessed an immortal soul, shared responsibility for his brother's guilt and ought to pity and relieve his distress, it tended, though slowly, to make the law more humane. It set its face against slave-raiding and slave-dealing, particularly the sale of slaves overseas, and did what it could to mitigate the slave's lot. It recognized his marriage as legitimate and denied its services to those who beat slaves to death, which the law, by refusing the poor creatures its protection, permitted them to do. And it encouraged the rich, by promises of remission of sin, to redeem and emancipate slaves. It used its influence, too, to substitute composition for the blood-feud. And it tried to protect the innocent by taking charge of the ancient pagan rites by which those who failed to purge themselves by compurgation were subjected to the judgment of the elements or Fate. The same forbearance towards the man rejected by society was shown in the Church's opposition to the death penalty. It did not question it out of any horror of death; on the contrary, its creed was founded on the conviction that death was only a temporary phenomenon. But it wished to give the criminal time in which to repent and save his soul. For the same reason it offered sanctuary at its altars to hunted men flying from vengeance: one that authority came to respect and which, though often abused, gave wrong-doers a second chance and the angry time for reflection.

The advance of Christianity was very slow. As always, it depended on individuals; on the human instruments through whom the Church worked. But during the century that followed Alfred's defeat of the Danes the process of rebuilding Christian society went on faster in England than in any other country. A great king had taught his people to defend their island home and had endowed it with a realm which was not for ever being partitioned among its princes. His descendants, the fair-haired athelings of the House of Wessex, produced in little more than half a century three other great rulers— Alfred's son, Edward the Elder, his grandson Athelstan, and his great-grandson Edgar. It was at Edgar's coronation that the earliest form of the service still used at the crowning of

England's kings was read by its author, the mystic saint and musician, Archbishop Dunstan. Behind the solemn rites—the royal prostration and oath, the archbishop's consecration and anointing, the anthem, "Zadok the Priest," linking the kings of the Angles and Saxons with those of the ancient Hebrews, the investiture with sword, sceptre and rod of justice, the shout of recognition by the assembled lords—lay the idea that an anointed king and his people were a partnership under God. After that sacramental act loyalty to the Crown became a Christian obligation. The ideal of patriotism first began to take vague shape in men's minds, superseding the older conception of tribal kinship.

It was this that helped to give England in the tenth century institutions stronger than those of any western land. Her system of taxation, of currency and coinage, of local government, of the issue of laws and charters were all in advance of those prevailing in the half-anarchical kingdoms and dukedoms of the former Frankish empire. As a result, though a country of little account at the world's edge, her wealth increased rapidly. It was part of her kings' policy to establish in every shire at least one town with a market-place and mint where contracts could be witnessed and reliable money coined. By the eleventh century there were more than seventy towns in the country. A dozen—Winchester, the royal capital, York, Norwich and Lincoln, Gloucester, Chester, Canterbury, Thetford, Worcester, Oxford, Ipswich and Hereford—had perhaps three or four thousand inhabitants, and one, the self-governing port of London, four or five times as many. Though most of them were ramparted, and a few walled, their real security and the source of their wealth was the king's peace and the confidence it inspired. The countryside was famous for beef, bacon and wheaten cakes, for ale, mead and perry, and for plentiful butter and cheese; a writer recorded that, while Italians cooked with oil, the English cooked with butter. Almost every village possessed a water-mill, and in the rich eastern counties of Norfolk and Lincoln often more than one. The Danish town of Derby had fourteen. The rivers swarmed with fish, and many places had eel-traps; the little Fenland town of Wisbech paid the abbot of Ely an annual rent of fourteen thousand eels. Chester sent its earldorman a thousand salmon a year, and Petersham in Surrey a thousand lampreys.

The heart of England's culture was no longer Northumbria

—now a wasted and depopulated province—but Wessex. Here, too, as in the northern kingdom that had welcomed Aidan and bred Cuthbert, Celtic blood and tradition mingled with Saxon. Even its early kings had borne names which were not Teuton, like Cerdic, Cynric, Ceawlin, and Celtic place-names were intertwined mysteriously in its western shires with English: Axe and Exe, avon for river, coombe for valley. The greatest Wessex figure of the age was Archbishop Dunstan, who, like his earlier countryman, St. Aldhelm, had been partly nursed in the tradition of Celtic Christianity. At Glastonbury, where as abbot his earliest work was done, legend went back far beyond the English conquest to the tiny wattle church which Joseph of Arimathaea was supposed to have built among the water meadows for the conversion of Roman Britain. Dunstan was a mystic, feeling his way to wisdom through visions and trances; he wrestled with fiends and monsters and heard mysterious, heavenly voices.

Wessex was now a settled land of villages, farms and fields whose names still figure on our maps. Its main outlines— church and parish boundary, mill, ford and footpath—were already what they were to remain for a thousand years. "See you our little mill," wrote a twentieth century poet,

> "that clacks
> So busy by the brook?
> She has ground her corn and paid her tax
> Ever since Domesday Book."

He might have added, earlier. Puttock's End, Cow Common, Crab's Green, Woolard's Ash, Doodle Oak—names of Essex fields and hamlets in the reign of Elizabeth II—were given them when the athelings of Wessex sat on the English throne. So were the boundaries of shire and hundred, and the cus-toms—themselves far older than their new Christian forms— with which men celebrated the changes of the year. Such were Plough Monday, when the village lads, with ribbons and cracking whips, resumed work after the twelve days of Christ-mas; May Day when they marched to the woods to gather greenery and danced round the May pole; Whitsun when the Morris dancers leapt through the villages with bells, hobby-horses and waving scarves; Lammas when the first bread was blessed, and Harvest Home when the Corn Dolly—effigy of a heathen goddess—was borne to the barns with reapers singing and piping behind. At Christmas the houses were decked with evergreen and the Yule candles lit.

With its fine craftsmen and the rule of its strong kings, England was beginning once more to accumulate treasures: to become a land worth plundering as she was before the Danes attacked her. Ivories and jewelled crucifixes, golden and silver candelabra, onyx vases and elaborate wood-carvings, superbly embroidered vestments, stoles and altar cloths adorned the churches and the halls and hunting lodges of the great. As they sat, in mantles of brightly coloured silks fastened with golden collars and garnet-inlaid brooches, listening to song, harp and minstrelsy, the princes and earldormen of Wessex were served from polished drinking-horns chased with silver and wooden goblets with gold. The century of Athelstan and Edgar saw a new flowering of Anglo-Saxon art. Archbishop Dunstan himself was a craftsman and loved to fashion jewellery and cast church-bells. He loved, too, to work in the scriptoria, as he had done as a young monk; in his day the illuminators of the monastic renaissance, with their gorgeous colouring and boldly flowing margins, reached new heights of achievement. So did the sculptors of the Winchester School who carved the angel at Bradford-on-Avon, the Virgin and Child at Inglesham, and the wonderful Harrowing of Hell in Bristol cathedral. The richer parish churches helped to house such treasures: small barnlike buildings, with primitive rounded arches, high walls and narrow windows and bell-towers crowned with weather-cocks—an English invention. A few survive, like the log church at Greenstead in Essex, flint and rubble Braemore in the Avon valley with its Anglo-Saxon text which no living parishioner can read, stone Barnack and broad-towered Earl's Barton in Northamptonshire.

In the depopulated north a simpler policy prevailed. Here Christian missionaries from harried Ireland were busy turning the Scandinavian settlements along the coasts and dales into Christian parishes. The wheel-head crosses that marked their open-air sites of worship show the transitional nature of the conversion: the carved Odin cross at Kirk Andrea in the Isle of Man with ravens croaking on a heathen god's shoulder, while on the other side Christ looks down in majesty; the Gosforth cross in Cumberland where the resurrected Saviour —Baldur the Beautiful of northern legend reborn—tramples the dragons and demons of Hell: Surt the fire-god, Fenris the wolf and Loki the serpent. The word "cross", derived from the Latin crux, was introduced by these Irish evangelists, gradually taking the place of the Anglo-Saxon "rood". It first appeared in northern names like Crosby and Crossthwaite. Other Scandinavian words were being woven into the map of northern England; gate a street and thwaite a clearing, fell a hill and thorpe a settlement, foss a waterfall and by a village. Similar Norse names—Swansea, Caldey, Fishguard, Gresholm, Haverford—appeared on the coasts of Anglesey, Pembroke- shire, Gower and Glamorgan.

Like their kinsfolk in the old Danelaw and East Anglia these northern dalesmen—pirates' brood though they were— had a great respect for law so long as they themselves made it. The very word entered England through their speech. So did the divisions or ridings into which they split the southern part of Northumbria, the juries of twelve leading men em- ployed in the administration of their towns and wapentakes, and their habit of majority decision. For it was a rule among these independent-minded men that, save in a boat or on the battlefield, they were all equal.

Yet all this polity and wealth depended in the last resort on the ability of English kings to keep the good order that Alfred had won. Not all the princes of the House of Wessex were great men or able to ride the tides of anarchy in an age still threatened by Viking invasions. Edgar's eldest son, a boy, was murdered at the instigation of his step-mother; the half- brother who succeeded him, Ethelred the Redeless, was a spoilt, petulant weakling. Under his inconstant impulses, and those of his brutal favourites, England's new-found unity dis- solved.

Once more, scenting weakness as vultures carrion, the Vik- ings returned. The European mainland was no longer the easy prey it had been; under the challenge of repeated invasion its divided peoples had learnt to defend themselves. Barred out of Europe, the Norsemen turned to England. For a generation they feasted on the carcass of a rich, leaderless land. Its monasteries again fell into decay, its farms were plundered, the peasants taxed into starvation and sold as slaves. The worst humiliation came in 1012 when the invaders pounced on Canterbury and carried off the primate, Alphege, and most of the monks and nuns. When the brave archbishop re- fused to appeal for a ransom, he was pelted to death with ox-bones by a pack of drunken pirates.

In the end, after a generation of rapine and bloodshed, a Danish conqueror, Canute, who had been converted to Christianity, was elected to the throne by the English Witanagemot or council of wise men. Ruling both England and Denmark he tried to make the North Sea and Anglo-Saxon lake and England part of a Scandinavian empire stretching from Ireland to the Baltic. But he died in 1035 with his work incomplete, and under his half-barbaric sons his realm disintegrated. Seven years later, when the last of them died "as he stood at his drink at Lambeth", the Witan chose as successor a prince of the old English line whose father had married a Norman princess. Edward "the Confessor" was a soft, devout, monk-like man, the chief interest of whose life was the building of an abbey—the "West minster" in the Thorney marshes near London on the model of a monastery in Normandy where he had spent his youth. Such was his piety that he even refused to give his wife an heir. Though his subjects greatly admired his saintliness and during his reign England suffered little from foreign invasion, under his flaccid, easy-going rule the feuds of the greater land-owners and earldormen kept her weak and divided.

CHAPTER III

THE NORMAN DISCIPLINE

THE DIFFICULTY that faced rulers in the Dark Ages was to make any system of government work except naked force. In tribal times a king could only impose his will when the horde was assembled for battle. When Clovis, conqueror of Gaul and the first king of the Franks, wished to preserve a chalice looted from Soissons cathedral, his sole resource was to split open the head of the head of the warrior who voiced the customary right of veto. The premature attempt even of a great ruler like Charlemagne to recreate an international empire based on law was shattered not only by the Norse raids but by the difficulty of keeping united large areas inhabited by primitive peoples. Without a trained bureaucracy the Roman system of raising revenue could not work; a Frankish king could only levy taxes by farming them out to local magnates.

Feudalism—the protection of the locality from predatory strangers by its stronger members—seemed the only answer until either the old imperialism could be recreated or a national order take its place. The local knight in his castle, with his horse, lance, shield and leather and chain armour, proved the answer to the invading hordes of Norsemen, Magyars and Moslems from which the West had suffered so long. His elaborate smith-made protection, his mobility and striking-power and his life-long dedication to arms made him despise mere numbers.

Yet, while he helped to save Europe, the feudal knight added to the problem of its government. If he was invaluable to his country's foes, he was equally so to its rulers and a scourge to everyone within reach of his strong arm. He lived for war and by it. His neighbours had to seek his protection or be ruined. The sole restraint on his power was that of the feudal superior from whom he received his lands. The knight's obligation to his overlord was the counterpart to the loyalty to the crown Alfred had tried to create in England. He did homage to him for his fief, swore *fidelitas* or fealty to him and gave him in war the precise measure of military service —neither more nor less—laid down in the terms of his enfeoffment.

It was the Church that took the lead in trying to discipline feudalism and harness it to constructive ends. It, too, had suffered from the anarchy caused by the invaders. Simony—the sale of sacred benefices—had become widespread; bishops paid kings and feudal lords at their consecration and recouped themselves from those they ordained, while patrons of livings exacted tribute from parish priests who in turn charged their parishioners for the Church's offices. At one time the papal throne was bought for a boy of twelve, who later sold it back to his godfather; at another there were three popes, all puppets of the feudal Roman nobility and one of them a man of notorious life. But in the eleventh century, when Edward the Confessor was governing—or rather failing to govern—England, a succession of great popes set themselves to reform the Church. Their aim was to rescue the Holy See from its dependence on local princes, to end the commerce in sacred benefices by enforcing canonical election, and to make the parish clergy a sacred caste apart by insisting on celibacy and continence. And in re-establishing law and order in ecclesiastical matters, they tried, also, to end the ravages of private feudal war. They set aside days and seasons for a "truce of God", when war was forbidden on penalty of expulsion from the Church's communion, and outlawed private fighting—at least in theory—from Thursday night till Monday morning. They sought, too, by an appeal to conscience, to present knightly power as a trust and to make knight errantry a Christian pursuit: to turn the aggressive, acquisitive Frankish freebooter, armed cap-à-pie, into a Christian champion, driving back the heathen, defending Holy Church and punishing iniquity. In chivalry, as it became called, the Church offered the military class a code of honour. It devised an elaborate ceremony at which the young knight, before being invested with arms, knelt all night in solitary prayer before the altar and, like the king at his crowning, took the Sacrament, swearing to use the power entrusted to him in righteousness and the defence of the helpless. And, for the sake of society, it invested the oath of fealty with mystery and sanctity. It was an offence against God, the Church taught, for a vassal to be false to his liege-lord.

In one State, in particular—the little warlike duchy of Normandy—the Church succeeded in establishing a working and mutually profitable partnership with the knightly class. A hundred years earlier, when Alfred's successors were creating a united England, a Viking pirate had secured from the ruler of West Francia or France—the western fragment of Charlemagne's disintegrated empire—a grant of conquered lands at the mouth of the Seine. Here, in what became named after them Normandy, intermarrying with the French and adopting their faith and language, a community of Norsemen established a dukedom whose disciplined chivalry of armoured knights evolved a technique of fighting from the saddle and stirrup that made them the arbiters of western Europe. They rode their horses through the waves of battle as their pirate forebears had sailed their ships. They loved fighting with lance and horse so much that, when they were not at war, they were for ever challenging one another in mimic tourneys where the victors held the vanquished to ransom and plundered their horses and armour.

They were masters, too, of law and rhetoric. They knew how to govern, just as they knew how to win battles, because they were quite clear what they wanted. They meant to get their way and, with harsh, logical insistence, they got it. Ruthless, almost entirely without sentiment, and though passionate, self-possessed and cool, they had the simplicity of genius. With their round bullet-heads, blue eyes and long aquiline noses, they looked like intelligent birds of prey.

Above all, they had energy. They were as restless as they were greedy and calculating. Like their Norse forebears they would go to the world's end for plunder. In the middle of the eleventh century a few hundred of them seized the south of Italy from the Byzantine Greeks. Then they went on to conquer the rich island of Sicily from the Saracens, the lords of the Mediterranean. An Italian who witnessed that astonishing conquest has left us their picture: dominant, harsh, revengeful, cunning, frugal, yet capable of lavish generosity when fame was to be won by it. "You never know," he wrote, "whether you will find them spendthrifts or robbers. . . . They are headstrong to excess unless they be curbed by the strong hand of justice. They are patient of cold if need be, patient of hunger, patient of hard work; they are passionately fond of hawking, of riding, of warlike armour and of splendid garments."

They had a genius for absorbing other civilisations. So thoroughly did they absorb that of the Frankish-Gaulish folk among whom they settled that within a century of their occupation of Normandy scarcely a word of their old Norse tongue was in use. They became a Romance or Latin speaking race and, having conquered a Christian land, fervent champions of the Church and the newly reformed papacy. Nowhere was the monastic reforming movement so enthusiastically supported by the laity, so many monasteries built and such learned and pious clerks appointed to well-endowed benefices. It was as though the Norman knights, the most acquisitive in Europe, were trying to offset their outrages by the orthodoxy of their ecclesiastical establishments and, while they stormed their way into their neighbours' lands, to buy an entry to Heaven. They became the greatest church-builders since the days of Charlemagne and even since those of imperial Rome, whose giant buildings they tried to copy. They were not delicate craftsmen like the English; their chief resource was to build immensely thick walls, and several of their grander achievements fell down.[1] But they had infinite ambition and a sense of space and grandeur.

Their buildings expressed their religion. Their patron-saint, standing above their churches with uplifted sword and outstretched wings, as the warrior archangel Michael, guardian of Heaven; their conception of God a feudal overlord, ready to reward those like themselves who kept the letter of His law. With the spirit they troubled themselves little; they were a practical folk who liked clear definitions. They built, not for comfort like the timber-loving Saxons, but in stone to endure. Their serried arches, marching like armies through space, the vast walls and pillars supporting them, the rude, demon-haunted figures gazing down from their capitals, symbolised the crude magnificence and vigour of their half-barbaric minds. With their grim massiveness and twin-towers rising into the sky like swords, such churches seemed designed, as Henry Adams wrote, to force Heaven: "all of them look as

---

[1] Dean Stanley used to say that when one went round the Norman churches of England, one was always safe in asking, "When did the tower fall?"

though they had fought at Hastings or stormed Jerusalem." [1]

After the collapse of Canute's empire the Normans turned their gaze on England. Its wealth, so much superior to that of Normandy, seemed a standing invitation. They viewed its easy-going provincials with a contempt they hardly tried to conceal: the words *pride* and *proud* first entered the English language to describe the arrogance of the Normans to whom the Confessor granted estates and bishoprics. As he had so conveniently refrained from giving his kingdom an heir, his great-nephew, the Duke of Normandy, formed the idea of claiming it for himself. He even succeeded in persuading his saintly uncle to promise it to him—though it was not by English law his to promise.

The English at that time were the most civilised people in western Europe. Their achievement in vernacular scholarship, poetry and literature was unique; their craftsmanship—in sculpture, embroidery, goldsmith's and coiner's work—most skilful and sensitive. They had evolved a union of Church and State for national ends which had no parallel outside the Byzantine empire; their bishops and earldormen sat side by side in the Witan and the provincial and shire courts. But to the radically minded Normans England was a land without discipline where the enthusiasm of saints and scholars had become lost in a sluggish stream of petty provincial interests; where married canons lived on hereditary endowments, and the very archbishop of Canterbury was a simoniac and uncanonically appointed, and where boorish nobles, sunk in swinish drunkenness and gluttony, sold sacred benefices, and bucolic warriors, too conservative to change, still fought on foot and with battle-axe. She had lost touch with the new world growing up beyond the Channel: with the international Church, with its reforming popes and disciplined monasteries, with the new ideals of chivalry, and the mailed knights, battle-trained horses, tall, moated castles which were now becoming the dominant features of the European landscape. She was living on the memories of the past, static, conservative, unimaginative. She had barred her mind to change; it remained to be seen if she could bar her gates.

The man who now set himself to conquer England was one of the great men of history. His mother was the unmarried

---

[1] Henry Adams, *Mont St. Michel and Chartres.*

daughter of a Falaise tanner; his great-great-grandfather had been a pirate. Left fatherless as a child, his boyhood had been spent amid the turmoil caused by the violence of his father's feudal barons. The ruin they unloosed had made an indelible impression on him. Far-sighted, patient, prudent, self-controlled, bold but thorough in all he did, and ruthless towards those who stood in his way, he made his little duchy, with its disciplined chivalry of armoured knights and ruddy-faced men-at-arms from the Normandy apple orchards, the most formidable force in Europe. Compelled to wage war in turn against his barons, his jealous neighbours in Maine, Anjou, and Brittany, and his feudal overlord, the titular king of France, he defeated them all. He never lost sight of his aims, never over-reached himself, and steadily increased his domains. When in his fortieth year he began to gather ships for the invasion of England, landless knights from every Frankish land flocked to his banners.

In that summer of 1066 England was assailed by two would-be conquerors. One, the king of Norway, seeking to re-incorporate her in a Scandinavian empire, was defeated on September 20th near his landing place in Yorkshire by Harold Godwinson, the Wessex earl whom the Witan, preferring to any of his jealous fellow earldormen, had elected to the throne on the Confessor's death. But when in October Harold hurried south to meet the other invader from Normandy he met his death in a desperate battle on the downs near Hastings, his house-carls dying round him to the last man. "In the English ranks," wrote the Norman chronicler, "the only movement was the dropping of the dead. . . . They were ever ready with their steel, those sons of the old Saxon race, the most dauntless of men."

The kingdom Alfred had made thus became a colony of a foreign dynastic empire—that of the dukes of Normandy, whose language and culture were French and who had little understanding of English ways. With a few thousand knights and men-at-arms William the Conqueror subjected a nation of between a million and a half and two million people. Duke of Normandy, he now became as well king of the English. At first, like Canute, he tried to govern them with the help of the native lords and prelates who accepted his conquest. Many of his earliest officials were English, and some of his first writs and charters were issued in their tongue—the last for three

hundred years. But he was faced by two inescapable difficulties. One was the need to reward the followers with whom
he had won and without whom he could not maintain his
throne; the other the obstinacy of the English and their hatred
of foreigners, particularly the French. He began by confis-
cating only the lands of those who had fought against him at
Hastings and whom, in keeping with his claim to be the Confessor's heir, he treated as traitors. But the discontent aroused
by the arrogance of his acquisitive barons and their rough
knights forced him to carry the process of confiscation further.
A widespread rising three years after the Conquest he suppressed with terrifying ruthlessness. During the next generation, seizing on every act of disobedience or rebellion, he
transferred the ownership of almost every large estate from
English hands to Norman. At the end of his twenty years'
reign there were only two major English land-owners left and
one English bishop. Almost every Englishman held his land
at the will of some Norman.

In this way William substituted for the old loose aristocratic
direction of the State a new and far more efficient one. He resumed the royal rights over the nation's land that his Anglo-
Saxon predecessors had improvidently "booked" away. He
kept a fifth for himself and his family, and a quarter for the
Church. Of the remainder he redistributed all but an insig-
nificant fraction among his hundred and seventy chief Norman and French followers on strictly defined conditions of
military service. Nearly half went to ten men. Having learnt
from his harsh life that no State or throne was safe unless
organised for instant war, the king attached to every grant of
land an inescapable martial obligation. In return for their
fiefs or "honours," as they were called, his tenants-in-chief,
including bishops and abbots, had to swear to support the
Crown with a fixed number of mounted and armoured
knights, to pay specified dues at stated times and to attend
the royal courts and councils. To meet these commitments
they in turn had to farm out their lands on similar terms to
professional knights or fightingmen, whom they "enfeoffed"
as their vassals.

Thus every substantial holding of land, whoever its im-
mediate occupier, was made to furnish and maintain an
armoured, mounted and battle-trained knight ready to take
the field at any moment. As well as serving the needs of its
peasant cultivators, who had to perform the same manual

services, or more, for its new owner as its old, it became a knight's fief or fee, itself part of some greater fief or "honour." If its feudal holder failed to perform his military services, it reverted to the overlord to whom he had sworn allegiance for it. It could neither be broken up nor sold without the latter's consent, and on its holder's death his heir, after paying a fine and doing homage, had to render the same services.

To a large extent this system had already been established in France and other parts of western Europe. Yet it was unique—a mark of William's creative genius—in its identification of the protection of the fief with that of the realm. It was the absence of this that had so troubled his own early life in Normandy and broken up the old English kingdom. In the Conqueror's new England the holder of every substantial military fief had to do homage for it, not only to his overlord, but to the Crown.

For after William had crushed two rebellions in which disloyal Norman tenants-in-chief had called out their vassals against him, and at a time when a new rising and a Danish invasion were theatened, he held, at the Christmas feast and council at Gloucester in 1085, "very deep speech with his wise men." Next year he summoned a meeting at Salisbury, not only of his tenants-in-chief, but of all principal landholders in the country. And by making them swear to obey him even against their own overlords, he made them directly responsible to the Crown as in no other State in Europe. By this simple device, he turned feudalism, without weakening its military efficiency, into an instrument of royal power. He became not only, like the King of France, the nominal lord paramount of the realm, but the actual one. He was able to do so because, having conquered England and its land, he started with a clean slate.

Nor did William make his nobles rulers of provinces like their English predecessors or their counterparts in France. Whether by accident or design, he scattered their estates about the country. This not only made it harder for them to rebel, but forced them to think in national as well as regional terms. Abroad the feudal count, like the old Anglo-Saxon earl, thought only of his county or province; in England, like the king himself, he had to think of the country as a whole. Henry de Ferrers, rewarded with 114 manors in Derbyshire, was given 96 in thirteen other counties. A still greater tenant-in-chief, Robert de Mortain, held his 793 manors in twenty different shires. The only exceptions were on the Welsh and Scottish borders, where the local magnates needed vast powers to keep the tribesmen of the Celtic west and north at bay. The prince bishop of Durham, and the earls of Chester, Shrewsbury, and Hereford, ruled what were later called counties palatine. Yet even these were small compared with the independent provinces of France, and the king appointed to them only men he could trust. He watched them very closely. Within half a century of the Conquest only two of these compact, semi-independent jurisdictions remained.

Within these limits—a framework of discipline in which every baron enjoyed his just feudal rights, but no more—William scrupulously respected the "liberties" of his nobles. They were the instrument by which he ruled. Less than two hundred French-speaking barons—closely inter-related and accustomed to working together—and five or six thousand knights became the principal land-holders of England. Having both a duty and incentive to protect the Conquest, they guaranteed its permanence. They formed a new ruling caste; a colonising warrior aristocracy that possessed not only privilege but creative energy. The names they brought from their Norman homes are writ on our maps and across our history —Montgomery and Mandeville, Warenne and Giffard, Baldwin and Mortimer, Mowbray and Beaumont, Neville and Lacy, Bohun and Courcy, Beauchamp and Percy.

Beneath this military superstructure the Conqueror had the sense to leave England much as it was. He kept the Witanagemot, which became the Great Council of his tenants-in-chief, lay and ecclesiastical. He kept the elaborate secretarial and financial machinery which the English kings had devised for raising gelds and land-taxes, and for sending out enquiries and orders to their officers in the shires. He kept the old divisions of shire and hundred; the shire-courts where, under the royal sheriff's eye, the freemen interpreted the customary law of the locality, and the hundred-courts where representatives of the villages—priest, reeve and leading peasants—settled their disputes and answered for breaches of the peace. He left unchanged the free communities of the Danelaw and the ancient tenures by which the Kentish cultivators were protected in their holdings. He left, too, with the Norman manor superimposed on it for military and taxing purposes, the midland English village, with its strip-divided fields, its hereditary rights of cattle-pasture and pig-pannage, its communal system of cultivation and wide variety of tenures. He left the Londoners the rights they had always enjoyed under their elected portreeve and burgesses. And he kept the old Anglo-Saxon shire fyrd or militia—an invaluable counterpoise to the Norman feudal array.

Wherever an English institution could serve his end, William improved on it. Having got rid of the independent provincial earls who under Ethelred and the Confessor had acquired the un-English right to own and rule land without relation to the service to the Crown for which it had been granted, he used in their place the sheriffs or royal officials with whom his predecessors had vainly tried to check the earls' powers. The Norman sheriff administered the royal estates in the shire, presided at its court, collected the taxes and led the shire militia in time of war or rebellion. This linked the Crown with the forces, so strong in medieval society, of local patriotism and self-interest and made for national unity. So did the system—possibly brought from France, but adapted also from Anglo-Saxon and Danish practice—by which sworn juries or panels of neighbours were made judges of local questions of fact. William used these repeatedly to discover the rights of the Crown against his powerful Norman followers and the taxable value of their estates.

For most Englishmen all this was a terribly painful process. "Cold heart and bloody hand," wrote a Norse poet, "now rule the English land." William was guilty, in his own dying words, of "the barbarous murder of many thousands, both young and old, of that fine race of people." [1] To many the Conquest brought bitter tragedy; the families of those who died in battle, the peasants on the line of march, the thanes whose lands were seized to provide fiefs for William's foreign barons and knights. All who made the least resistance were ruthlessly stripped of their estates in pursuit of the royal policy. Most of the old English nobles and thanes who sur-

---

[1] "I have persecuted its native inhabitants beyond all reason. Whether gentle or simple, I have cruelly oppressed them; many I unjustly disinherited; innumerable multitudes, especially in the county of York, perished through me by famine or the sword." Ordericus Vitalis, The Ecclesiastical History cit. *English Historical Documents,* I, 286.

vived Hastings and the later rebellions in the west, north and midlands became mere farmers; at Marsh Gibbon in Buckinghamshire—the Conqueror's great tax-survey records—Aethelric, the former owner, "now holds it of William, the son of Ansculf, in heaviness and misery." [1] Some fled to Scotland, where they strengthened the Saxon elements of that wild land, or took service in the Varangian bodyguard of the Greek emperor at Constantinople. A few brave men, preferring liberty to life, took to the marshes and forests as outlaws, like Hereward the Wake, a small Lincolnshire landowner who held out in the Fens till 1071. "Most", as William Fuller wrote six centuries later, "betook themselves to patience which taught many a noble hand to work, foot to travel, tongue to entreat."

Humbler folk were left in possession of their holdings; Norman and English alike would have starved otherwise. Yet many of them were subjected to the tyranny of the special courts which the Conqueror set up in the forests, still covering more than a quarter of the land, to preserve the red and fallow deer for his hunting. "He loved the tall stags like a father", we are told. To guard them his forest officers put out the eyes of any man found killing hart or hind, and mutilated poor peasants caught in the woods with dogs or arrows. In these sacred precincts even the lopping of a bough was punished. Rich and poor alike murmured at the king's forest laws, but "he was so sturdy that he recked nought of them."

William was hard and ruthless: "so stark a man," an English monk called him. After the second rising of the northern counties in 1070, when five hundred Norman knights were massacred at Durham, he so harried the countryside that along the road from York to Durham not a house remained standing. Even the northern capital and its famous minster were burnt. It took the north generations to recover. Seventeen years later the royal commissioners, surveying the tax capacity of Yorkshire, entered against place after place the grim word, "Waste."

Above all, the Conqueror was a merciless taxer. His first act after his coronation was to "lay on a geld exceeding stiff." Close-fisted and grasping—a monk complained that, while the

---

[1] *"Graviter et miserabiliter"*—one of the few human touches in that grim, invaluable record.

Saxon kings gave their courtiers four meals a day, he gave his only one—he had compiled after 1085, mainly that he might tax his realm more closely, a record of all feudal holdings directly or indirectly liable to the Crown. "So narrowly did he cause the survey to be made," wrote an English chronicler "that there was not one single hide nor rood of land, nor —it is shameful to tell, but he thought it no shame to do— was there an ox, cow or swine that was not set down in the writ." Using commissioners to hold local enquiries or inquests in every shire and hundred, he had recorded, with meticulous efficiency,[1] the ownership and taxable value of every manor or village under lordship, both at the Conquest and at the time of the survey. This included the number of its ploughlands or hides,[2] of the freemen, villeins, cottars and slaves living on it, of its mills, fish-ponds and plough-teams, the extent of its woodland, meadow and pasture—everything, in short, that was capable of being taxed. Originally drawn up on long parchment rolls stored in the Treasury at Winchester, the survey was copied into two volumes christened by the English "Domesday" because there was no appeal against it. It was the most remarkable administrative document of the age; there is nothing like it in the contemporary annals of any other country. It enabled the king to know the landed wealth of his entire realm; "how it was peopled and with what sort of men," what their rights were, and how much they were worth.

The taxation William imposed fell directly on the rich, but, as the rich could pass it on, even more severely on the poor. The peasants' burdens, the labour and boon-services demanded of them by their lords, became heavier. The English thane, who had taken part of the village produce as his due and occasionally summoned its reluctant young men from the plough to serve in the earldorman's levies, was supplanted by a Norman or Frenchman. There was a new face—and a new tongue spoken—at the manor house. It is never pleasant to have to pay taxes and rent. It is far worse to have to pay them to a foreigner. And these foreigners were great sticklers for their rights. They left no one in any doubt that they were the masters of the country and regarded the natives as a con-

[1] He employed a second body of commissioners to check the findings of the first. F. M. Stenton, *Anglo-Saxon England*, 609.

[2] Usually reckoned at about 120 acres, though its size varied in different parts of the country.

quered race. In those harsh years when Norman knight and
English churl were learning uneasily to live together, many
an English back must have smarted from the lash of a French
man-at-arms. So must many a sullen English heart.

Behind the Norman knight's bailiff, with his bullying ways
and grasping demands, was the castle which his master built
to house his retainers and overawe the neighbourhood. Everywhere, on strategic hill and vantage point, the castles rose—
little islands of foreign power in a subjected countryside: the
high, circular, moated mound, raised by English labour and
crowned by a wooden, and often later stone, keep or tower;
the outer bailey with its earthwork enclosure and barracks,
whence knights and men-at-arms rode forth to police and
terrorise the countryside; the moat with its drawbridge. Even
proud London was overawed by its Tower, begun in wood
immediately after the Conquest and in stone a generation
later.[1] The heavily armoured Norman retainers—*cnihtas* or
knights, as the English called them—who garrisoned these
strong-points had the whip-hand of the countryside. A poor
man, if he was to live and till the soil in peace, had to make
what terms he could with them. Otherwise he might find his
house burnt over his head, his wife and children driven into
the woods, and himself thrown into a stinking dungeon.

Yet the Norman Conquest brought compensations to the
underdog. William conquered more than the English. He used
the heritage of Alfred to curb his own turbulent nobility. He
brought feudalism under royal control. The stark king fastened his English version of the feudal system, with all his
Norman thoroughness, on the free-booter barons and knights
who had so long kept western Europe in an uproar with
their selfish civil wars. It was this that completed the work
that Alfred had begun. It made England a disciplined land,
disciplined not only at the base but at the summit. A man
could cross her, it was said, with his bosom full of gold.

By making England one, William saved her, too, from
future conquests. He closed the door on the northern barbarians who had ravaged her for three centuries and who now
withdrew into the Scandinavian mists. Twice during his reign
the Danes were invited by rebellious subjects to land on the

[1] The White Tower, with its 15-feet thick walls, is the only surviving part built by the Conqueror. The words *castle* and *tower*
both entered the English language at this time.

east coast, and twice were driven out with no profit to themselves and disastrous consequences to their sympathizers. Though, with Norsemen settled round her northern and western shores, Scotland still looked for another generation to the barbarian North, England ceased to be a frontier land between the Viking world and the reviving civilisation of western Europe. Henceforth her lot lay with the lands that had inherited the memories and traditions of Rome. Having under Canute been part of a Scandinavian empire spanning the North Sea, she became part of a Norman-French empire spanning the Channel.

CHAPTER IV

MONKS AND FRIARS

IT HAD BEEN the monks who had first taught the English and Normans the arts of civilisation. Five hundred years before the Conquest, when the Anglo-Saxons had been rooting out the last traces of Roman and Christian civilisation from southern Britain, the Italian St. Benedict had founded at Monte Cassino the monastic rule that for the next six centuries was to be the spearhead of human progress. With his Roman passion for order he had established his "little rule for beginners," based on vows of obedience, poverty and chastity. He laid down times for prayer and work, ordering every hour by the monastery bell, and insisted on the importance of manual labour. Idleness he denounced as the enemy of the soul. "The brethren must work with their hands, and at other times must study holy books . . . Let them serve in turn and let none be excused the work of cook. If possible let the monastery be so that all necessary work, in mill, garden and bakehouse, can be done within it . . . Let no-one have any property—not a pencil, nor a pocket book, nothing whatsoever—for there are they whose bodies and wills even are not their own. In a monastery none follows the will of his own heart."

The Benedictine monasteries had become islands of example in a confused, ignorant world. Their black-gowned monks built churches and granaries, converted and taught the heathen, farmed and made gardens and practised the, but for them, forgotten arts of music, painting, carving and sculpture, metalwork, bell-casting and organ building, and laboriously, with loving and beautiful skill, copied books and manuscripts. And when the frail plant of civilisation had been all but destroyed by the Viking invasions, it had been Benedictine monks from Cluny in Burgundy who had revived it, re-establishing their founder's neglected rule in the ruined monasteries of the western kingdoms. In the days of King Edgar and Archbishop Dunstan, Worcester, Bath, Cerne, Winchcombe, Eynsham and Abingdon, Thorney, Crowland, Ely and Peterborough had all been restored as beacons of light and learning.

Though, by the time of the Norman Conquest, in most of the larger houses the monks had ceased to do menial work, they were still dedicated men, living lives of disciplined worship and contemplation apart from the world. They rose from their pallets in the dormitories after midnight to troop down cold corridors to celebrate Matins and Lauds in the chapel; assembled for admonition or punishment and to discuss the business of the day in the chapter house—so called because every day a chapter of St. Benedict's rule was recited aloud there—dined in silence in the refectory, where the officers and their guests sat in state on the dais and the monks at long tables below, as in an Oxford college today, while one of the brethren read a Latin homily; laboured in the monastic fields, gardens and workshops or copied and illuminated books in the scriptorium, whose desks looked through unglazed arches on to the grass garth of the cloisters; taught the novices and prescribed to the sick until the hour of Vespers recalled them once more to their devotions. From the first moment of the day to the last, when Compline was sung before they withdrew at dusk to their dormitories, their lives were ordered by the chapel bell—a sound familiar in every part of Christendom.

It would be hard to exaggerate the part played by the monastic houses in forming English institutions. Our schools, universities and charitable foundations all grew out of their ordered life. The names of their officers still survive in our societies and collegiate bodies: the precentor in charge of the music, services and books, the chamberlain of the clothing and bedding, the sacristan of the church fabric and sacred vessels, the cellarer of the provisioning and the bursar of the finances, the infirmarer of the hospital, the almoner of the charities. In that simple rustic world there was nothing to compare with these establishments, with their libraries, dormitories and guest-houses, kitchens, butteries, bakehouses, breweries, laundries and dairies, their workshops, granges, barns, fish-ponds, orchards, vineyards and gardens—the first to be made in Britain since Roman times—their water-pipes, drains and filter-tanks. Far in advance of the richest layman they even possessed lavatories, with long stone or marble washing-troughs, brass water-cocks and towels. And in their infirmaries, where the monks were periodically bled, bath-houses were provided for bathing the sick and aged and, before the great Christian feasts, the entire chapter.

Such institutions were teachers and exemplars, not only of learning and piety, but of the arts of life. In the Customary of St. Augustine's, Canterbury, which William the Conqueror's Italian archbishop, Lanfranc, restored to its ancient monastic constitution, the monks were enjoined not to crack nuts with their teeth, make signs across the refectory or lean on the table. "The dishes are not to be broken or dirty or smeared on the underneath," ran the Rule of Barnwell priory; "the brethren ought all to be careful not to wipe their noses or rub their teeth on the napkins or tablecloths." [1] Every three weeks the monastic linen was washed, and in summer every fortnight. In the guest-house, where travellers were entertained, the hosteller kept a store of clean towels and sheets, well-scrubbed salt-cellars and porringers, silver spoons and basins, fresh rushes for the floor and straw for the beds, candles, candlesticks and writing materials.

The wealth and prestige of the monasteries grew with every generation. At the magnificent services which were held at their shrines—the greatest events of the medieval year—offerings were showered on them by multitudes of deeply moved Christians. Most visitors left donations with the houses that sheltered them; every rich man wished to win prestige on earth and a mediator in Heaven by some gift or legacy to the saint or martyr commemorated by the local shrine: blessed Alban or Edmund, Peter or Paul, or the tender, merciful Virgin. In men's minds the monasteries were personally identified with these divine personages. Their jewelled shrines and crosses, golden and silver vessels and candlesticks, embroidered altarcloths, chasubles and dalmatics, their rare books bound in gold and the hallowed relics brought from afar by visiting kings and princes were the glory of neighbourhood and kingdom. Their wealth was immense. An abbey like St. Albans or Bury St. Edmunds might have estates in a dozen counties. Its officers were constantly travelling to collect its rents and dues. Every fortnight Ramsey drew from the village

[1] D. H. S. Cranage, *The Home of the Monk*, 23–4.

whose turn had come to supply its kitchens twelve quarters of flour for the monks' and guests' bread, 2000 loaves for its servants, ten fat pigs, fourteen lambs, 120 hen, 2000 eggs, and vast quantities of malt, honey, lard, cheese, butter, beans and horse-fodder.

Monks were members of exclusive, self-renewing societies. Subject to the rules of their Orders, and except where their church was a bishop's throne—where it became the custom in England for them to accept the king's nomination—they elected their own heads and admitted to their privileged circle only those they approved. An abbot or presiding prior of a great monastery was lord of a vast property. It was not enough for him to be, like old Abbot Hugh of Bury, "a good and kindly man, a godfearing and pious monk but in temporal matters unskilful and improvident." If he was, the abbey soon fell into debt to the Jews—forever, before their expulsion from England at the end of the thirteenth century, offering tempting loans on its treasures—or was cheated of rents and services by grasping knights and cunning peasants. When in Henry II's reign Samson, the sub-sacristan of Bury, was elected in Hugh's stead, the holy Edmund himself was said to have appeared to one of the brethren in a vision, predicting that the new abbot—unlike his senile predecessor—would be "constant in labour, alike when disputing with the archbishop of Canterbury about the pleas of the Crown, when striving with the knights of St. Edmund for the payment of scutage, with the burghers about encroachment on the market or with the sokemen for the suits of hundreds." Samson proved all that the saint had foretold, holding inquests into the abbey's rights on every manor and into the obligations of all its villeins and freeholders. He cleared wastes and brought them into cultivation, made and stocked parks and fishponds, rebuilt halls, granges and chapels, replaced reed and straw roofs with stone and lead and paid off the abbey's soaring debts to the Jews, entering all in a book which he kept daily "as if he saw in it the image of his probity in a glass."

Many abbots left such minor details to their subordinates; Samson was an exceptional man. An abbot normally had enough to do without being an accountant. He was the father confessor of a community whose influence was nation-wide. He might sit in the great council of the realm; he presided regularly over the feudal court of the abbey's barons, knights and freeholders. He played a leading part in the affairs, not only of the monastery but of the neighbourhood, acting as a judge in a wide range of secular affairs. When, for instance, a poor girl begging her bread from door to door was assaulted by one of the sons of Richard FitzDrogo, it was Abbot Samson who imposed a heavy fine to compound the wrong and settled it on the girl and a passing pedlar who agreed to marry her. And, like the monastery itself, he had to provide hospitality for a constant succession of great travellers, including the king. Samson, we are told, "whenever any important guest arrived, used to sit with his monks in some retired grove and watch the coursing for a while." For an abbey played as large a part in the social life of the nation as in the religious, political and economic. Its prestige, and that of its saint's shrine, was a matter of widespread concern. A broil between the burghers of Bury and the abbey servants during the Christmas feast led to the abbot discontinuing his customary hospitality and threatening the offenders with excommunication, whereupon "they all went out from the church and, having taken counsel, stripped themselves and, naked except for their underclothes, prostrated themselves before the door." Even the smaller houses were the leading institutions of the countryside in which they stood; when, after a riot, the mayor of Oxford surrendered the keys of the town to the prior of St. Frideswide's, he did so on bended knees.

In days when there were no hotels, newspapers or posts, the monasteries, with their international organisation, were the means of communicating news, learning, crafts, and discoveries. They provided the schools, hospitals and libraries of the age. They trained its artists, scientists, physicians and writers. A monk of Malmesbury invented a flying machine that flew a furlong; the same house had a medical school started by an Italian to which patients came from every part of the country. Most of the larger abbeys maintained a succession of historiographers who compiled elaborate, if somewhat inaccurate, chronicles of their times; William of Malmesbury, Florence of Worcester, Eadmer and Gervase of Canterbury, and the two thirteenth century chroniclers of St. Albans, Roger of Wendover and Matthew Paris, are among the fathers of English history. And from the cloisters the Christian kings, who were slowly creating England and the other infant states of Europe, drew officers trained in regular habits of routine, business and accountancy, and, still more important, in ideals of public service. The monastic officers were called "obedientiaries"; they commanded because they obeyed. Nowhere else could those who had to keep order over large areas find men so fit for their business. For the Church offered a far wider choice of trained servants than the feudal families whose sons were usually taught only to hunt and fight. Through its hierarchy unaccounted men could rise to the proudest posts in Christendom; could become bishops and abbots, justiciars, chancellors and royal ministers. So the great statesman, Suger, who, as minister to two kings, laid the foundations of French monarchial power in the second quarter of the twelfth century, began his career as an acolyte, serving the altar of the monastery for which his father had worked as a serf. His contemporary Adrian IV—the only Englishman to become pope—had begged his boyhood's bread at the gates of St. Albans abbey.

The Norman conquest coincided with a monastic revival throughout western Europe. In 1066 there had been only thirty-five monasteries in England, and only in two or three had the monk's habit been worn. One alone—Burton—lay north of the Trent. During the next half century, not only were the older Benedictine houses revitalised by the French and Italian abbots whom the Conqueror imported from the Cluniac foundations on the continent and from the monastic schools of Normandy, but for the first time since the Danish invasions, monasteries reappeared after a lapse of two hundred years in the ravaged lands beyond the Humber.

But the real revival of monastic life in the north occurred in the reign of Henry I with the coming of the Cistercians. The splendour, wealth and magnificent ritual of the Benedictine houses, even after the Cluniac reforms, had left the more austere spirits of the age unsatisfied, and during the twelfth century a movement began in France to restore the simplicity and poverty of early monastic rule. In 1128 the first Cistercian house in England was founded at Waverley in Surrey. But is was among the desolate Yorkshire hills and the remote valleys of the Welsh Marches that the Order made its chief settlements. It was part of its Rule that its monks should live far from the haunts of men, in silence and austerity, and support themselves by their own labour. Even their rough, homespun woollen tunic and cowls were undyed, giving them their name of white monks in contrast to the black monks of the older Rule.

Their simplicity of life and love of solitude and country pursuits made a deep appeal to the English. By the middle of the century there were twenty Cistercian monasteries in Yorkshire alone, and forty in the kingdom. Fountains, founded in 1132 on waste ground in Skeldale by a dozen pioneers from St. Mary's, York, grew from a few huts under an elm tree into the great abbey of St. Mary's. Rievaulx, Jervaux, Byland and Kirkstall, Tintern, Valle Crucis, Neath, Abbey Dore and Margam, raised in the twelfth and rebuilt in the thirteenth and fourteenth centuries, were among the grandest achievements of the Middle Ages. Bare today of ornament, sculpture and painting, their grave, simple outlines have still the power, even in ruin, to stir the heart. Equally impressive were the woods the monks planted round their homes and the sheep-runs the lay brethren or *conversi*—drawn from the peasant class—made on the bleak northern and western hills. They were the most enlightened landlords and finest farmers of the age, sowing alternate corn and grass leys and transforming scrubby wilderness with flocks that grazed by day on the uplands and folded at night on the barley ploughlands. Theirs was an instinctive genius for blending the works of God and man; in the Great Coxwell barn in Berkshire we can still see the reverence and skill with which they turned nature to human ends while enriching and beautifying it. *"Laborare est orare"*, was their founder's motto: to work is to pray. They built roads and bridges, drained marshes and planted trees, quarried stone, wrought in wood and metal, laid out gardens and vineyards and bred fine horses, cattle and sheep. To them England owed the noble Lion breed whose golden hoof raised the Cotswold towns and villages. They made her wool as famous as their brother monks of Citeaux made the vineyards of the stony *Côte d'Or*. And if the great names of Chambertin and Clos de Vougeot still recall for lovers of wine the skill of the French Cistercians, their brethren in England are commemorated by the homely cheese which the monks of Jervaux made from ewe's milk in lonely Wensleydale.

Nothing gives a clearer idea of the might of the medieval Church than to stand in one of the cathedrals, still towering above the roofs of our modern towns, that were first raised as monastic churches. They express the universal sense of the importance of religion and the soaring imagination and practical genius of men who had mastered the lost Roman art of vaulting great spaces in stone. Most of them were originally built on the site of smaller Saxon churches by English masons in the massive Norman style under the prelates whom the Conqueror imported from Normandy, and rebuilt in a still more ambitious style under their successors in the latter twelfth and early thirteenth centuries. Canterbury, whose choir Lanfranc started to build with Caen stone in 1072, Rochester begun five years later, Ely, with its magnificent nave, in 1083, Worcester in 1084, and the incomparable Durham in 1093, with its ribbed vaulting—the earliest of its kind in Europe—and its still surviving Norman nave and choir; Norwich, Winchester and Coventry—were all made for monks. So were the abbey churches of St. Albans—built partly from Roman tiles and stones—Westminster, Gloucester, Peterborough, Bath, Chester, Malmesbury, Tewkesbury, Pershore, Sherborne and Bury St. Edmunds, whose nave, over 300 feet long, surpassed that of our largest cathedral today.

These vast edifices were miracles of construction. So were the non-monastic cathedrals served by secular canons, which the Normans raised in London, York, Old Sarum, Lichfield, Lincoln, Exeter, Carlisle, Chichester, Hereford and Wells. They were built without any but the most elementary mechanism for moving and lifting large weights, by men whose wealth consisted almost entirely of crops, flocks and herds and whose sole means of transport were wheeled carts drawn by oxen. To realise the magnitude of their achievement one has only to reckon what it would cost even with modern machinery and power, to rebuild in stone every cathedral and parish church in England. Yet this is what the men of the twelfth and thirteenth centuries did at a time when the population was only a small fraction of its present size. "It was as though," a chronicler wrote, "the very world had shaken herself and cast off her old age, and was clothing herself everywhere with a white robe of new churches."

The architecture of these cathedrals expressed the unity of existence in which their builders believed: the ordered vaulting; the pillars rising out of the earth like trees; the stone walls and arches carved with flowers and leaves, animals and men; the light of heaven flooding in through windows, at first plain but later painted, like the ceilings, in brilliant colours; the arches soaring into the sky, and the whole made one by the idea, implicit in every image and symbol, of God over all and judging all, and Christ and his Mother, the Virgin, pitying and loving all. Great sacrifices were made by clerics and laymen alike to raise these monuments to their faith; one abbot gave the entire woolcrop of his manors for a year to provide a tapestry hanging, while the monks of Abingdon sold the gold and silver from their shrines to build their new church. Relics of saints and martyrs—the monasteries' most precious possessions—were taken on tours round the country to raise money from the laity, who gave, not only gifts in money and kind, but even sometimes their labour to help the travelling bands of professional masons and craftsmen to whom the work of construction was entrusted.

Though maintained by native endowments many of the monasteries were subject to the rule of international organisations and responsible, through their chapters-general, to the pope as the head of Christendom. For the monks were the "regulars" of Christ's army in contradistinction to the "secular" and local clergy of the diocese and parish. So after their foundation in the thirteenth century were international Orders of a different kind, whose members, also following a disciplined Rule, served God, not like monks in the cloister, but in the street and field. Bound by vows of chastity and poverty, the mendicant friars or brothers, abjured the static, conventual life of the monastic Orders. The black-gowned Dominicans or preaching friars were founded by the Spaniard, St. Dominic, to combat the heresies which had swept southern Europe at the close of the twelfth century. The Grey friars or Franciscans—sometimes called Minorities because they were *minores* or "lesser brethren" who served the poor—were founded a few years later by a rich Italian clothier's son, Francis of Assisi, who abandoned a life of wealth and gaiety to minister to the lepers and paupers of the cloth-manufacturing cities of northern Italy.

The first Franciscans, including three Englishmen, landed at Dover in 1224. Penniless, barefoot and bare-headed, in coarse grey gowns with girdles of rope, they made their way, like St. Augustine and his monks six centuries before, to Canterbury, and thence to London and Oxford, begging their bread along the highway and preaching to the poor. They took up their abode in the strongholds of vice and misery; their diocese was the lazar-house door, the stews, the stinking hovels along the stagnant ditches outside the town walls; their pulpit the dunghill and garbage-pit, the pothouse and brothel. The location of their first settlements—the Greyfriars in Stinking Lane, Sheer Hog and Scalding Lane—testify to the nature of their work. Here they built huts of mud and sticks, and "when it was time to drink at collation, they put a little pot on the fire with dregs of ale, and dipped a cup into the pot and drank in turn, each speaking some work of edification."

The all-embracing charity, cheerfulness and courtesy and the heroic example of these humble evangelists made a profound impression on the English. They revived memories of Aidan and the Celtic saints. Despite the haunts of wretchedness they chose, they were so merry that they were known as God's jesters. To the rich monks of the conventual houses, they seemed only vulgar sensationalists and interlopers, "utterly shameless and forgetful of their profession and Order." To the neglected masses of the city slums, they appeared as heavenly messengers. Their sermons, racy, eloquent, charged with fervent emotion and illustrated by lively, colloquial tales that the simplest could understand, went straight to the hearts of uneducated men and women whose knowledge of the Christian story had been hitherto derived from services conducted in a tongue intelligible only to the learned. They introduced into the vernacular English speech words of faith like mercy, pity, patience, comfort, conscience and salvation.

By reminding men that Christ was poor and lived among the poor, the friars started to deflect Christian alms and legacies from the over-endowed monasteries to institutions that relieved want, sickness and suffering. Till now these had tended to be somewhat spasmodic, like the annual distribution of flour—still made today after eight centuries—to the Hampshire villagers of Tichborne. London's two greatest hospitals—St. Bartholomew's founded by Rufus's courtier, Rahere, in the Smithfield marshes, and the even older St. Thomas' in Southwark for sick and needy travellers—had been established by Augustinian canons in the twelfth century. The Franciscans following the example of their founder, made a cult of lazar houses, often establishing their friaries beside them and making their novices undergo a period of training in them. They were enthusiastic practitioners of medicine—a science recently revived by contact with the Moorish and Jewish scholars of southern Spain [1]—and administered it free to the poor among whom they worked. It was a ministration desperately needed,

---

[1] Arabic symbols are still used by doctors for prescriptions.

for the slums of medieval cities, situated mostly by the swampy side of streams outside the walls, were dreadful haunts of disease and wretchedness.

Above all, the friars were teachers, and played a leading part in the universities which had grown during the previous century out of the cathedral schools. Their eloquence made them the natural leaders of the young students, as penniless and ragged as themselves, who, living in crowded garrets and taverns, flocked to the lectures of the learned doctors of theology, law and grammar in their hired rooms or schools and endeavoured to earn from the chancellor or bishop's representative the Church's licence to teach. These turbulent communities, for all their poverty, were intensely alive—gay, ardent and speculative. Though little accounted by the rich and powerful, it was with them, rather than with the sedentary and devotional monks of the Benedictine and Cistercian houses, that the future of Christendom and European learning lay. The friars, in touch with common humanity, had the perception to see this and, through their work in the universities, to mould that future. The famous Dominican house in the Jacobin convent at Paris was for the next half century the inspiration of Europe's greatest university. It gave her the two most eminent schoolmen of the age—Albert the Great, the Swabian Regent Master who made Aristotle, rediscovered by Arab commentators, the basis of western scholasticism; and Thomas of Aquinas, "the big dumb ox of Sicily", who, seeing natural law as "the mind and will of God," sought to harmonise Christian faith with reason. In the disputations in which they maintained their theses against all comers, these Dominican schoolmen tried to prove God by logic—a heroic feat of mind that in the end proved almost as dangerous to faith as to intellectual freedom.

In no land was the impact of the friars' teaching greater than in England. It gave a new and European importance to the schools of Oxford—founded in a small stone building in the churchyard of St. Mary's after Henry II, during his dispute with Becket, had recalled the English scholars from Paris. Both Dominicans and Franciscans established missions there, and at the East Anglian university which had arisen at Cambridge, on the site of a "little waste chester," following a murderous affray in 1208 between town and gown at Oxford. For a time, too, there were nascent universities at Stamford, Northampton and Reading. The exposure to vice and possibly heresy of the indisciplined youths who herded together in such places was a challenge to the friars. The school which the Franciscans built in their friary at Oxford formed the model for the university's earliest halls and colleges, William of Durham's charitable foundation for theological students that grew into University College, Sir John de Balliol's slightly later one that became Balliol, and Merton, founded between 1264 and 1274 by one of Henry III's chancellors "for the perpetual sustenance of twenty scholars living in the schools," were all inspired by the discipline and communal industry of the friars' house. The lectures and disputations held there drew such crowds that the secular masters were left, we are told, at their desks "like sparrows alone upon the housetops."

One of the earliest triumphs of the Franciscans was to persuade the great Regent Master of the Oxford Schools, Robert Grosseteste, to become their Lector. Until his election in 1235 as Bishop of Lincoln—the diocese in which the university lay—he was the inspirer of a group of young Franciscan scholars, whose experimental approach to the problems of the universe constituted the first serious Christian challenge to the authoritarian cosmology of the Middle Ages. A Suffolk farmer's son, Grosseteste was a mathematician and physicist, as well as a theologian and grammarian, and was famous for experiments with lenses. His methods, unlike those of most medieval philosophers, were experimental and inductive. The greatest of his pupils, Roger Bacon—"the marvellous doctor" —a Franciscan from Ilchester in Somerset, carried his practice even further, making an investigation of natural science that brought him at times into conflict with the ecclesiastical authorities for unorthodoxy and even suspected heresy. He was a man consumed with wonder at the mechanism of the universe. His mind, reinforced by his study of Arabic scientific writers, was for ever voyaging into the unknown, dreaming of boats without oars, self-propelled carts, and bridges which hung suspended over space. His *Opus Majus,* written and secretly published at the request of the pope, is the greatest scientific work of the thirteenth century and possibly of the entire Middle Ages.

For a century, during the long reign of Henry III and the first two Edwards, a succession of great university doctors from the British Isles, lecturing in the schools of Paris and Oxford, contributed to the most remarkable flowering of abstract thought since the days of ancient Greece. Alexander of Hales, Adam Marsh "the illustrious doctor", Thomas of York were among the foremost philosophers of the age; three other famous English scholastics, two of them friars. St. Edmund Rich, Kilwardby and Pecham, sat in turn on St. Augustine's throne at Canterbury.[1] An even greater scholar, Duns Scotus—a Franciscan from Roxburghshire who inferred the rational probability of an Infinite Being by proving mathematically that infinity existed—revolutionised philosophical thought by successfully challenging the conclusions of the great St. Thomas Aquinas. Another Franciscan born in a Surrey village at the beginning of Edward I's reign, William of Ockham, by proving, with razor-like logic that no-one could refute, the impossibility of bridging the gulf between reason and faith, made a permanent separation between natural philosophy and theology and, leaving the Church the embarrassing legacy of thinking one thing and believing another, established ecclesiastical authority as the sole basis for religious conviction: a proposition loaded with peril should an age of scepticism arise.

The friars' success changed the character of their ministry. By the reign of Edward III they were no longer the selfless and penniless saints who had "followed the naked Christ" at their first coming a hundred years before. As their founders had bade them, they still begged their way wherever they went, but the need to do so had vanished. Their four great international Orders—Dominicans, Franciscans, Carmelites and Austin Friars, all with forty or more houses in England—controlled immense wealth, owning, through a system of trusts, friaries and churches, some of them like the famous three-hundred-foot-long Greyfriars church in London almost as splendid as those of the larger abbeys. For more than a century the benefactions and bequests of the rich had flowed into their coffers and, as the confessors of kings, nobles and merchants, they enjoyed vast influence.

Though strongest in the trading and wool towns, whose burghers thronged the great new preaching naves which were raised from their wealth, the friars were everywhere, minstering to rich and poor alike and employing popular and even

---

[1] "Any list of the dozen or so most influential masters of the period of 1200–1350 would be found to contain the names of more Englishmen than of any other nationality." M. D. Knowles, *The Evolution of Medieval Thought*, 279.

sensational devices to win converts to their faith and sub-
scribers to their Order. They were to be seen in the king's
court, in the baron's hall, in the merchant's counting-house, on
the village green, in the haunts of vice and poverty. Wherever,
it was said, there was a fly, there was "eke a friar." Their
appeal arose partly from their popular style of preaching—
an art in which they were carefully trained and in which they
far excelled the uneducated and untravelled parish priests—
and partly from the understanding and ingratiating way in
which they heard confessions and the readiness with which,
according to their many critics among the secular and monastic clergy, they granted absolution, especially to those with
money to compound for their sins. They were active at both
ends of the social and cultural scale, playing a leading part
in the theological and philosophical speculations of the universities and tickling the fancy of the credulous and uneducated by their racy and crude stories and similes. Their genial,
man-of-the-world approach was combined with a highly emo-
tional appeal, and they were particularly popular with the
ladies, to whom their gaiety, good humour and here-today,
gone-tomorrow approach much endeared them—according to
their enemies far too much.

Because their sermons were changing the character of popular worship, pulpits, perched on long narrow stems like in-
verted wineglasses and covered with painted canopies—formerly only to be found in cathedrals and beside open-air
preaching crosses—became part of the internal furniture of
the richer town churches. From these, hooded friars declaimed
with lively gestures to rapt congregations, the ladies in wimples
and 'kerchiefs grouped around on benches while their hus-
bands stood behind or leaned against the pillars and humbler
folk squatted on the rush-strewn stones. In an age when there
were no newspapers and few could read, such sermons proved
immensely exciting, being spiced not only with dramatic tales
and jests but with news of the outside world. Their preachers
had a way both of delicately flattering their auditors, even
when they rebuked them, and of castigating the failings of
others which made what they had to say—at its best great and
profound oratory—not only a religious experience but de-
lightful entertainment. In the manuscript collections, some in
the vernacular and some translated into more decorous Latin,
that have come down to us one can follow their technique.
"Do you want me to talk to you about worthy womanhood,"

says one, possibly with a wink to take the sting out of his rebuke: "I'm going to say something instead about that old dame whom I see asleep over there . . . For God's sake if anyone has a pin, let him wake her up." Another preacher tells of "the little black imp" that runs round in sermon time and "puts his fingers over the ears and eyes of the people, making them deaf and sleep", or the small industrious devil who fills whole sacks with the words of those who "jangle and yap" in church and skip the prayers and responses.[1] One can see him doing so on a misericord in Ely cathedral; the craftsman who carved it must have heard just such a sermon.

This preaching had far-reaching social consequences. In days of wide regional differences it helped to create a common national sentiment, idiom and speech. Far more than the writers of books could do before printing, the mendicants, with their similes, sayings and jests, familiarised men and women of all classes with words drawn from half the languages and dialects of the West. And at a time of staggering social injustices and ever-widening divisions of wealth, they produced a climate of thought in which the inequality of man could no longer be taken wholly for granted. The Church did not teach that all men were equal; on the contrary, it insisted that the world, like Heaven, was a hierarchy in which every man had his appointed place and must give reverence and obedience to those in authority. Yet the friars' vivid portrayal of the fate that awaited the unrighteous great made it clear to even the most humble-minded that no-one, from the king downwards, could hope to escape the pains of Hell if he flouted justice. The rich, the great fourteenth century Dominican preacher, Dr. Bromyard, declared in a sermon, were deceived in thinking that they were the masters of their riches, since they were only for a short time its guardians. "All are descended from the same first parents, and all come from the same mud." Where, he asked, were the evil princes of the world, the kings and lords who had lived with pride and possessed great palaces, manors and lands, who ruled harshly and cruelly to obtain the pleasures of the world? "Of

[1] G. R. Owst, *Preaching in Medieval England*, 175–8, 186. His name was Tittivullus, and once, when caught at his business, he explained that he had to present daily to his master, the Devil, "a thousand pokes full of failings and of negligences and syllables and words that are done . . . in reading and singing, or else I must be sore beaten." Eileen Power, *Medieval People*, 70.

all their riches, their delicacies, they have nothing, and the worms have their bodies. Instead of palace, hall and chamber their soul shall have the deep lake of hell . . . In place of scented baths their body shall have a narrow pit in the earth and a bath more black and foul than any bath of pitch and sulphur. In place of inordinate embraces they will have there the embraces of the fiery brands of hell . . . Instead of wives they shall have toads, instead of a great retinue and throng of followers their body shall have a throng of worms and their soul a throng of demons." The friars were the pace-setters of the age, pointing to a world very different to that around them, where presently brother would no longer be able to ignore the claims of brother.[1]

By the middle of the fourteenth century the great conventual houses which had transmitted the legacies of Christianity and Latin civilisation to the warrior classes of western Europe had ceased to be proselytising agents. No longer recruited from men with a burning sense of mission but mainly from the younger sons of the lesser landowners and wealthier burgesses, the monks were far removed from the lives of the townsmen and peasants at their gates whose rents and tithes sustained their magnificent institutions. In their churches they still kept up a continuous sequence of services, prayer and chanting. But, though royal and noble personages frequently visited the more famous houses, making their stay and devotions memorable by benefactions of jewels and relics, except in a few of the larger abbeys, where part of the church was screened off for parochial use, the ordinary laity had no part in their secluded life. Apart from those who lived inside their franchises and liberties and were so subject to their jurisdiction, the public's contact with such great monasteries was confined to the payment of rent, tithes and services to their officers and bailiffs, the carefully graded hospitality they offered to travellers, and the broken meats their almoners distributed to the poor at their gates. Their premises—which included most of the largest habitable buildings in the land—were also used for sessions of parliament; the chapter house of Westminster Abbey was the usual meeting-place for the knights and burgesses of the Commons. At Gloucester the monks had to vacate their home and encamp in an orchard when a parliament met there.

[1] G. R. Owst, *Literature and Pulpit in Medieval England*, 293–4.

Except in a few secluded priories and cells, where monks with a vocation for solitude were wont to retire for contemplation, and in the few houses of the Carthusians—a hermit Order where the old strictness and monastic silence still prevailed and whose motto was, "Never reformed because never deformed"—monks were no longer dedicated men living austere lives, but comfortable members of a rich bachelor fraternity, proud of their corporate traditions and treasures and exceedingly jealous of their rights. Though their lives for the most part were decorous and orderly, they were seldom ascetic. In theory, vegetarian diet, silence at meals and strict fasts were still the rule; in practice, the "pittances" of meat and luxuries formerly only allowed to monks in sickness had become part of the normal monastic dietary, though, to avoid desecrating the refectory, meals on "flesh days" were usually taken in a parlour or in the misericord of the infirmary. The table of a rich, well-found monastery was like that of a nineteenth century Oxford or Cambridge college, a by-word for good food and drink. Even in a little priory like Bicester twenty-five menials looked after eleven canons. In many of the larger houses servants outnumbered the brethren by three to one. At Durham the prior's staff, in light green and blue liveries, included a butler, a cup-bearer, valets, pages, grooms, gardeners, washerwomen, even a jester. Nor were monks any longer confined to the cloister. In a large house, with numerous manors and distant estates, there was ample scope for travel for any brother with a flair for affairs. The fourteenth century poet, William Langland, depicted such a one as

"a rider, a roamer by streets,
A leader of law-days and a land buyer,
A pricker on a palfrey from manor to manor,
An heap of hounds at his arse as a lord were."

His contemporary, the monk in Chaucer's *Canterbury Tales,* whose passions were inspecting farms and hunting, had "many a dainty horse in stable"; his bridle, when he rode, jingled

"so clear
And eke as loud as doth the chapel bell
Where that this lord was keeper of the cell.
The rule of St. Maur of St. Beneyt,
Because that it was old and somewhat straight
This ilkë monk let pass the oldë day
And held after the newë time alway."

"A lord full fat and in good point," with sleeves rounded with the finest fur, his favourite food was "a fat swan roast."

The age of monastic saints had passed for ever. What was now admired in conventual circles was a dignified, shrewd man of the world who combined the conventional Christian virtues with a keen eye for his house's interests. There is a picture of one in Knighton's chronicle: William of Clown of the Augustinian abbey of St. Mary's in the Meadows, Leicester. The friend both of the famous soldier, Henry of Lancaster, and Edward III, he ruled it for thirty-three years to its great enrichment.

> "He was a lover of peace and quiet, a reformer of quarrels and wrongs, . . . kind and obliging to his underlings and persons of the lower orders, unspeakably amiable to great men and the magnates of the realm . . . In his days two churches were appropriated, . . . two manors acquired, likewise rents and possessions. He also obtained a charter from the king for himself and his successors, excusing them from attending parliament . . . To this kindly abbot, God gave so great grace in the eyes of all men, lords and others, that there was scarce a man who could deny him what he asked. On such good terms was he with the lord king that he asked him in jest to grant him a fair for buying and selling harriers and hounds of all sorts. The king actually thought that he meant it seriously and granted him the fair; but he would not insist on the matter. In hunting of the hare he was reckoned the most notable and renowned among all the lords of the realm, so that the king himself and his son, Prince Edward, and divers lords of the realm had an annual engagement to hunt at his entertainment. Nevertheless he would often say in private that the only reason why he took delight in such paltry sports was to show politeness to the lords of the realm, to get on easy terms with them and win their goodwill in matters of business." [1]

Such dignitaries lived in palatial lodgings, entertained princes and, like bishops, had parks, studs and country manor-houses where from time to time favoured members of the

[1] A. Hamilton Thompson, *The English Clergy and their Organization in the later Middle Ages,* 168–70.

chapters were invited to stay for recreation and sport. At St. Albans the abbot dined on a dais fifteen steps above the rest of the hall, while the monks who served him sang a grace at every fifth step. Yet sometimes such great men, who for the honour of their houses kept a lord's state, in secret lived austere and devout lives, fasting, rising for the midnight office, sleeping on penitential beds and wearing horsehair under their magnificent garments, like Richard of Wallingford, the black-smith's son who became abbot of St. Albans at thirty-one and died of leprosy, and Thomas de la Mare who reigned over the same house for nearly half a century and built its great gateway and king's hall. To enrich the architectural heritage of his house was still a favourite occupation for an abbot; Simon Langham of Westminster, the last monk to become archbishop of Canterbury, endowed the Abbey with its cloisters and much of its present nave.

Paradoxically, despite their wealth monasteries were often in financial trouble, especially the smaller ones. With the falling rents and farming profits of the fourteenth century—the result of war, famine and plague—and with growing royal and papal taxation, even the greater abbeys had difficulty in maintaining their costly expenditure and were forced to borrow at exorbitant rates. The open house they kept for itinerant lords—for no place was so comfortable as a monastery—was a heavy strain on their resources; often some pious prince or earl would descend on his favourite abbey for the Christmas or Easter feast with two or three hundred retainers and a pack of hounds. In many cases, too, monasteries were saddled with what were called "corrodies," compelling them to maintain a number of idle and sometimes highly embarrassing pensioners, either of founders' kin or the nominees of some benefactor. It was a common practice for houses in need of cash to sell for a lump sum such an annuity to be paid in the form of food, drink, clothing and lodging during the pensioner's life, sometimes even with remainder to his widow.

All this tended to make the monks harsh landlords, enforcing their rights against their tenants and villeins and the burghers at their gates with more than ordinary rigidity, which they were the better able to do owing to their habit of keeping records. They were great sticklers for the privileges which had come down to them from their historic past and which they regarded as the private property of the saints in whose honour their houses had been founded; as Tyndale wrote shortly before their end in the sixteenth century, "It is God's, not theirs, they say; it is St. Hubert's rents, St. Alban's lands, St. Peter's patrimony." This rendered them unpopular, except in the remoter, wilder parts of the country where their houses were still the chief centres of local culture, piety and charity. Though their magnificent churches and famous relics were still a source of regional pride—

> "In Holland in the fenny lands
> Be sure you mark where Croyland stands."

they had become, in southern England at least, a synonym for easy living. The "Order of Bel-Ease" was the name given to the regulars in one satire.

What was true of monasteries was true, on their much smaller scale, of nunneries. Most of them were very small, though a few like Wilton, Romsey, Wherwell and Sempringham were rich and famous; it was a saying that if the abbot of Glastonbury were to marry the abbess of Shaftesbury their heir would be richer than the king. Convents did a good deal of teaching, though seldom of a very strenuous kind, taking young girls of good family as boarders and sometimes keeping an infant school for their neighbourhood.[1] They were renowned, too, for their needlework—the much coveted *opus Anglicanum*. They provided dignified places of retirement for dowagers of the upper class, a vocation and home for unmarriageable daughters and a devout finishing-school for young ladies. The cachet given by membership of a fashionable convent was considerable, and rich merchants and franklins would pay high premiums for their womenfolk's admission. The prioress of such was a woman of distinction and breeding, like Chaucer's Madame Eglentine who wore an elegantly pleated cloak, a coral bracelet, two necklaces of green breads—for saying her prayers— and a gold brooch engraved with the words, *Amor vincit omnia.*

> "Full well she sang the services divine
> Entunëd in her nose full seemëly.
> And French she spoke full fair and sweetëly
> After the school of Stratford-attë-Bowe,
> For French of Paris was to her unknowe.

[1] "Abstinence, the abbess, taught me my A.B.C." *Piers Plowman.*

At meatë well i'taught was she in all;
She let no morsel from her lippës fall,
Nor wet her fingers in her saucë deep.
Well could she carry a morsel and well keep
That never drop upon her breast should be,
For all her thought was set on courtesy"

The poet's picture of the little dogs she kept as pets and on whom she lavised such affection seems to have been drawn from the life. An episcopal visitation revealed how Lady Audley brought to the convent at Langley "a great abundance of dogs, in so much that when she comes to church there follow her twelve who make a great uproar." As was to be expected in such purely female establishments, there was often more love of fine clothes than was compatible with a life of religious dedication, and an incurable tendency to tittle-tattle and back-biting. When during an episcopal visitation the nuns accused the prioress of Ankerwyke, Godstow, of making a private room for herself in the dormitory, she retorted that she had been kept awake at night by their chattering to Oxford scholars loitering on the river bank. And a fifteenth century prioress of Eastbourne, who might have been Madame Eglentine's sister, was accused by her flock of putting the convent into £40 debt because "she frequently rides abroad and pretends that she does so on the common business of the house—although it is not so—with a train of attendants much too large, and tarries too long abroad; she feasts sumptuously both when abroad and at home and is very choice in her dress so that the fur trimmings of her mantle are worth 100s." [1] Visiting bishops were always trying, though in vain, to moderate such shortcomings in the ladies religious.

The truth was that after the thirteenth century both monasteries and nunneries were fighting against the trend of a thriving, vigorous age in which the instinct of the ordinary individual was to mingle with the world and emulate its rising standards of comfort and elegance rather than, as in earlier and more barbaric times, to seek refuge from it in the communal dedication of the convent. It was symptomatic that in many houses, not only the abbot and prior, but most of the obedientiaries had separate apartments. At Launceston, Bishop Grandisson of Exeter found every canon in possession,

---

[1] Hamilton Thompson, 172; P. Kendall, *The Yorkist Age*, 269–70.

not only of a room, but of a page, a herb-garden, a dovecot and a dog of his own. Cash allowances to monks for personal expenditure, for spices, clothes, even for work done for the monastery, were all eroding the selfless spirit of the cloister; monasteries were approximating more and more to the less rigid ideals of the secular cathedral and collegiate chapters. It was symptomatic that most of the conventual houses founded in the fourteenth century partook of this looser character. Side by side with the monasteries, whose population was slowly declining, were springing up a growing number of collegiate chapters, whose prebends offered their founders a patronage similar to that of the secular cathedrals and which no monastery, with its basic rule of residence, could offer. Some of these, like St. George's, Windsor and the royal "peculiar", Wimborne Minster, possessed churches which rivalled the monastic cathedrals.[1]

The real charge against the monasteries was that they no longer fulfilled any essential part in the country's polity or justified the huge proportion of the national wealth they controlled. They had even ceased to set its artistic standards, for, except in a few of the greater Benedictine houses like Gloucester and Ely, they were now surpassed as architectural patrons and innovators by the rich statesmen-bishops of the royal court, and most of the lesser arts, like the illumination of manuscripts, were executed by lay professionals instead of in the cloister. Only in the keeping of historical chronicles were the monasteries still leaders. They survived for another hundred and fifty years, continuing until their dissolution by Henry VIII to exercise great social, and to a lesser degree political, influence because they were an integral part of the ruling establishment and fabric of society and, as such, constituted an irremovable vested interest.

[1] In his *English Cathedrals* John Harvey reckons that before the end of the Middle Ages there were more than a hundred churches of cathedral type in England, a quarter of which have been totally destroyed while others survive only in ruins.

CHAPTER V

THE MAKING OF THE LAW

> "The King is under no man, but he is under
> God and the Law."
>
> BRACTON

FOR THREE HUNDRED years after the Conquest England remained to outward appearance a country of two races—a ruling and landowning aristocracy of French descent and speech and a servile native majority speaking a despised vernacular in a diversity of local dialects. Yet even from the start two forces tended to draw ruler and ruled together and blend them into a single nation, One was the Church, the other the Crown. For, though the kings were Frenchmen and England itself only a province of their foreign dynastic empire, they were always ready to use their humble English subjects to tame recalcitrant French lords. It was with the aid of his "brave and honourable English," as he called them, that the Conqueror's heir, William "Rufus", had a rebellious cousin seized, whipped in every church in Salisbury and hanged as a traitor. And it was the English who, forty years after Hastings, enabled the Conqueror's youngest son, Henry, to wrest Normandy from his brother Robert. Though he was as grasping as his father, Henry proclaimed his adherence to English law, swore in his coronation oath to maintain justice and mercy and promised to "abolish all the evil practices with which the realm was unjustly oppressed." He even taught himself English and claimed that he had been called to the throne in the old electoral way "by the common counsel of the barons of the realm." He married a daughter of the Scots king, who through an English mother was descended from Edmund Ironside and Alfred, and, in later years, loved a

Welsh princess, Nest—wife of one of his Marcher barons—who helped him to understand, not only his English subjects, but his British.

Henry I, "the Lion of Justice" as they called him, deserved his people's confidence. "There was great awe of him", wrote the Anglo-Saxon chronicler; "no man durst misdo against another in his time; he made peace for man and beast." For thirty-six years this squat, avaricious, smooth-spoken man gave the English that political stability which those who have known anarchy most value. He was a man of business who could read Latin, understood the importance of administration and introduced into government regular habits and routine. His father had given England a taxing system more accurate than any in Europe; building on his foundations, Henry gave it a permanent officialdom. He made it out of the domestic officers of his household—the treasurer; the chamberlain who looked after the bedchamber; the constable of the knights and the marshal of the stables; the steward who presided in the hall where scores of ushers kept order with rods; the reverend chancellor with his seal and writing-office—an innovation of the Confessor's—where writs were prepared for the sheriffs.

The greatest of the royal servants was the justiciar, who deputised for the king during his absences abroad in his other dominions. He and his fellow officers formed a standing inner court of the Great Council called the Curia Regis, to which both judicial appeals and affairs of State were referred. With their staffs of trained clerks and their chambers where suitors could wait on them, they were the first fathers of our civil service. In the great stone hall of Westminster—today the oldest public building in England—which William Rufus raised over the marble bench where the English kings had done justice in the open air, public business continued even when the Court was travelling. Here twice a year, under the chairmanship of king or justiciar, officials called barons of the Exchequer sat at a table with counters and a chequered cloth, carefully checking with the sheriffs the taxes, rents, fines and debts due to the Crown. Every penny had to be accounted for. There was nothing else like it in western Europe.

This capacity for organisation, for creating institutions which continued irrespective of persons, made a deep impression on Henry's subjects. They admired the unhurried regularity and dignity with which he did business: his daily reception before the midday meal of all who came for justice, the sober recreation after it, the carefully planned arrangements for State progresses through his dominions. He made his influence felt in every county, where his sheriffs were kept perpetually busy, receiving writs, making records and collecting the revenue under the scrutiny of the royal officers at Westminster. After his death, when his weak successor, Stephen of Blois, let the country lapse into anarchy, the good order he had kept was remembered with gratitude. It was his grandson and namesake—by his daughter Matilda's marriage with Geoffrey Plantagenet, count of Anjou—who, assuming the throne in 1154 after a generation of civil war, re-imposed on the feudal baronage the restraints of strong administration. Having got rid of their mercenaries and unlicensed castles, the second Henry—ruler by inheritence and marriage of more than half France—subjected them, like his grandfather, to fiscal discipline, recalling to their old work of punishing infringements of royal rights the Exchequer officials whom the latter had trained.

The methods of these watchdogs were described in the *Dialogue of the Exchequer*, written by a son of Henry's treasurer, Nigel of Ely. Its guiding principle—still enshrined in Treasury practice—was "devotion to the king's interests with a single mind, due regard being paid to equity." In its pages we can watch the presiding justiciar, with the treasurer, chancellor and barons of the Exchequer, sitting on the covered benches round the black-and-white squared table, as each sheriff presented his accounts, and the official calculator, as in some gigantic chessmatch, moved the piles of coins or counters that represented money. We see the humbler officials of the Lower Exchequer—silverer, melter, ushers, chamberlains and tellers—receiving and weighing the cash, and sometimes assaying or "blanching" it in the furnace, while the tally-cutter notches and splits the wooden talleys which serve for receipts. And we can still read the Latin entries on the sheepskin pipe-rolls on which were recorded the state of the sheriffs' annual account with the Exchequer, the debts due to the Crown, the farms and rents of royal estates and woods, the legal fines, the escheats of those whose fiefs had become vacant and the year's feudal reliefs and tallages. Among the latter was a war-tax on knights' fees called scutage or shieldmoney, initiated earlier to meet the case of ecclesiastical tenants unable to serve in the field and which Henry adapted to give lay tenants an alternative to accompanying him on his foreign campaigns. It suited both them and him, for, by using the proceeds to hire mercenaries, he partly freed himself from dependence on his baronage.

But the field, above all others, in which Henry II mastered his barons was law. At his accession there were at least four different systems of jurisdiction in England. There were the great franchises of the baronial honours, and the village manorial courts, both private property. There were the old public courts of shire and hundred, presided over by the sheriff—nominally a royal officer, but in practice a local magnate who farmed their profits and the taxes of the country and who, during Stephen's lax rule, had often encroached on the Crown's rights and, in some cases, even tried to make his office hereditary. And there was the king himself, who not only sat in his *curia regis* as supreme feudal overlord, but, as successor of the athelings, was the traditional fount of national justice.

Henry first sought control of the shire and hundred courts. He revived his grandfather's practice of sending out Exchequer barons on circuit to sit beside the sheriffs and enforce his fiscal rights. Before long he had made these progresses annual events. And since there was then little distinction between the profits of jurisdiction and jurisdiction itself, he empowered his officers, not only to look into revenue matters but to hear and try local pleas of the Crown. To these he added offenses which had hitherto been dealt with by the sheriffs. By two assizes or royal councils—one held at the Wiltshire hunting palace of Clarendon in 1166 and the other ten years later at Northampton—trials of murder, robbery, larceny, rape, forgery, arson and harbouring criminals were reserved to the justices *in eyre*. The criminal jurisdiction of the Crown—formerly confined to *lèse majesté* and breaches of the king's peace on the royal domains and highways—was made nationwide, and the sheriffs' chief judicial powers transferred to officers under the sovereign's eye.

These Henry chose carefully for their loyalty and impartiality, and, as he and they gained experience, for knowledge of the law. At first he had to rely on bishops, Exchequer officials and minor barons temporarily executing judicial commissions. But by experiment he gradually created a body of trained judges whose business it was "to do justice habitually." Some were clerics, others laymen, but all were drawn from the lesser Anglo-Norman families whom he used as a counter-poise to the feudal magnates. They were assigned to six, and later four, regular circuits of counties, round which, escorted by sheriffs and javelin men, they rode on annual progresses. Others, sitting on the bench in Westminster Hall, formed a permanent judicial tribunal of the *curia regis,* which later grew into the courts of King's Bench and Common Pleas. One of its members, Ranulf de Glanvill—or, possibly, his clerk, Hubert Walter, who succeeded him as justiciar—wrote the nation's first legal classic, a Latin treatise on the laws and customs of England and the procedure of the royal courts.

It was through such procedure that Henry traversed the power of the feudal jurisdictions. One of the commonest sources of disorder during the civil wars of Stephen's reign had been the baronial habit of forcibly seizing land on some trumped-up excuse. The victim had two alternatives: to counter-attack with like force if he could command it or to appeal in his overlord's court to the only process recognized there, trial-by-battle. In this, whether fought by the principals or by professional champions, victory almost invariably went to the strongest and richest, the largest purse securing the longest lance.

By adapting the old English principle—enshrined in the coronation oath—that it was the king's duty to see that justice was done and that every freeman had a right of appeal to him Henry and his judges devised writs or royal commands restoring possession to any freeman forcibly dis-possessed of his land. They offered these for sale to all, Norman and English alike, whose tenures were free from servile services: to all, that is "free to go with their land where they would." A writ of summons called *praecipe* di-rected the sheriff to order the overlord of any land seized to restore it immediately or answer for his failure in the royal court. Another called *novel disseisin* commanded him to reinstate any dispossessed freeholder pending trial and summon "twelve & free and lawful men of the neighbor-hood" to "recognise" and declare, under oath before the king's judges, to whom its possession had belonged. A later writ called *mort d'ancestor* similarly protected the peaceful pos-session of a freeholder's heir against all claimants not able to prove a superior right in the royal courts.

These possessory writs, as they were called, had three effects. They protected a man's right to possession as distinct from his legal ownership—a matter which might otherwise be disputed for ever. They made everyone with a claim to a freehold plead it, not in the court of the feudal overlord, who was powerless against a royal writ, but in the king's. And, through the procedure laid down for investigating such claims, they substituted for the barbarous custom of proof-by-battle a sworn inquest or "recognition" by "twelve free and lawful men of the neighbourhood", summoned by the sheriff to "recognise" with whom the disputed possession lay.

These "recognitors" or jurymen were not the doomsmen of the old formalistic English law, swearing in support of a neighbour's oath. Nor were they necessarily witnesses to acts that had happened under their eyes. They were men of substance assembled to answer questions of common knowledge put to them under oath by the king's judges. The Conqueror had used such inquisitions for fiscal purposes. His great-grandson used them for judicial. It is immaterial whether they derived, as some think, from a long-disused device of Charlemagne's or from that of the twelve thanes of the Anglo-Danish wapentake swearing to accuse no innocent man and conceal no guilty one. What matters is that, imposed by the royal prerogative, they were at once accepted in a country where presentment and judgment by a man's neighbours had been part of popular law from time immemorial. Through the ingenuity and good sense of this strong, subtle-minded and original ruler, the corporate conscience of a group of neighbors, acquainted with the persons and facts involved and sworn to speak the truth, was substituted for the unpredictable arbitrament of battle. It seemed a more sensible way of ascertaining God's will, in other words the truth. And it was certainly a better way—and this may have appealed even more strongly to Henry—of keeping the peace.

The same procedure was extended to actions to determine legal ownership. By a process called the grand assize a free-holder whose title was challenged could decline trial-by-battle in his overlord's court and, opting for a trial in the king's, put himself "upon the testimony of the country." In this, twelve knights of the shire declared in the presence of the royal judges which of the litigating parties had the better right. Once determined, such recognition by grand assize was final. "So effectively does this procedure," wrote Glanvill, "preserve the lives and the civil condition of men that every man may now legally retain possession of his freehold and at the same time avoid the doubtful event of the duel."

Through these writs—"infinitely diversified for different causes"—Henry achieved a major and peaceful revolution. He did so under the guise of restoring "the good old laws." Appealing to native English tradition, he used the prerogative to bring the whole system of freehold tenure under national law. By making the smaller landowner's right to his property dependent on the royal instead of the feudal courts, he struck at the root of the great lord's power over his military tenants. And he dealt a death-blow to trial-by-battle and private war. He did not abolish the feudal courts and their processes; like the lesser, and very active, private manorial courts they survived for centuries. He merely drove them out of such business as imperilled the unity and safety of the State by offering their clients cheaper, surer and quicker justice in the royal courts. His writs attracted to the latter an ever-growing volume of litigation and revenue. "The convincing proof of our king's strength and justice," wrote a grateful subject, "is that whoever has a just cause wants to have it tried before him."

Henry's enemies—the great and strong—complained that he wore out their patience with his perpetual assizes and cunning legal formulas: his "mousetraps", as one of them called them. His justification, in Richard Fitzneal's words, was that "he spared the poor both labour and expense." Selfish, crafty, unscrupulous, the great lawyer-king wielded the sword of justice "for the punishment of evil-doers and the maintenance of peace and quite for honest men." His judges made his remedies available in every corner of the realm. With the precedents they enshrined in their judgments, they little by little created a common law for all England. Even that of the shire and hundred courts had varied from district to district; Kent, Wessex, Mercia, the Danelaw, London and the Celtic West had all had their separate customs and practices. Henry's judges established the same system for north, south, east and west, for town and country, for Norman, Englishman and Welshman. They nationalised, as it were, the Law.

In doing so they drew from the principles which Italian jurists had recently rediscovered in the great legal codes left behind six centuries before by the Emperor Justinian. But, while the continental lawyers who studied Roman jurispru-

dence in the new universities of Bologna and Paris had little
chance of applying it except in the church courts, law in England, thanks to Henry's triumph over the feudal jurisdictions,
was no academic study confined to learned doctors and
pursued only in palace courts, but a practical, day-by-day
business affecting the whole nation. However much they
might admire the logical maxims of imperial Rome, Henry's
judges had to administer the kind of law to which ordinary
Englishmen were accustomed. In their judgments, based on
the decisions of their predecessors, they embodied from popular and local custom whatever seemed compatible with a common national system.

The growth of such case-law, as it was called, was a two-
way process. It was not merely imposed from above but
grew from below. It was, above all, a collaboration between
professional judges stating the law and laymen drawn from
different classes of society, deciding questions of fact. The
classic example, pregnant with far-reaching consequences for
the future of England and the ocean nations that sprang from
her, was the use in criminal jurisdiction of the old Anglo-
Saxon principle of enlisting local worthies to sift local accusations. The assize of Clarendon directed the itinerant
judges to enquire of twelve "lawful" men from every hundred and four from every township whether any of their
neighbours were reputed to have committed felony. Only those
so presented were to be put upon their trial. So resolved was
Henry to stamp out the violence unloosed by civil war and
such the weight he attached to the verdicts of these local
worthies that even when those they accused were proved innocent by the customary "judgment of God" or trial by water,
they were banished the realm.

This principle of allowing representatives of the neighbourhood to decide questions of fact in criminal law was applied
to the trials not only of Englishmen but of Normans. So was
the rule—unknown to ancient Rome—that every case should
be tried in public, as in the presence of the Anglo-Saxon
tribe. The secret tribunal, that instrument of imperial tyranny,
was never allowed a lodgment in English Common Law.
When, long afterwards, the kings of other lands brought the
feudal jurisdictions under their control, the authoritarian
maxims of Roman civil and canon law, deeply rooted in the
minds of continental royal lawyers, often became instruments
of despotism. In England, where law was founded on

popular custom and the open participation of the ordinary man in its processes, it proved a bulwark of public and private liberties.

Henry's achievement was far in advance of his age. No other ruler could offer his people such a system of national justice. So unique was it that when the kings of Castile and Navarre became involved in a quarrel about one another's lands, they brought an action in his court like a pair of English knights seeking a remedy by grand assize or inquest of *novel disseisin*. By the end of Henry's reign there was no major offense against the public peace which could not bring the offender within range of a royal writ. Even the killing and maiming of villeins and cottars were punished by his courts. Within five years of his death an ordinance of his greatest disciple, Hubert Walter the justiciar, created in every county officials called coroners to hold inquests on all sudden and suspicious deaths.

All this prepared the way for the rule of law that was to become the dominant trait in England's life. Henceforward, whoever gave law to her, was to have a machinery by which it could be enforced—against the strong as well as the weak. The professional judges Henry trained, the regular courts in which they sat, the writs they devised to meet popular needs, and the judgments they left behind to guide their successors, helped to ensure that justice should be done even in the royal absence or in the reign of a weak or unjust sovereign. By making the Common Law the permanent embodiment of a righteous king sitting in judgment, the great Angevin established the English habit of obedience to law which was to prove the strongest of all the forces making for the nation's peaceful continuity and progress.

In the century after Henry's death the legal institutions he had created continued to grow. It was an age of fertile judicial invention, when a little group of royal justices—sitting on the bench of Common Pleas at Westminster, travelling the country on eyre or attending the sovereign's person in the court of King's Bench—were devising and offering the subject an evergrowing number of writs and building up by their judgments a body of law that made England the justest land in Europe. Among them were some very great men—Martin Pattishall, whose tireless industry on assize wore out all his fellow judges, William Raleigh of Devonshire who became bishop of Norwich and Winchester, and his still more famous pupil, Henry de Bracton—another west-country man who held the rectorships of Coombe-in-Teignhead and Bideford and who lies buried in Exeter cathedral of which he was chancellor. His text-book on litigation, *The Laws and Customs of England,* citing more than five hundred decisions collected from the plea rolls of the royal courts, was the most germinating legal work of the century.

Though case-law was not yet binding on the courts, it was fast becoming so, for the professional judges were the sole interpreters of the "custom of the king's court" which became through them the common law of England. Its strength lay in its popularity with all classes of free Englishmen. It was in the thirteenth century that the words judgment and plea, inquest, assize and heir, acquit and fine first became part of English speech. Even the poorest freeman felt that he could get justice from the royal courts and at a cheaper rate than that offered under any other system of law. For it was a point of honour with the king's judges that, while the sale of writs formed an important source of revenue, a poor litigant should be able to obtain an essential writ for nothing.

In their work of enforcing the law the king's ministers were faced by a decision—made in 1215 at an international Church Council held at the Lateran palace at Rome—that the clergy should no longer take part in the practice of ascertaining legal guilt by the time-honoured ordeal of fire or water. This sign of growing reliance on human reason, which the Church, through its educational institutions, was slowly if unconsciously creating, robbed the primitive "judgment by God" of its religious sanction. It presented courts of law throughout Christendom with the problem of finding some alternative method of reaching verdicts when there was a clash of evidence. In southern lands, where there were plenty of clerks trained by the law-schools of Ravenna and Bologna in the re-discovered principles of classical jurisprudence, resort was had to the Roman rules of evidence. In England, far removed from the fount of classical learning, a simpler native substitute was found. In 1218, the king's Council issued to itinerant justices a direction that, sooner than keep persons charged with felonies indefinitely in jail, they should use their discretion. They were to experiment and make use of their experience in ascertaining and estimating local opinion. Just as Henry II's judges had accepted, as proof of a man's right to

his lands, a sworn oath from an assize or jury of his neighbours, so his grandson's judges met the Lateran Council's
repudiation of trial-by-God by summoning similar, though
humbler, juries to resolve the guilt of those accused of felony.
Juries of presentment, drawn partly from the knightly class
and partly from representatives of the villages, were already
presenting suspected criminals to the king's justices. The latter
now adopted the idea of using the small freeholders or sokemen assembled by the sheriffs for this purpose to resolve, with
a simple yes or no, whether those presented were actually
guilty of the crimes of which they had been accused. They
took counsel, as the saying was, of the neighbourhood.

Thus for the supposed verdict of God through the elements
was gradually substituted the conception—a curiously English
one—of a verdict through the inspiration of a dozen decent
honest freemen, equipped with local knowledge and sworn
under a solemn religious oath to speak the truth in open
court. *Vox populi*—not of an anonymous mob but of a group
of "worthy and lawful" men who knew their neighbourhood
—was to be accepted as the voice of God. The accused could
take his choice of submitting to such a verdict, of putting himself, as it was called, upon the country, or of remaining in
gaol. It was a rough and ready way of getting at the truth,
but one whose roots lay deep in English history. And in the
course of their everyday practice—though it was a process
that took centuries to complete—the trained judges of the
Crown contrived methods of making evidence available to
such petty juries that eventually proved more realistic than
all the elaborate rules of Roman Law. The judges expounded
and interpreted the law, and the jurymen, who began their
long career as corporate witnesses to the opinion of the locality, became in the end judges of fact and assessors of
evidence.

The English chain of law was a partnership between Crown
and people: between, that is, the hall of justice at Westminster and the local courts, officers and jurymen of the
shire, hundred and vill, and the delegated jurisdictions and
franchises of the feudal landowners. These last remained as
numerous as ever but now derived their strength, not, as in
other feudal States, from their separateness but from their
participation in the royal machinery of government. The
sword and rod of equity with which the king did justice were

the earls and barons of the realm, the sheriffs and knights of the shire, the constables of the hundred and vill. And they in their turn depended on the royal authority for the peace, order and growing prosperity of their society.

Behind the royal courts lay "the community of the realm." It consisted, not only of barons and prelates but of the lesser landowners of the shire, of the petty freeholders of the villages and the burgesses of the free towns. The first, increasingly styled knights of the shire, performed a multitude of duties. They served as sheriffs, escheators and coroners, and as justices on special commissions of gaol-delivery to relieve the overworked royal judges; they sat in judgment in the shire court at its monthly meetings in the countytown, and attended the two great annual assemblies when the lord, knights and freeholders of the shire gathered to meet the justices on eyre. They served on the committees which scrutinised the presentments of the hundreds and villages, and carried the record of the shire court to Westminster when summoned there by the king's judges. They acted as jurymen on the grand assize, assessed, as elected representatives of their fellow knights of the shire, any taxes due from each hundred, and investigated and reported on local abuses and grievances. They were constantly being called on for their views in questions put to them on oath by the king's judges and council. So were the humbler freeholders and sokemen who also, as elected representatives of their neighbours, assessed the village taxes. Even outside the privileged ranks of "free men," the community of the unfree was represented by the six *villani* or villein-farmers who presented, with the parish priest and reeve, the local malefactors and answered for the village's offences and omissions before the terrible, all-enquiring eyre.

Co-operation between central officials, paid and trained, for their specialist functions, and unpaid and part-time amateurs representing the interests, property and good-sense of the local community was the means by which the Plantagenet kings both ordered and unified their realm. By the end of the thirteenth century, with the growing complexity of legal procedure, the royal justices had become something more than temporary deputies delegated from baronial or episcopal bench to try particular cases in their sovereign's place. They were now permanent royal officials. They still performed a multitude of services, hearing assizes, delivering county gaols on eyre, acting as commissioners of array, supervising the collection of subsidies and sitting on the royal Council. Some were in clerical orders like John le Breton or Britton, the bishop of Hereford who is believed to have written a condensation of Bracton's treatise on the laws of England, the much-used Martin of Littleburn, and the Norfolk-born Ralph de Hengham, canon of St. Paul's and arch deacon of Worcester, who began his legal career as a clerk to one of Henry III's judges and rose to be chief justice both of the Common Pleas and King's Bench, leaving behind two important tracts on procedure and pleadings. Others were laymen, county knights and local notables or legal specialists who had practised as lawyers in the courts before they became judges. Of the fifteen members of the King's Bench appointed during Edward I's reign seven were clerics and eight laymen, including both the chief justices of his latter years.

Below them were the attorneys, who represented clients, prosecuting their writs and entering their pleas by proxy, and the skilled narrators, pleaders, and serjeants-at-law—successors of the professional champions of trial by battle—who composed the pleas and narrated and argued the pleadings, so saving suitors from the verbal slips which could so easily unsuit the untrained.[1] For the rules of an action-at-law before the king's judges were most strictly enforced; the very language, a kind of bastard French interlaced with Latin and designed to ensure the utmost precision of meaning, was almost impossible for a layman to understand. Any freeholder who had been dispossessed or kept out of his land could buy from the Chancery clerks a writ addressed to the sheriff of his county directing him to summon the dispossessor to answer the plaintiff in an action-at-law. The number of such writs had been steadily increasing in order to cover all conceivable causes of action over freehold-land. Yet, unless the exact one appropriate to the wrong complained of was chosen, the

---

[1] "Pleaders are serjeants wise in the law of the realm who serve the commonalty of the people, stating and defending for hire actions in court for those who have need of them. . . . When the declaration of the plaintiff has been heard, the adversary is concerned to make a good answer. And because folk do not generally know all the 'exceptions' which can be used by way of answer, pleaders are necessary who know how to set forth causes and to defend them according to the rule of law and the usage of the realm." *The Mirror of Justices,* (Selden Society) VII, 47, 90.

action was bound to fail. The forms of pleading and procedure of the particular remedy sought had to be meticulously observed by both plaintiff and defendant, even to the minutest details of wording. How essential this was can be seen from the defence made on behalf of the Bishop of Lichfield to a writ of *darrein presentment* affecting the right of presentation to a Cheshire church. Because the words "who is dead" had been omitted, the plaintiff would have been unsuited had not "a certain John of Wettenhall, who was sitting among the doomsmen of the county court, made answer that the Earl Ranulf"—the owner of the Palatine court before it had lapsed to the Crown—"delivered to them a register of original writs, and in that register that word neither was nor is, nor up till now has it been used in the county court of Cheshire, wherefore, if that word had been put in the writ, by that addition the writ must according to the custom of Chester be quashed." [1]

The Exchequer enforced the king's fiscal rights, the King's Bench tried pleas of the Crown and heard appeals from other courts, the Common Pleas sat permanently in Westminster Hall to adjudicate, with the help of local juries from the shires, disputes between the owners of freehold land. Below them, though also subject to the king's overriding writ, were local courts of an older kind, administering the customary law of the neighbourhood. The most important of these was the shire court, presided over by the sheriff, which met one a month in the south and every six weeks in the wilder north. Held in some spot hallowed by immemorial usage and dating back to days when the shire had been almost an independent province, it was attended, not only by litigants, but by all, either in person or deputy who, holding freehold land in the county, owed it suit. For it was the basis of Anglo-Saxon and Danish law—long adopted by England's French-speaking kings and lords—that all freemen should by "witness of the shire" share responsibility for the administration of justice in the county where their lands lay.

At this great concourse of neighbours and men of substance, held either in the open air or, more often now, in a fine new hall of plea, like the one Edmund of Cornwall built for his duchy at Lostwithiel, royal ordinances and statutes were pro-

---

[1] *Select Cases in the Court of King's Bench under Edward I.* Vol. I. 43 (Selden Society, 1936).

claimed, officers and bailiffs were sworn in, inquests were held into disputed rights, and presentments made on matters relating to pleas of the Crown for trial by the itinerant justices. The suitors of the court also elected those required by the king to "bear the record of the shire" in the courts at Westminster or in parliament, and the coroners whose business it was to keep a record, independently of the sheriff, of all crimes and incidents affecting the Crown's rights and to hold inquests on sudden deaths, shipwrecks and discoveries of treasure trove. Sentence of outlawry was passed, too, in the shire court on anyone who had failed on four successive occasions to answer a summons to a criminal charge. Though its work was being increasingly superseded by the king's courts, it still had cognizance of cases in which the accused elected to be tried by the older methods of compurgation. Sometimes, too, when neither party wanted a jury, a plea of land would remain in the county court to be resolved by two professional champions contending all day with minute horn-tipped pick-axes until one or other yielded as "craven." [1]

Below the sheriff's court was the hundred court, held once every three weeks by a bailiff to whom the sheriff or the owner of the hundred jurisdiction had sublet its profits, but who, as a royal officer, was responsible to the sheriff, or, in a few special cases, directly to the Crown. It was usually held in the open air, the suitors of the court—freehold tenants of certain parcels of land—sitting on benches round a table occupied by the bailiff and his clerk. Its business was of a petty kind—claims for services arising out of land, detention of chattels and small debts, complaints about the maiming of beasts, and personal assaults and brawls not amounting to felony. The most common plea was trespass—an elastic offense which it was often easier to bring home to a neighbour in the hundred court than to compass in the rigid limits of a Chancery writ. It is doubtful, for instance, if Robert Kite could have obtained redress at Westminster from Stephen Winter whom he sued in the court of Milton hundred for coming into his garden, breaking down his hedges and carrying off his roses "against the peace," or John Malkin from Maud-atte-Hythe and her son for beating his pig and egging on their dogs till they bit off its tail! [2] There were other pleas,

[1] H. Cam, *The Hundred and the Hundred Rolls.*
[2] *Idem,* 181–2.

like verbal contracts and slander, for which the royal courts offered as yet no remedy, but under which rustic litigants could sue one another in those of the hundred.

Twice a year, at Easter and Michaelmas, the sheriff visited every hundred in the shire to hold a tourn or criminal court. Everyone who held freehold land in the hundred except the greater magnates had to attend or be fined for absence. In the tourn or "law-hundred," peasants of villein blood as well as freemen, played a part. For by Anglo-Saxon law every lay-man without land that could be forfeited for felony had to belong to a tithing—a group of neighbours responsible for one another's good conduct. Before the sheriff's annual view of frankpledge, as it was called, the bailiff checked the tithing lists of every village in his hundred, crossing out the names of those who had died since the last view and swearing in any lad who had reached the age of twelve and so become, in the eyes of the law, a responsible citizen. With his hand on the Bible the boy had to promise to keep the peace and be neither a thief nor helper of thieves. "I will be a lawful man," he swore, "and bear loyalty to our lord the king and his heirs, and I will be justiciable to my chief tithing man, so help me God and the saints." Then he and every other villager paid his tithing-penny, which constituted, with the various court fees and assized rents, the profits of the hundred jurisdiction.

At the sheriff's tourn every village or township was repre-sented by its reeve and four men who answered for any omission in its public duty and for such offences as ploughing up the king's highway or executing a thief caught red-handed without first securing the official witness of a royal bailiff or coroner. They were responsible too, for the township's pay-ment of fines imposed on it for breaches of the regulations for baking of bread and brewing of ale. They had to report to twelve freeholders called the jury of presentment all crimes that had been committed within the township. The tourn dealt, also, with nuisances like washing clothes in wells and pol-luting drinking-water. More serious offences were presented by the jury to the royal justices for trial on their next visit to the shire. When this happened the humble representatives of the village found themselves answering questions put to them under oath by the king's chief legal officers.

After Henry II no king did so much to make England a law-abiding land as his great-grandson, Edward I. Like his predecessor he took his legal responsibilities very seriously. As a boy he had studied law under his tutor, Hugh Giffard, one of his father's justices. The hero of his youth had been his uncle, the great French king, St. Louis, who had loved to sit under the oak at Vincennes dispensing justice to his subjects. His ideal and that of his age was of a delicately poised balance between conflicting claims, one in which every man's right to his own could be ascertained, weighed and enforced. For to the medieval mind, haunted by the memory of dark centuries of barbarism, justice was the highest earthly good, a mirror of the heavenly state in an imperfect world. It had nothing to do with equality, a conception then unknown. Its purport was expressed by a phrase in a legal treatise called *The Mirror of Justices,* written, it is believed, by a London fishmonger who held the office of city chamberlain: that "folk should keep themselves from sin and live in quiet and receive right according to fixed usage and holy judgments." The goal was a society in which every man was offered the peaceful means of enjoying his particular rights. Law was the mechanism provided by the Crown for ensuring him that opportunity.

Edward's sense of justice was of a narrower, less altruistic nature than that of St. Louis. He was resolved to do justice to all, but he did not except himself. Lordship to him was the first prerequisite of a Christian society—a right to be exercised justly and firmly and, wherever possible, extended. His duty to God and his people, he conceived, was to hold fast to his royal prerogative. He was always appealing to his coronation oath against suggestions that he should part with any of his rights, real or imagined; he held them, he said, in trust for his people. While endorsing the dictum of his subject, Andrew Horn, that "the law requires that one should use judgment, not force," he saw it as a contest, like the older trial-by-battle, in which a man was justified in using every technical nicety. He observed the full rigour of the game. Of its hard, intricate rules he showed himself as much a master of war, seizing every advantage and never yielding a point without the clearest necessity. The courts were his, established to ensure not only that justice was done but that the kingdom was firmly ruled. Though after one or two early attempts he refrained from insisting that his judges should act as his advocates in disputes with the subject, he kept special pleaders or serjeants to "sue for the king," like William of Gisleham and Gilbert of Thornton, the earliest-known king's serjeant. They and his attorney, Richard de Bretteville—forerunner of our attorney-general—were kept incessantly busy. "O Lord," wrote a clerk at the foot of a membrane recording that officer's many activities, "have pity on Bretteville!"

Yet Edward abided by his own rules. He used them to further his kingly ends but respected them. His favourite motto was, "Keep troth." And though he was a strict upholder of his legal rights, his judges were not afraid to take their stand on his law rather than on his will. There is a story of Chief Justice Hengham turning in the royal presence on two of his fellow judges who had upheld a royal writ of summons which failed to specify the charges against the defendant—an incorrigibly litigious countess. "The law wills," he declared, "that no-one be taken by surprise in the king's court. If you had your way this lady would answer in court for what she has not been warned to answer by writ. Therefore, she shall be warned by writ of the articles of which she is to answer, and this is the law of the land." Though thwarted, the king accepted his chief justice's objection, adding characteristically, "I have nothing to do with your disputations but, by God's blood, you shall give me a good writ before you arise hence!" [1]

It was this growing acceptance of law by king and subject that made justice a more realisable commodity in England than in any other land. To offer relief to the subject and strict and impartial justice to all in their degree, to ensure that under the Crown both the obligations and rights of a feudal society were observed, to unify and strengthen the realm, these were Edward's objects, tirelessly pursued. His instruments were the prerogative, the common law and royal courts of justice that had grown out of it and the periodic assemblies or parliaments of magnates, prelates, shire knights and burgesses that he had taken to summoning whenever he needed common counsel and consent in support of his measures. His three great statutes of Westminster of 1275, 1285, and 1290 were the crowning heights of his achievement. Each was a comprehensive code framed to amend, clarify and supplement the law and enable him to control the many-sided life of a passionate, turbulent and conservative people, rooted in ancient ways and divided by regional loyalties, rights and customs.

[1] *Select Cases in the Court of King's Bench under Edward I.* Vol. I. LXX (Selden Society, 1936).

The summer of 1285 saw the most intensive piece of law-making in medieval history. Drafted by the chancellor and judges, it bore the impress of the king's authoritative, unifying mind. In accordance with his favourite adage that "that which touches all should be approved by all," it was submitted to the magnates and representatives of the counties and boroughs at his Whitsun and Michaelmas parliaments. Like all his reforms of the law, it dealt with things in a severely practical way. It made great changes, yet never for the sake of change, only for clarification and greater working efficiency. Its object was to make the law operate justly and expeditiously.

First place, in that hierarchical age, was given to the grievances of the larger landowners. At a time when revenue from land was almost the sole source of livelihood for everyone except a few merchant speculators, its owner had to make provision during his lifetime, not only for his heir, but for his other children and his widow after his death. To prevent them from being left penniless he had to carve out of the family inheritance subsidiary estates to support them and their children and children's children. Yet if his own heirs were not to suffer, he had to ensure that such offshoots from his main estate should revert to it after they had fulfilled the purpose for which they were intended. In his gift to a son when he came of age or a daughter on her marriage a donor would stipulate that the land should return to him or his heirs if the donee's issue failed within so many generations.

Such settlements were immensely complicated by the rules of feudal enfeoffment. And during the thirteenth century the common law lawyers with their fine and subtle definitions, adopted the view that, if land had been given "to X and the heirs of his body," this must mean to X and his heirs absolutely as soon as an heir of his body was born. By availing himself of this interpretation an unscrupulous person—the husband, say, of a daughter to whom a conditional estate had been given—could dispose of the property as though it was his own fee simple and not a mere life-interest. In this way both the issue of the marriage could be deprived of the gift intended for them and the donor's estate of the reversion.

Naturally donors and their heirs, unversed in legal subtleties, regarded such alienation as a species of fraud. It particularly outraged the magnates, who, as tenants-in-chief of the Crown, had still to find out of their truncated fiefs the feudal services and aids due for the whole. Their plea that the king should redress the wrong that the operation of his own law had made possible was now met in the second Statute of Westminster. This did not seek to establish a perpetually enduring entail—a thing the Common Law regarded as unreasonable and unattainable. Its aim, as stated in the preamble, was to ensure that where a gift had been made on certain conditions to provide what were called estates of curtsey, dower or frank marriage, the rights of both beneficiaries and reversioners should be respected and that "the will of the donor expressed in the charter of gift should be observed."

Named after its opening words, *De Donis Conditionalibus* established what was to be the basic principle of English land law for seven centuries. Not only did it protect the reversion to the donor's heirs, but by forbidding alienation by the donee and so safeguarding the rights of his issue, it gave recognition to a new kind of heritable estate, inalienable as long as there was issue in tail of the original donee. Within practicable limits it ensured the primogenitary principle in the descent of both the parent estate and its offshoot. Owing to a flaw in one of its clauses, a generation later a loophole was found in the statute that enabled not the donee but his son to alienate the land and so disinherit his issue. But a great judge of Edward II's reign, Chief Justice Bereford, who had known what was in the mind of Edward I and his chief justice, Hengham, when they framed *De Donis,* insisted in a famous judgment on looking to the spirit instead of the letter of the statute and restored the entail in the grandson's favour, so establishing a precedent that was followed by the courts. And though, a century later, lawyers had found other ways of enabling tenants-in-tail to bar the entail, by that time it had become established that the principle of English landed inheritance, in families of modest wealth as well as large, should be primogeniture and not, as was the case in other western kingdoms, partition. Instead of being divided among younger sons, landed property in England was to be transmitted dynastically.

The effect of this on the nation's future can scarcely be exaggerated. It did not render the alienation of entailed estates impossible—for the ingenuity of lawyers proved inexhaustible—but it made it difficult. At a time when the rigid feudalism of the past was giving place to more elastic forms of tenure, a new land-owning class was encouraged by the common law to adopt the feudal military device for preserving landed property intact by transmission through the eldest son. Read aloud in Westminster Hall on June 28th, 1285, the second Statute of Westminster subordinated the promptings of personal affection to the long-term interests of the realm. It helped to create landed families whose estates and traditions, preserved from generation to generation, formed a school for training men for public service and the capacity to rule. The heads of such families looked after and enhanced their estates, making England in time to come the wealthiest farming country in the world, while relays of energetic and ambitious younger sons, educated for wealth but not endowed with it, went out from homes rich in transmitted standards of living and behaviour to make their fortunes and serve the State. *De Donis* helped to prevent the landed gentry from becoming, as on the continent, an exclusive caste divorced from responsibility. It made for an elastic as opposed to a rigid system of government, for enterprise and adventure instead of stagnation.

It was from this new landowning class, standing between the greater feudal magnates and the mass of the nation, that Edward created a new local judiciary. In every shire a number of trusted knights and landowners were appointed to act, in an unpaid capacity, as conservators or keepers of the peace. This was an extension of the Plantagenet system of dividing and broadening the exercise of provincial authority, formerly centred in the hands of the sheriff. For, in days of feudal delegation and inadequate communication, it had been found that too much power in a sheriff's hands ended in his becoming an irremoveable and even hereditary official, as ready to defy the Crown as those he was appointed to control. It had, therefore, been the policy of every king since Henry II to entrust every new power of the Crown, not to the sheriffs, but to other officers—to county coroners, justices of assize, commissioners of array and taxes, knights of the shire, and now conservators or, as they became in the next century, justices of the peace. In the reign of Edward's grandson, Edward III, these were given power to try felonies and misdemeanours and, in their courts of quarter sessions, to take over much of the criminal jurisdiction hitherto performed by the shire courts. Working within the traditional unit of local government, with all its binding ties of neighborhood and regional sentiment, they were subject, not to some provincial satrap whose interest it was to defy the Crown, but to the king's courts and officers at Westminster by whom they were appointed and in whose hands lay the power to dismiss them.

The source of their authority was the king, the terms under which they exercised it the Common Law, the link between them and the government the royal judges on their periodic visitations of inquest and gaol delivery. This interplay of central authority and local representation, of the rule of law and popularly delegated self-government, is the key to much of England's history.

If, thanks to her strong line of kings, the law and its subtle complex processes had taken the place of the sword, it was employed, by Crown and subject alike, with the ruthlessness of the battlefield. And it was often grossly abused. In a medieval State without a police force and only a minute administrative service, corruption and maladministration of justice were inevitable. Twice in his reign Edward I was forced to take drastic action against his own officers for abuses of the law. Sheriffs and their servants took bribes, were extortionate, refused writs or sold them at extortionate prices, and imprisoned men under legal pretences to make them pay for their release. Judges and their clerks let it be known that success in their courts would never attend a suitor who did no fee them. In 1289, on his return to England after three years in his French dominions, Edward found no less than seven hundred officials guilty of malpractices. Only two of the eight judges of the King's Bench and Common Pleas escaped disgrace, while five justices of eyre were found guilty and dismissed.

As some extenuation of the judges' conduct must be set the very modest salaries they received. The Church having refused to allow its members to plead in the lay courts because it regarded advocacy as a perversion of truth,[1] the Crown could no longer maintain a sufficiently experienced judiciary out of ecclesiastical benefices. Since it could not afford to pay adequate salaries, it let its judges supplement their income by fees. In an intensely litigious age, when every landowner was almost continuously engaged in the courts, rich suitors felt no compunction in supplementing the fees of judges and their clerks. Between such bonuses and bribery was only a step.

The most important result of these judicial scandals was a

---

[1] As early as 1217 Bishop Poore of Salisbury laid down in a *constitutio,* "Neither *clerici* nor priests are to appear as *advocati* in a secular tribunal unless in their own cases or those of poor persons." H. Cohen, *History of the English Bar,* 159.

reorganization of the legal profession. The task was entrusted to the new chief justice of the Common Pleas, John de Metyngham—one of the two members of the original bench to escape the purge. In 1292 he and his fellow judges were commissioned to choose from every county a number of the more promising students of law to be officially attached to the courts either as attorneys or as apprentices to the serjeants or *servientes ad legem* who pleaded before the king's judges. They were to enjoy a monopoly and their numbers, fixed at first at a hundred and forty, were to be left to the judges to add to as required. In other words, the profession was to regulate its own recruitment, education and rules of practice.

It was the beginning of a new form of learned education, one outside the Church and independent of it. A century after Henry II had been forced to concede immunity for clerics from lay justice, his great-grandson established secular training for the common law as an alternative to the study of civil law which, like every other form of learning, the Church in its universities reserved exclusively for its own members. It was an education based on the practice of the courts and necessitating great precision of thought and speech. It was taught, not by theorists in lecture rooms and libraries, but in crowded courts of law where, under the eye of the king's judges, quick and trained professional wits were pitted against one another, as the masters of forensic science, thinking and arguing on their feet, sought to fit the conflicting facts of their clients' disputes into the sharply defined framework of Common Law writs and procedures.

These tyros or apprentices assisted and devilled for their seniors as they do today, attended their consultations and listened to the thrust and parry of their contests from enclosures called "cribs" built at the sides of the courts. In the year in which the king entrusted their education to his judges there appeared the first of the Year Books—manuscript notes of cases, pleadings and forensic argument made for young advocates to help them master the intricacies of the law. Written in the legal French of the courts, they set out in staccato jottings the arguments and altercations, exceptions and answers of the great serjeants who dominated the courts at the end of the thirteenth and beginning of the fourteenth century—Lowther, Heyham, Howard, Hertpool, Huntingdom, Spigornel—and the interruptions and, often, caustic comments of the judges. "Leave off your noise and deliver yourself from his account," Chief Justice Hengham interrupts an over-persistent pleader. "Get to your business," his successor, Bereford, enjoins, "you plead one point, they about another, so that neither of you strikes the other." And when learned counsel tried to gain the day by arguing, "We have seen damages awarded in similar circumstances," Bereford replied: "You will never see them so long as I am here." "Where have you seen a guardian vouch on a writ of *dower*," asked another judge, and, when the incautious serjeant answered, "Sir, in trinity term last past, and of that I vouch the record," there came the crushing rejoinder, "If you find it, I will give you my hat!"

The interest of these early Year Books—and no other nation has anything like them—is the greater because, in those formative years, judges were helping by their judgments and the precedents they created to shape the future course of the law. Some of them, like Hengham, had even drafted it in the king's council chamber; "do not gloss the statute," he remarked on one occasion, "we know it better than you, for we made it." "The judgment to be by you now given," council reminded the court in another case, "will be hereafter an authority in every *quare non admissit* in England." For all their insistence on the rigid rules of pleading and procedure, such judges were very conscious of the immense discretionary power to do justice and equity delegated to them by their royal master. "You wicked rascal," Staunton, J. interrupted a dishonest attorney who had prayed for a *postea* in defiance of the rules of just dealing, "you shall not have it! But because you, to delay the woman from her dower, have vouched and not sued a writ to summon your warrantor, this court awards that you go to prison." [1]

The apprentice pleaders did not only learn together in the courts. They lived together in inns or hospices presided over by their senior members. In the leafy suburb of Holborn and in the Thames-side meadows between Westminster Hall and London's western walls there sprang up, during the years of expanding litigation that followed Edward's legislative reforms, a whole colony of such bachelor establishments. Keeping an inn seems to have become a highly profitable source of revenue for leaders of the legal profession, for some of them kept several; a Chancery clerk named John de Tamworth

---

[1] Selden Society XXII, Year Book Series IV, 195.

had, in the reign of Edward's grandson, no less than four in the neighbourhood of Fetter Lane. Similar inns were kept for the clerks of Chancery. Nearly all were rented from the ecclesiastical corporations or dignitaries—Templars, Hospitallers, Black Friars, the priory of St. Bartholomew, the convent of Clerkenwell, the abbey of Missenden, the Bishop of Ely— who owned most of the land to the west of London. Though never formally incorporated like the Church's residential colleges and halls at Oxford and Cambridge, they helped to create esprit de corps and standards of professional conduct among those studying and practising the law. Many of them adopted a practice of holding legal debates or moots; when in 1344 Clifford's Inn was demised to a society of apprentices of the law, one of its rules was that "every member shall be obliged in his turn to carry on all manner of erudition and learning in the said inn that appertains to an outer barrister." [1]

After Edward I had placed the education of the legal profession under his judges and divorced it from the Church, its wealth and influence grew rapidly. In an acquisitive and evolving society in which litigation had taken the place of private war, the brethren of the coif—the white silken hood worn by the king's serjeants-at-law and the judges who were chosen from their ranks—constituted a new aristocracy; "law," wrote the poet Langland, "is grown lord"! Their wealth was a phenomenon; in the poll-tax on 1379 the judges of the King's Bench and Common Pleas were assessed at more than earls and more than twice as much as barons, with whom the serjeants and greater "apprentices at law," or barristers, as they later became called, were grouped as equals. Even "lesser apprentices who followed the law" had to pay as much as aldermen.

By the end of the fourteenth century the judges in their scarlet robes trimmed with white budge or lambskin and the serjeants in their long parti-coloured gowns of blue, green and brown, cut almost as great a figure as the magnates and prelates. Their splendour did not make them or their profession popular. To a simple Christian mind there seemed something indecent in making a livelihood, let alone a fortune, out of influencing judgment by forensic subtleties. "Whosoever speaks the truth for a price," declared a preacher, "or

[1] E. Williams, *Early Holborn and the Legal Quarter of London*, I, 15.

does justice for reward sells God who is himself both truth and justice." [1] Lawyers were regarded as special pleaders who championed any cause for a fee and unsuited the innocent with technical tricks and quibbles in a jargon that no man but they could understand. In his epic on Christian justice, Langland depicted the serjeants-at-law in their hoods of silk hovering like hawks at the bar,

> "Pleading for pence and pounds the law,
> Not for love of Our Lord unloosening their lips.
> Thou mightest better measure the mist on Malvern hills
> Than get a mumble out of them till money were shown."

They seemed to him outside the pale of salvation.

To a lawyer, absorbed in a fascinating intellectual pursuit and a member of a professional brotherhood which had already developed a sense of tradition and *esprit de corps,* all this appeared in a very different light. How different is shown by Chief Justice Thirning's claim that in the reign of Edward III "the law was of the greatest perfection that ever it was." Yet, though most of the judges and serjeants were men of probity, proud of their calling and of the law they administered,[2] to the layman the law for long continued to seem incomprehensibly complex and formalistic. Suitors found their writs abated and themselves unsuited for minute errors in Latin or even spelling, or quashed by the judges because they did not closely enough resemble those that already existed, however inadequate these were for the needs of a developing society. Earlier in the century a great judge like William de Bereford could still look beyond the letter of the law and insist that, if it outraged natural justice, the court should offer redress to a suitor injured by such formalism. "This is not properly a debt but a penalty," he told a plaintiff who was demanding the last penal ounce from his bond; "what equity would it be to award you the debt when the document is tendered and when you cannot show that you have been

---

[1] Master Ralph of Acton, G. R. Owst, *Literature and Pulpit,* 344.

[2] Like Chaucer's "man of law"—believed to have been drawn from his friend, Thomas Pynchbeck, who, admitted serjeant in 1376, became chief baron of the Exchequer:

> "In terms of law had he the judgments all
> That from the timës of King Will were fall, . . .
> And every statute could he plead by rote."

damaged by the detention?" Yet before long, judges were laying it down that equity was one thing and the common law another and that they were exactly bound by the wording of statutes and their predecessors' decisions. If as late as 1345 Chief Justice Stonor, who had first practised in the days of Edward I, could still declare that "law is that which is right," the spirit of the bench in the second half of the century was put by Hillary J., when he said, "We will not and *we cannot* change ancient usages." [1]

In the long run there was to be gain as well as loss in this, for, by walking closely in well-trodden steps, judges and pleaders were building up a body of precedent so strong that, so long as they stuck closely to it, even the king and his ministers would presently have difficulty in forcing them from it. This was to prove a safeguard for men's rights against tyranny. But at the moment the threat to the ordinary man was not from the king but from the over-powerful neighbour who, with the help of force and fraud, could use formalistic legal processes and the letter of the law to trick him out of his rights and property. From this inflexibility of the Common Law courts the only appeal was to the king and his Council—the original source from which the judges derived their power. As the remedies of a system of law made for a rural and feudal society became increasingly inadequate, the Council took to referring petitions for relief and redress to the chancellor who, as the chief executive officer of the Crown, possessed in the Chancery staff a body of clerks accustomed to framing and issuing writs. Usually himself a cleric and trained in the canonical principles of equity and, in theory, the "keeper of the king's conscience," he seemed the natural channel through which the discretionary prerogative powers of justice could be granted. There thus began to grow up, side by side with the ordinary courts, a Chancery court of equity transcending and overriding their rules wherever these manifestly outraged conscience and reason. Those who sought the king's grace could petition the Crown for a remedy, on which, if the chancellor considered the petition or "bill" justified, he would issue a writ to compel the party whose wrong was complained of to return a sworn answer under penalty—or *sub poena*—of a heavy fine. By examining the petitioner and re-

[1] *Year Books* 2 and 3 Edw. II (Selden Society) xiii, 59 cit. T. F. Plucknett, *A Concise History of the Common Law*, 639.

spondent and allowing them to interrogate one another under
oath he would then adjudicate the case without the aid of a
jury as natural justice dictated. For it needed the royal prerogative of doing justice and equity to temper the harsh
rigidity of the Common Law.

Yet though the courts at Westminster in the latter Middle
Ages were often narrow and inflexible—and in ways that the
great twelfth and thirteenth century lawyers had never en-
visaged—and though, being tied by inherited serfdom to the
soil they cultivated, nearly half the English people could not
yet sue in the royal courts in respect of their "villein" land,
livestock or property—all of which in the law's eyes belonged
to their lords—the Common Law operated imperceptibly to
widen the bounds of justice. For its spirit did not favour serfdom. However strong the class bias and interest of its officers,
it leant instinctively towards liberty. In this it differed from
the civil law of the continental kingdoms which derived from
Roman imperial law and a civilisation whose economic basis
had been slavery. The English ideal was the "free and lawful
man"—*liber et legalis homo*—entitled to equal justice, answerable for the acts of others only if he had commanded or con-
sented to them, and presumed by the law to be a rational and
responsible being and, as such, expected to play his part in
administering justice by representing the local community
before the king's judges and assisting them in the determination of fact. Though vast numbers of once free peasants had
become tied to the soil during the feudal anarchy of the Dark
Ages, and their liberties been further eroded under their
grasping Norman conquerors, even before the Peasants' Revolt of 1381 the genius of the Common Law was granting to
the bondsman rights which it regarded as the heritage of all.
It treated him as free in his relation to everyone except his
lord, protected him against the latter's crimes and gave him
the benefit of the doubt in questions affecting feudal status,
holding, for instance, that the illegitimate child of parents, one
of whom was free, must be free too, contrary to the practice
elsewhere. Though it enforced serfdom where serfdom could
be proved, it construed every sign of freedom as a proof of
freedom. It allowed a lord whose bondsman had fled from his
"villein nest" a writ, *de nativo habendo,* bidding the sheriff
hand over the fugitive, but it allowed the latter another, *de
libertate probanda,* which set him at liberty until the lord had
proved in the king's courts a right to his return. "In the begin-

ning," said Justice Herle in a judgment of Edward II's reign, "every man in the world was free, and the law is so favourable to liberty that he who is once found free and of free estate in a court of record shall be holden free for ever unless some later act of his own makes him villein." [1]

It was this sense that the law in England made for a freedom unknown elsewhere that caused the great fifteenth century lawyer, Chief Justice Fortescue, in his *De Laudibus Legum Angliae*, to write, "The King of England cannot alter nor change the laws of the realm at his pleasure. . . . The law, indeed, by which a group of men is made into a people, resembles the nerves of the body physical, for, just as the body is held together by the nerves, so this body mystical is bound together and united into one by the law, . . . and the members and bones of this body, which signify the solid basis of truth by which the community is sustained, preserve their rights through the law, as the body natural does through the nerves. And just as the head of the body physical is unable to change its nerves, or to deny its members proper strength and due nourishment of blood, so a king, who is head of the body politic, is unable to change the laws of that body, or to deprive that same people of their own substance uninvited or against their wills."

[1] *Year Books*, 3 Ed. II, 94 (Selden Society), cit. H. S. Bennett, *Life on the English Manor*, 309.

CHAPTER VI

COMMON COUNSEL AND PARLIAMENT

BY THE BEGINNING of the thirteenth century a remarkable thing had started to happen. The people of England, conquered a hundred and fifty years earlier by a foreign aristocracy who had seized their land and despised their language, were becoming more conscious than ever before of their unity and nationhood. And though their kings and lords still spoke French and boasted French descent, even they had begun to think of themselves as English and of their country as England. Within a generation of the Conquest an Italian archbishop of Canterbury was writing of "we English" and "our island."

For there seemed to be something in the land that naturalised foreigners and, adapting their ways, absorbed them. It was due largely to its being cut off from Europe by sea, so that its diverse folk gradually came to think of themselves, not merely as barons or knights, churchmen, merchants or peasants, but as members of a distinct community that was both part of western Christendom and yet apart from it. Before Frenchmen had come to regard themselves as Frenchmen, Germans as Germans or Italians as Italians, Englishmen, including the Normans settled in England, thought of themselves as Englishmen. This sense of separateness was aided by their kings' insistence on the unity of the realm and on a common system of law. And it was stimulated by the difficulty the conquerors—a few thousand warriors speaking a foreign tongue—experienced in ruling so stubborn a race. A hundred years after Hastings there were still Englishmen who persisted in going unshaved as a protest against the Conquest. Living in this misty land of rain and deep clay forests among an alien population, the Norman knights could only exploit their conquest by meeting the natives half, and more than half-way.

They needed English men and women to plough their fields, tend their homes, nurse their children and help them in battle. And the English did so—on terms: that their conquerors left them English and became in the end English themselves.

Since their numbers were so small, the conquerors soon became bilingual. They continued to think and converse among themselves in French, but spoke English with their subordinates. They learnt it from their nurses and servants, reeves and ploughmen, and, after the conquest was complete, from their men-at-arms. Abbot Samson of Bury—head of the richest monastery in the land—preached to the common people in the dialect of Norfolk where he had been born and bred. And by the end of the twelfth century even Normans were coming to take a pride in the history and traditions of the country they had won and to treasure the legends of its saints and heroes. The monkish historians, Henry of Huntingdon and William of Malmesbury, collected the ballads and tales of old England, and Gerald de Barry, the Marcher's son, loved to boast of his Welsh ancestry and the beauties and antiquities of his Pembrokeshire home. It was a Norman—Geoffrey of Monmouth, bishop of St. Asaph—who wrote the romantic tale of King Arthur and his British court and made it almost as favourite a theme with the French-speaking ruling-class as the exploits of Charlemagne and the Song of Roland. It helped to make Britain's inhabitants—Normans, Welsh and English alike—believe that they had a common history.

French and English place-names were blended on the map; English place and Norman owner grown English—Norton Fitzwarren, Pillerton Hersey, Sturminster Marshal, Berry Pomeroy. And the marriage of Church and State, spiritual and secular, was consummated, too, in this land where everything ultimately merged and became part of something else: Abbots Bromley and Temple Guiting, Toller Monachorum and Salford Priors, Whiteladies Aston and Whitechurch Canonicorum. The great bishop, Richard le Poore, who built Salisbury cathedral, left his heart to be buried in the little Dorset village of Tarrant Crawford.

From all this sprang a new force with which kings and barons and even the Church had to reckon: that of national opinion. Its chief repositories were the men who were growing up between the greater feudal barons and the inarticulate peasant mass of the nation. It was an upper middle-class composed mainly of descendants of the Norman knights who had been enfeoffed as owners, or rather feudal holders, of the soil and whose fiefs, though originally granted for life, had become, like other property, hereditary. As their military functions fell into abeyance, they became, instead of professional soldiers, landed gentlemen with administrative responsibilities. They served on the new juries of the grand assize and in the "oversight" of the royal forests, performed the customary duties of suit of court in the shire and hundred courts, and gave testimony on oath in the periodical inquests of kings and sheriffs. They intermingled increasingly with the wealthier English freemen and landholders and with the Anglo-Norman traders of London and the new towns. Many of our oldest families—Berkeleys and Nevilles, Lumleys, Leghs and Clavells —sprang from this twelfth century knighthood rising into gentility. It found its natural leaders in the officials and judges whom the kings had set up as a counterpoise to the higher feudal aristocracy and ennobled with grants of land. It was employed by the Crown for an evergrowing host of local administrative and legal tasks. It provided laymen of trust and character with the time for public service, and ecclesiastics with sufficient personal status to make the Church in England rather more independent of foreign control than elsewhere.

The Norman and Angevin system of common law and central administration helped to train this new upper or upper-middle class. So did the ancient Anglo-Saxon institutions of local government. The shire and hundred courts, the juries impanelled to pronounce on questions of fact, the larger towns beginning to win rights of self-government from their overlords, all gave men opportunities of learning to act in co-operation, of administering corporate affairs and finance, and of reaching practical decisions after ordered discussion. As the nation grew in wealth and civilisation, more and more public business was left to local men of worth rich enough to take communal responsibility under the Crown yet not strong enough, like the greater feudal lords, to act without it. After Henry II's death the judges and officials he had trained continued to enforce justice even under his crusader successor, Richard Coeur de Lion, who during his ten years' reign was almost continuously out of the country. But the real test for them came during the reign of Henry's youngest son, John. This erratic and moody tyrant, who inherited much of his father's genius but none of his creative capacity, used the legal and administrative machinery he had inherited to subject the English landowning classes to intolerable and arbitrary taxation. He levied scutage after scutage—the composition which tenants-in-chief and their military vassals had to pay in lieu of the service in the field by which they held their lands—not only after his campaigns but before them, so getting the money whether he incurred the expenses of a war or not. While his father in thirty-five years levied only eight scutages and his crusading brother two, John in fifteen years imposed eleven, several for service on campaigns that never took place. Hitherto the extent of such service and of composition for it had been limited by feudal custom. John varied it at his pleasure. The rate at which it was assessed was almost double that of his brother's day.

As well as scutage and the customary feudal aids from his tenants-in-chief, John imposed levies on the capital value of all personal and moveable goods—an impost originally instituted for Richard's crusade to recover Jerusalem—and at least seven general tallages on the manors and boroughs of the royal demesne. Some of these, like Worcester, Northampton and Oxford, had to pay three or four times as much as they had paid before. When his tenants' estates, through death or other cause, fell into his custody John stripped them by special tallages of almost their entire realisable capital. He seized men's children as hostages and trafficked the wardships of minors and the marriages of heiresses to the basest agents. He made mercenary captains sheriffs and simultaneously allowed them to hold judicial office, so enabling them to blackmail property-owners with vexatious writs and false accusations. Summonses were issued in order to extract fines for non-attendance, writs were withheld or sold at exorbitant rates, crushing penalties imposed without regard to the nature of the offence or means of the accused, justice delayed or even denied altogether. The elaborate fiscal and legal system of the two Henrys and the great justiciars was turned into a merciless machine for extortion.

In the light of his son's use of it Henry II's achievement had presented England with a terrible dilemma. The great Angevin had convinced the nation and even its feudal magnates that, after the disorder of Stephen's reign, happiness and prosperity for all depended on the supremacy of the Crown. He had created a legal and financial machinery for making that supremacy effective and a self-renewing school of trained administrators to operate it. But when his son proved a diabolical maniac, who used the royal power to make life intolerable for his subjects and alienated everyone in turn, those whom Henry had made the agents of that power were, little by little, driven into making a choice. They had either to destroy it, and with it the order and unity on which the prosperity of the realm depended, or subject the wearer of the crown himself to it. The first course might have been easy; the second was superlatively hard. It is the supreme measure of Henry II's achievement in educating his greater subjects that the best of them chose the second, and carried their reluctant fellows with them.

Yet the very cunning and ability of his son also impelled men to that wiser choice. Had John been a weakling as well as an impossible king, the monarchical power which had become the expression of England's unity could scarcely have survived the storms raised by his misdeeds. Yet for all his periodic lethargy, when driven into a corner he fought back with a fury that made even the most reckless or arrogant opponent chary of going to extremes. It was no child's play to dash from his hands the sceptre and rod he misused. The alternative of restraining and controlling him—and with him the royal power—was thus kept open.

It was an alternative, too, to which Englishmen now instinctively turned. It was of the Crown that they thought when they used the word England, for without it there would have been no England. Ever since the days of Alfred the monarchy had been implanting in them the habit of acting together. The great alien princes who had grasped in their strong hands the athelings' sceptre—Canute the Dane, William and Henry the Normans, Henry the Angevin—had all strengthened it. It had become natural even to Anglo-Norman barons to act with and through the Crown. They still tried to do so when its wearer of the hour became their oppressor and enemy.

Only the barons, with their armour, horses, castles and men-at-arms, had the means to withstand such a tyrant. Even for them it involved intense danger. But they had been driven to desperation. Some were reactionaries who sought to restore the untrammelled rights of provincial feudalism. Others were selfish bullies who wished to free themselves from royal control in order to oppress their weaker neighbours. Most, however, were members of the new aristocracy of office which

Henry II had used to discipline the older nobility and fashion the administrative machine that had now been turned into an instrument of irresponsible tyranny. They were strongest in the north, where authority had always been left to the man on the spot and where local magnates were used to defending themselves against Scottish raiders. It was these northerners, who, goaded beyond endurance, in the summer of 1213 refused a royal demand for scutage. In this they were acting beyond their rights, for it was part of the feudal law that an overlord could tax his tenants-in-chief to support his wars. But they maintained that such a right could be denied if it was not used justly and within the limits set by custom.

Others felt that their first duty was to the Crown, irrespective of its wearer. The king's majesty had become more important to them than the king himself. The tenure of their lands, their dignities and honours, the functioning of their local institutions and the administration of justice and order were all inextricably bound up with it. The nation was drifting into war, not only between its best elements and its worst, but between the best themselves. Men were appealing from the king to the king's law and taking their stand, in the name of the just laws of the king's father, against the king's government. The perils inherent in the situation were intense.

To resolve it called not only for loyalty and selflessness, but for the most subtle, comprehending statesmanship. And in its primate, Stephen Langton, the nation found what it needed. Langton was a scholar trained in the close logic of the medieval Church, with a vision that embraced all Christendom. His temper was essentially moderate, conciliatory and unassuming. He had the kind of good sense and quiet, rather whimsical humour that takes the hysteria out of strained situations. He was always seeking to achieve what men of goodwill, after calmly hearing and debating all the arguments, considered both just and expedient. His aim was reasonableness even more than reason. In this he was most English. So was he in his respect for established custom and dislike of extremes.

It was not Langton's wish to see the Crown overthrown, the law ignored, the realm divided, the barons petty sovereigns as in the days of Stephen. For two years—amongst the most crucial in English history—he struggled, not only with his treacherous and tyrannical sovereign, but with the factious interests and violent passions of those who were trying to use the resentment the latter had aroused to destroy the peace and the unity of the realm. He repeatedly urged them not to carry things to extremes, while reminding the king of his coronation oath and the solemn compacts to govern justly of his predecessors. All that was needed to restore justice and peace to England, he claimed, was to renew such compacts. "A charter of Henry I has been found," he told the barons, "by means of which, if you desire, you may regain your lost liberty." And he tried unceasingly to induce them to base their demands on its terms.

Langton's wisdom and moderation failed to save England from the civil war he feared—one in which John, after ravaging his own country, met his death after a disastrous march through the flooded Nene. But before war broke out, on June 15th 1215 in a Thames-side meadow called Runnymede the armed barons, with the archbishop's aid, forced the reluctant monarch to set his seal to a document which became a blueprint for England's future constitutional development. Ostensibly a restatement of ancient law and custom, it promised that the king should not without "general counsel," that is without the consent of the great council, demand any scutage or aid from his tenants-in-chief other than the three regular aids long recognised by feudal custom; that the heirs of earls and barons should be admitted to their inheritances on payment of the customary reliefs; that the estates of heirs-in-ward should not be wasted during their infancy nor widows robbed of their dowries or forced against their will to marry royal nominees. It laid down that no free man should be imprisoned or dispossessed save by process of law and the just judgments of his equals; that he should not be taxed or fined unreasonably or to his ruin; that his means of livelihood, including the merchant's stock, the craftsman's tools and the peasant's wainage, should be free from amercement; that London and the chartered boroughs should enjoy their ancient liberties; that merchants should come and go safely in time of war; and that the foreign mercenaries should be dismissed. It provided for the regular administration of the judicial system; ordered that the common pleas should be held at Westminster and not follow a perambulating court; that none should be made justices, bailiffs or constables who did not know the law of the land; that sheriffs should not sit in judgment in their own shires; that two justices with four knights of the shire should hold assizes in every county every quarter; that royal writs should not be sold at exorbitant prices or withheld from those entitled to them. "To none," the king was made to swear, "will we sell, to none will we deny or delay right or justice."

In all this the Charter, which consisted of more than sixty clauses, was a recital of the wrongs suffered by Englishmen under a tyrannical king. And, as men of property—and, above all, landed property—were the only subjects with rights enforceable in the king's own courts, it confined itself in the main to setting out particulars of the redress granted them. It was a charter of "liberties," and to the medieval mind a liberty was a right to the enjoyment of a specific property. It was a freedom to do something with one's own without interference by the king or any other man.

Called Magna Carta because of its length, the Charter was not, therefore, a declaration of general principles, let alone of human rights. Medieval men thought of these only in connection with religion. The Charter enunciated no theories; it was nothing if not specific and practical. Yet, though its chief beneficiaries were tenants-in-chief of the Crown, it was a national as well as feudal document. It made no distinction between Norman and English and guaranteed the liberties of small property-owners as well as large. Thirty-two of its sixty-one clauses dealt with the relations of the king and his subjects and not merely his tenants-in-chief. "We grant," it declared, "to all the freemen of our realm, from us and our heirs forever, all the undermentioned liberties to have and to hold for them as our heirs from us and our heirs." And it established two precedents of immense significance for the future. One was that when an English king broke the feudal compact and gave his vassals the right—universally recognised by feudal law—to renounce their allegiance, it was not necessary to dissolve the bonds of political society and disintegrate the realm. Magna Carta was a substitute for deposition: a legal expedient to enforce customary law that left the king on the throne and the sword of civil war undrawn. Government in England, though exercised by the king, was to be rooted in justice and based on law, or it was not to be accepted as government at all. Magna Carta was the first great political act in the history of the nation-state—itself an institution of which the English had been the pioneers.

The barons' unity in the face of John's injustice, and their decision to act within the law had created a new phenomenon: a corporate estate of the realm to prevent the unjust exercise of power by the realm's ruler. The taxpayers had combined to control the tax-imposer. Magna Carta was the product not of a rebellion, as it seemed at the time to the king and his more bitter opponents, but of a revolution carried out by process of law. By the provisions for summoning the great council before any new aid or scutage could be granted, it made a representative assembly of feudal tenants a preliminary to taxing those tenants. This was something wholly new. And in establishing the principle that the king must conform to the law which he administered, it created a constitutional device for compelling him to do so. In addition to provisions for regulating the summons of lords to the council—archbishops, earls, bishops and greater barons by individual writ, and lesser barons by collective summons through the sheriffs —the Charter contained a clause by which twenty-five representative barons, chosen by their Order, were to become its guardians. They were to "observe, keep and cause to be observed, with all their might" the liberties it guaranteed. Should any of them be infringed, and just redress be refused, these twenty-five lords—almost all of whom had served, or were the sons of men who had served, as royal officials—were empowered to take up arms against the king to enforce the Charter. The indignant John was made to admit his subjects' right to restrain the wearer of the Crown whenever he infringed their liberties. "These barons," he had to announce on behalf of himself and his heirs, "with all the commons of the land shall distrain and annoy us by every means in their power; that is, by seizing our castles, lands and possessions, and every other mode, till the wrong shall be repaid to their satisfaction, saving our person, our queen and our children. And when it shall be repaired, they shall obey us as before."

By this device, though a clumsy and primitive one, the men who had wrung Magna Carta from the king sought to ensure its permanence. It was dictated by fear and the just belief of the barons that the moment their force was dispersed John would try to destroy both them and their settlement. Its dangers were clearly foreseen by Langton who tried, though in vain, to introduce a mediating body between the king and the barons' council. "They have given me," declared the furious monarch, "twenty-five over-kings!" Yet the pattern of constitutional thought thus set was to be reproduced in a thousand forms in the history of the English nation. It is still enshrined, after seven centuries, in the words of the national anthem:

> "May he defend our laws
> And ever give us cause
> To sing with heart and voice
> God save the king!"

It was a prayer that the best of those who stood by the king's shoulder at Runnymede had tried to realise.

Several times during the 56 years' reign of John's son—who succeeded to the throne in 1216 at the age of nine—the Charter was re-confirmed. Henry III was a good, weak, obstinate, unreliable man who got himself and the country into grave financial difficulties through an ambitious foreign policy which he was incapable of implementing. In 1255, at the Easter feast at Oxford, he appealed to the assembled magnates—the country's chief taxpayers with whom he had been quarrelling —to rescue him and the administration from his almost bottomless debts. The barons' leaders took counsel of one another and at the end of April came to the council armed. They left their swords at the door—a custom still enshrined in the ritual of parliament—but made the king and his eldest son, the young Lord Edward, swear to abide by their advice. It was agreed that a committee of twenty-four, half chosen by the barons and half by Henry, should draft proposals for a plan of reform to redress the nation's grievances and restore the ancient co-operation between Crown and magnates.

That summer, at a meeting at Oxford of the great council, the reforming committee's provisions were announced. They were accepted by the king who saw in them his only hope of obtaining the aid he needed. They were of a most drastic kind. An *ad hoc* Council of Fifteen was to "have the power of advising the king in good faith concerning the government of the kingdom . . . in order to amend and redress everything that they shall consider in need of amendment or redress." If its members failed to agree or were not all present, a decision of the majority was to bind all—a principle of great future significance. It was to have authority over the justiciar, treasurer and chancellor—who was to seal nothing by the king's will alone without the Council's knowledge—to reform the royal household, to place the castles in the hands of native-born custodians, and to appoint sheriffs annually from men of the counties they administered.

Of these measures the most important was that which regulated the meetings of the great council of the realm or parliament as it was now beginning to be called—the enduring embodiment of the ancient English custom that a king should take counsel of his chief men and have "deep speech" with them. Parliament was a French word for such deep speech, for talking things over. Magna Carta had indicated the means by which the magnates—earls, barons, bishops and greater abbots—were to be summoned to meetings of this body. It was now enacted that parliament should meet regularly three times a year, at Michaelmas, Candlemas and in June. "To these three parliaments," it was declared, "the chosen councillors of the king shall come, even if they are not summoned, in order to examine the state of the kingdom and consider its common needs and those of the king." And to them were to come twelve representatives of the general "community"—that is the general body of barons. Their approval of whatever the Council decided was thereafter to bind the community.

The reforming Fifteen acted quickly. While parliament received and investigated hundreds of judicial petitions, it began with furious energy to reform the kingdom's internal wrongs, appointing four representative knights in every shire to draw up for the consideration of the royal judges lists of grievances and unjust administrative practices. For, with all their limitations, the barons had learnt the lesson that Langton had taught them at the beginning of the century. Their attitude was now not only feudal but national; their business, as they saw it, not only to defend their interests, but to champion those of the community as a whole. "We wish," their spokesmen had declared in the council as far back as 1234, "to keep in mind the common welfare of the realm and not to burden the poor." They had made provision in their periodic meetings for relieving poor suitors from a ruinous attendance on the royal courts by permitting them to plead by attorney, and had sought to protect merchants from royal purveyors, and widows and minors from grasping overlords. Now, at a time of widespread hardship and discontent, when a succession of bad harvests, with famine and pestilence, had brought many to the verge of ruin, they proclaimed their intention of investigating the complaints of the lesser freeholders, even the poorest and most obscure.

Yet in doing so, their movement lost its unity. The zeal of the more ardent reformers outran the disinterestedness of the more conservative. The barons had been united in their resolve to check the king's extravagant foreign adventures, to rid the government of aliens and to take their rightful place in the control of the realm. But when it was proposed that, having reformed the abuses of the royal administration, the Council of Fifteen should investigate those of the baronial courts—in other words, the grievances of their own tenants—many barons, led by the great Marcher earl of Gloucester, Richard de Clare, felt that it was time to call a halt.

Yet, as much as the magnates, the lesser landowners of the shires had been politically awakened by the growing efficiency and extortionate power of the royal officials. They, too, had to unite to control them or lose their self-respect. And the very use the barons were making of them and the part they already played in the kingdom's administration rendered them a force to be reckoned with. They had been called upon in the past year to elect four of their members in every shire to ensure that the sheriff observed the law and to report his misdemeanours to the justiciar. They had now been given the duty of electing in the county courts four men from the shire from whom the exchequer was to choose the sheriff of the year. And, they were accustomed in a humble and attendant capacity, to send representatives or knights of the shire to the king's courts at Westminster, and had occasionally been summoned to meetings of the great council or parliament to answer questions on oath on local matters of taxation or justice.

Had king, barons and prelates—the privileged ruling Orders of the realm—been united, these rustic knights, or bachelors as they were called, would have counted for little. But in the revolutionary situation that now existed they were able to make their voice heard. They did so—in no uncertain fashion—for the first time in English history in the autumn of 1259, when at the royal feast of St. Edward held at Westminster before the meeting of parliament they addressed a corporate protest to the Lord Edward, the king's son and heir. In this document, known as the "protest of the Community of Bachelors of England," they complained that, while "the lord king had performed and fulfilled all and singular that the barons had ordained, . . . the barons themselves had done nothing of what they had promised for the good of the realm; but only for their own good and to the harm of the king elsewhere."

The twenty-year-old prince—the future Edward I, whose ardent, noble head as a youth can be seen carved in stone above a capital in the north transept of Westminster Abbey—responded to this tactfully phrased appeal with characteristic frankness. Though devoted to his father, he was in his directness his complete opposite. He had sworn, he declared, a solemn oath at Oxford and, though he had made it reluctantly, "he was not on this account less prepared to stand by it and to expose himself to death for the community of England and for the advantage of the State." [1] He, therefore, informed the barons that, unless they fulfilled their oath, he would support the "community" of bachelors and help to enforce it.

As a result, further reforms entitled the Provisions of Westminster—the complement of the earlier Provisions of Oxford—were enacted in parliament. These provided among other things that no-one except the king and his ministers should levy distraints outside his fief, that no-one without a royal writ should compel his free tenants to respond in his court to any matter concerning their free tenements, that none but the king should hear appeals of false judgments, and that no charter of exemption from assize or jury service should exempt a man, however great, from the obligation to testify on oath in the royal courts if his doing so was essential to justice.

The reforms for which the Council of Fifteen had been set up were now complete. A wilful, vain monarch had been taught the lesson that England could only be ruled with the assent of her leading men. And unlike his father, he had learnt it without bloodshed. Moderate and informed opinion, therefore, began to veer towards the Crown, feeling that the nation should return to the form of government to which it was used.

Yet England had a further lesson to learn and a harsher. Her sovereign's obstinacy had awoken feelings that could not be easily resolved. There was a strange ferment in the air: of vague, vehement talk of justice and treason, not to the king

[1] *Annals of Burton*, cit. B. Wilkinson, *Constitutional History of England*, I, 171.

but to the community; of friars preaching apocalyptic sermons in streets and on village greens; of cities arming their men and watching their gates; of war in the Marches where the prince of Gwynnedd, Llywelyn ap Gruffydd, enraged by the encroachments of English officials, was making a new nation of the Welsh and burning the lands and castles of the Marchers.

All this might have come to nothing in that politically immature age but for one circumstance. That circumstance was a great man. Simon de Montfort had come to England from France thirty years earlier to claim the earldom of Leicester and marry the king's sister. He had little liking for the English and never really understood them.[1] But he was obsessed with the belief that power should be exercised as a sacred trust and that it was a Christian noble's duty to enforce justice. It was this conviction, and his dynamic capacity to communicate it to others, that won him the devotion of all whose hopes of a juster society had been quickened by the baronial reforms. He appealed to the discontented, to the hothead young lords and bachelors, to the men outside the Constitution, to the merchants and apprentices of the eastern towns, particularly of London and the Cinque Ports, to the preaching friars who went among the poor, to the ragged scholars and simple craftsmen and artisans who wanted to see God's kingdom made on earth. The son of the crusader who had crushed the Albigensians and won Provence for the French Crown, he invested every policy he championed with a passionate religious earnestness. He was a man, it was said, who watched more often than he slept; "Sir Simon the Righteous," they called him. The Provisions of Oxford which he had helped to frame had become in his eyes divine commandments. "He stood firm like an immoveable pillar," wrote a monkish admirer, "and neither threats, promises, gifts nor flattery could avail to move him .... to betray the oath which he had taken to reform the kingdom."

The trouble was that Simon did not attach the same meaning to that oath as either the king, who had subscribed to it, or the ordinary conservative-minded Englishman of his day.

---

[1] That "coward" people, he once called them. "An Englishman, he said, would put you in a hole and then turn tail, and when he said this he was thinking of the legend of which Frenchmen made a favourite gibe, that the English had tails." F. M. Powicke, *Henry III and the Lord Edward,* 409.

He maintained that the Council of Fifteen set up at Oxford was no mere temporary expedient to reform abuses and re-establish government by assent, but a permanent executive council to rule in the king's name. Yet the throne had always been the medium through which England had been governed, and it was hard for Englishmen to conceive of any other and still harder to devise a substitute for it. To constrain an English king to rule with the assent of his magnates was one thing, to exercise his functions for him another. De Montfort, in the name of reform, was advocating a form of government wholly foreign to English tradition.

Without this provocative challenge Henry, an ageing man who had learnt his lesson, would almost certainly have acquiesced in the baronial reforms. They had been demanded by the entire nation. But this oligarch, with his haughty claims to subject him to a council of nobles and summon parliament in his absence, aroused all his obstinacy and petulance and his most treacherous, dangerous mood. And the jealousy and alarm which the proud, unbending Frenchman awoke in his associates, and in moderate and conservative men generally, created a party for the king which had not before existed. For Simon's violence and intransigence sooner or later alienated everyone who tried to work with him as an equal. He was incapable of sharing power: he could only give orders and be obeyed. Compromise—the breath of self-government—was alien to him. He wished to establish the rule of righteousness on earth and viewed everyone who opposed him as the agent of unrighteousness.

That winter a final attempt was made to avert disaster by an appeal to the arbitration of the king's brother-in-law, the saintly Louis IX of France. But when his award in Henry's favour was published at Amiens early in 1264, de Montfort refused to accept it. "Though all should forsake me," he declared, "I will stand firm . . . in the just cause to which my faith is pledged." On May 14th, to the amazement of everyone, his army defeated the royal array on the Lewes downs in Sussex. It was a triumph of youth over numbers, of the towns over the country, of the greenclad archers of the weald —prototypes of the yeoman infantry of England's future— over the glittering but old-fashioned feudal chivalry of the Court. Both Henry and his son were taken prisoners, and de Montfort became virtual dictator.

For a year he ruled England in the king's name, with the

help of a nominated council of oligarchs. He proved no more
capable than Henry of simultaneously founding the rule of
justice on earth and pleasing everyone. His dilemma was that
his only legal claim to authority in a land inherently monarchical was either the captive king, in whose name he governed
and who could not be permanently constrained by force, or
a conception wholly repugnant to a nation which liked law
without a sovereign as little as a sovereign without law. Yet,
though his triumph at Lewes was ephemeral and the civil war
itself unnecessary—since the king had already accepted the
principle of government with baronial counsel—the representative conception of parliament was enlarged through de
Montfort's need to obtain wider support for his rule. In
January, 1265, he summoned to a parliament, not only the
greater barons and prelates by separate writ, and two knights
elected in the shire court of every county, but two burgesses
from each of the larger towns to represent the urban freemen
and taxpayers. This was revolutionary, for at law no burgess
had any right to refuse consent to a tallage demanded by the
Crown. Only a few years earlier such a claim had caused
Henry III to imprison some rash London citizens who made
it. By this step de Montfort unconsciously placed what was
to prove, in a precedent-loving nation a barrier across an
avenue of taxation that might, as commercial wealth grew,
have made the Crown independent of a parliament of landowners.

The rule of the great champion of oligarchy lasted little
more than a year. His difficulties and critics multiplied; the
one made the other. In the spring of 1265 he fell out with his
chief supporter, the young Earl of Gloucester. At the end of
May Prince Edward—whose political stature had been growing fast—escaped from his captors at Hereford and, joining
the Marcher lords with whom he had been secretly negotiating, routed and destroyed de Montfort at Evesham.

Yet, though the royal party had triumphed, there was no
going back on the principle for which so many had striven:
that the government of England, though primarily and funda-
mentally monarchical, should be with the counsel and consent of the realm expressed through frequent meetings of its
chief men in parliament. The real victor in the war was the
Lord Edward, who was a man of his word and understood England. Unlike his father he was a prince of dominant
personality who wished to rule a strong and united people and

instinctively saw that the only way to do so was through frequent counsel with their leading representatives. It was this knowledge, learnt from the tragic experience of his father's reign, that made him, when his time came, one of the greatest of English kings. And seeing how bitter and stubborn was the resistance of de Montfort's defeated followers, when the first feelings of triumph and bitterness were over he took a leading part in their reconciliation. In the "Dictum of Kenilworth" in 1266, he offered the right to the "disinherited" to buy back their estates at a judicially assessed rate. A year later he was the moving spirit in the great Statute of Marlborough, by which the king in parliament, while subordinating once more and for all time the baronial franchises to the royal, formally confirmed the Provisions of Oxford and Westminster and made them part of the main-stream of English law.

Nor did de Montfort's influence end with his death. In a sense it became stronger when his over-powerful personality had been removed. Thousands of simple Englishmen sympathised with the disinherited; it was this that had made Edward offer them reconciliation. During this time there seems to have first arisen the popular legend of Robin Hood and his merry men, lurking in the green wood to war against the rich and proud and seize their wealth to help the poor. Sung as ballads and passed from mouth to mouth in hedgerow and ale-house, such tales constituted a new ideal of chivalry: a chivalry so far unknown in feudal Europe, for it glorified the lowly against the great. Simon's own memory was venerated by the poor as that of a saint and martyr. His ideal of the rights of the "universitas" or "commonalty," of an imaginary community of the whole realm to which even village craftsmen and petty traders and peasants could appeal in the name of justice, struck deep roots in the English heart.

It was Edward I's supreme achievement—more even than his legal reforms—that he took the nation into a kind of partnership and, by regularly consulting its representatives and seeking their consent, laid the foundations of the greatest of all English institutions: a royal parliament in which king and subject could meet to treat, co-operate and, if necessary, dispute over matters of common concern. When his father died in 1272 he was out of England on crusade, but as soon as he returned, after appointing commissioners to make an exhaustive inquest and report on the grievances of the subject, he called his first parliament. To it he summoned the magnates, lay and ecclesiastical—the earls and barons, archbishops, bishops and abbots who were his tenants-in-chief—and, through the sheriffs, four elected and representative knights, "discreet in law", from the shire-court of every county and four merchants or burgesses from the burgemote or borough court of every important town. They were to come without arms and under the king's peace and protection and to be immune from the ordinary processes of law while the court of parliament was in session. "And because elections ought to be free," ran the writ to the sheriffs, "the king commandeth upon great forfeiture that no man by force of arms nor by malice nor menacing shall disturb or hinder any to make free election." [1]

For, having learnt through his inquest what was wrong with his realm, Edward had resolved on great changes. For these he needed his subjects' witness and approval. For in the Middle Ages there were laws that were seen, not as something that could be changed at will, but as sacred and immutable. However unquestioned a king's right to act, ordain and give judgment, the ancient law of the kingdom was a public inheritance which it was his duty to preserve and enforce. [2] His ordinances might have the force of law but only while he himself could impose them. After his death, if they were contrary to custom, they could be ignored or forgotten. Even in England, where the power of the locality had been far more strictly subordinated to the State than on the continent, the king's word was law only in his lifetime.

If society was to progress, some authority, associated with the Crown yet more enduring than the king's life, was needed

[1] "If we seek the origins of the parliamentary privileges of later times, like freedom of speech and freedom from arrest, it is in the peculiar sanctities accruing to a court of law that we must look for them." G. O. Sayles, *The Medieval Foundations of England*, 453.

[2] "The only law recognized in the Middle Ages, Professor Kern has shown, was the 'good old law,' the inherited custom of the people which was above and superior to the State and which none, not even the king, could alter. The business of the State was to maintain and to preserve the law, to restore it where it had fallen into disuse, and even to 'declare' it; but none, save God, could 'make' the law, which had existed from time immemorial, concrete, all-embracing and beyond human touch." G. Barraclough, "Law and Legislation in Medieval England." *Law Quarterly Review*, LVI, 76.

to register the nation's acceptance of major changes in the law. In an age of isolated and intensely localised communities the tendency of custom to ossify was a mountain in the path of a reforming king. *"Nolumus leges Angliae mutare"*— "we do not wish the laws of England to be changed"—Henry III's barons had replied at the Council of Merton to Bishop Grosseteste's plea for a more humane attitude towards children born out of wedlock. Edward could not overcome this traditional inertia merely by devising ingenious legal writs and directives to his judges as his great-grandfather, Henry II, had done. But with his strong practical sense he saw that a royal ordinance or judgment could be given a sanction more than ordinarily binding by having it publicly witnessed and approved in a session or parliament of the *magnum consilium* —that supreme national council or court of royal officials and judges, feudal tenants-in-chief, prelates and magnates to which his father in times of need had had resource for "colloquy and treating" and to which in his later years both he and Edward, as his deputy, had increasingly referred the vast mass of petitions and appeals to the Crown from those unable to obtain justice from the ordinary courts. In the Statute of Marlborough of 1267 Edward himself, in his father's name, had legalised the baronial reforms of the past decade by a solemn public act of the Crown, issued in parliament under the great seal and enrolled in writing as a permanent national record. By this means he had given to the royal decisions that resolved the controversies of the civil war an enduring validity which, despite his unchallenged right to declare law by ordinance, they could have had in no other way. Henceforward such statutes, as they became called, were cited in pleadings in the royal courts. Like Magna Carta they became part of the continuing life of the nation.

When after their slow, laborious and reluctantly undertaken journeys the magnates and the representatives of the local communities met the king and his council at Westminster, they were presented with a document drafted by the royal judges in French—the speech of their knightly class— and read to them by Chancellor Burnell. Its object was to define, clarify and, where found necessary, reform the law. "Because," ran its preamble, "our lord the king hath great desire to redress the state of the realm in such things as require amendment for the common profit of holy Church and the realm, and because the state of holy Church hath been

evil kept and the people otherwise entreated as they ought to
be, and the peace less kept and the laws less used and
offenders less punished than they ought to be, the king hath
ordained by his council and the assent of the archbishops,
bishops, earls, barons and all the commonalty of the realm the
acts under written."

The fifty-one clauses of this royal enactment covered a vast
field. They set forth, in easy, almost conversational, speech, a
legal remedy for most of the worst abuses the king's commissioners had noted in their winter's visitation. The ideal
of securing, by a specific remedy, the just rights of every man
according to his status ran through the whole enactment.
Drafted by practising judges, it reflected the preference, always marked in English law, for concrete remedies over
abstract principles.

Copies of the act—the "new provisions and statutes . . .
ordained for the good of the realm and relief of the people"
and known as the first Statute of Westminster—were sent,
like Magna Carta, to the sheriffs. It was proclaimed in the
courts of every county, hundred, city, borough and market-
town, and all judges, sheriffs and bailiffs were ordered to
enforce it. It was the first of a long succession of parliamentary statutes enacted by Edward in council in the presence
of the assembled magnates and representatives of the nation.
Such statutes both changed and became part of the common
and customary law. They derived their authority, not from
verbally transmitted custom, but from a written document
issued under royal seal and preserved in the rolls or records of
parliament, which, before the end of his reign, Edward
ordered to be kept at Westminster. Copied by pleaders into
handbooks that became part of every practising lawyer's
equipment, they were cited in the courts and accepted as
evidence of law by the judges.

The parliament which Edward held at Westminster in the
spring of 1275 was not only summoned to endorse his proposals for reforming legal procedure. It was called to approve
a new kind of tax. With changes in the landed and economic
structure of the country most of the older feudal sources of
revenue were drying up, and the king, to support the growing
charges of State needed new and extraordinary aids. Sixty
years earlier the Great Charter had forbidden the levying
of additional aids on land save by consent of the assembled magnates—a thing always hard to obtain. In its search for new

revenue the Crown had been forced to turn increasingly to the taxation of movable or personal wealth, which had not the same sanctity as land in the eyes of the ruling class. Its chief possessors in a taxable form were the merchants of the chartered towns and the flock-masters and wool-exporters who during the past century had been creating a new form of national wealth out of the downland sheep.

Legally the king was not obliged to consult merchants before taxing their goods. From time immemorial feudal lords had tallaged the towns and markets of their demesnes; it was for this that they had founded them. But times had changed, and merchants were no longer the helpless, half-emancipated villeins they had been before the crusades had introduced the feudal nobility of Europe to the luxuries of the East. Ever since they had been driven into the rebel ranks by his father's insistence on his right to tax them at will, Edward had wooed the traders of the capital and south-eastern ports, seeing with his realist's eye the power that came from control of cash and credit. He saw that a freely-negotiated agreement under which the merchant community assumed corporate responsibility for its own taxes was likely to prove more valuable to the Crown and, in the elementary administrative conditions of the time, provide a more readily accessible revenue than any forced imposition.

It was this that had caused him to follow de Montfort's revolutionary precedent and to summon to his first parliament the proctors or representatives of all the cities, boroughs and "towns of merchants." He did not call upon them to take part in the discussions about his new land-laws—matters far above them—but to grant him a share of the increased trading profits which his strong rule and wise foreign policy were helping to create. In return for a standing duty of half a mark, or 6s. 8d., on every sack of wool exported and 13s. 4d. on every last of leather, he offered to surrender the royal prerogative of imposing direct taxation on merchandise. This gesture was as far-reaching as it was imaginative and generous. The "Great and Ancient Custom," as it became called, "granted at the instance of the merchants" and approved by the magnates, was the beginning of the Crown's permanent customs revenue. Henceforth it took its place, with the older "tonnage" on wine-imports, beside the feudal aids and dues, the rents of the royal estates—now much reduced by the grants of earlier sovereigns—the sheriffs' "farms" of the shires and the proceeds of justice.

Later that year, in a second parliament summoned to Westminster at Michaelmas and attended by knights of the shire as well as by the feudal and ecclesiastical magnates, the king obtained an "aid" of a fifteenth on all other lay moveables. The idea of representation, of the right of those present to bind the absent and of the majority to outvote the minority—a conception which the friars in their provincial assemblies had first introduced into England—was beginning to take shape under Edward's guidance. In his writs to the sheriffs he insisted that elected knights and burgesses should have full power of attorney to bind their fellows to "whatever should be ordained by common counsel." Needing his subjects' co-operation, he pursued every means of obtaining it.

In the last part of his reign after conquering Wales Edward, in an abortive attempt to unify the British Isles, became involved in wars against Scotland and France. In turn they involved him in growing financial difficulties and clashes with the principal taxpayers, the magnates and the Church. When in 1297 the representatives of the shires—who lacked the strength to stand up to him—voted him a subsidy on personal property, the earls of Norfolk and Hereford, Roger Bigod the marshal and Humphrey de Bohun the constable, forbade its collection during the king's absence abroad on the grounds that the consent of the magnates had not been obtained to what, without it, was a mere "tallage at will". However much they have been influenced by their own grievances, they took their stand on the "community's" corporate right to be consulted according to traditional forms and usages before any innovation affecting its liberties became law. After Edward's death in 1307 the breach between the Crown and the magnates—temporarily repaired during his lifetime—widened dangerously. Instead of governing with the advice and counsel of his "chief men", as the latter urged was his constitutional duty, the young Edward II allowed himself to be guided by an irresponsible favourite named Gaveston—"the king's idol", as the people called him. In the course of the quarrel Gaveston was captured and murdered by the magnates, the army of a divided England was routed by the insurgent Scots at Bannockburn, and a reforming council of

"Lords Ordainers" was set up by the armed barons to advise and restrain the young king and "ordain and establish the estate of the realm and household according to right and reason."

Their Ordinances transformed the king into an official of state committed to carrying out the will of the magnates through officers controlled by parliament. They sought to transfer the royal power from Edward and his existing household officers—the chamberlain and the keepers and controllers of the Wardrobe—to their own nominees who were no longer to be responsible to the king personally but to the king in parliament, an abstraction which they made the corner-stone of their reformed system of government. The Ordainers were an aristocratic body but, by their insistence on ministerial responsibility to parliament and their reliance on that institution to make an erring king fulfil his obligations to the community, they took a first step on the long stony road to parliamentary control of the executive. They ordained that the king should not engage in any foreign war or leave the country without consent of parliament which was to meet in some convenient place at least once a year. All his officers were to swear to maintain the Ordinances, and a committee of lords was to hear and adjudge complaints against them in every parliament.

Yet in his own eyes and those of the great mass of his subjects the king remained a king. The magnates could constrain him by arms, but they could only permanently prevent him from exercising his functions by depriving him of his liberty as their predecessors under de Montfort had deprived his grandfather. Whatever titles and offices they might compel him to grant them, the royal prerogatives remained his and his alone. In 1322, availing himself of a popular reaction in his favour, the king turned the tables on his enemies, defeating and executing their leader, his cousin, Thomas earl of Lancaster—Gaveston's murderer. Having avenged the latter, Edward summoned to York a parliament of royalist sympathisers—magnates, knights of the shire and burgesses—who annulled the Ordinances on the ground that the Ordainers had acted without the king and were therefore no true parliament. Instead, they laid it down that all matters affecting "the estate of the king and his heirs" should "henceforth be granted and established in parliament by our lord the king and with the consent of the prelates, earls and barons and of the commonalty of the kingdom, as has been accustomed in times past."

But the Statute of York was an attempt to stabilise the realm, not by a compromise embodying the best of two opposed principles like the Statute of Marlborough after de Montfort's death, but by a denial of everything for which the magnates had been contending. The sovereign alone was to "treat, grant and establish" laws in parliament. The only function of "the prelates, earls, barons and commonalty of the realm" was to "consent". The statute harked back to the benevolent paternalism which had worked so well and with a broad measure of agreement in Edward I's early years but which had broken down under a successor as idle, irresponsible and easily swayed as his son. It postulated a just and active king and a willing people. But it made no attempt to deal with the question of what was to happen if the king was not just and active and the subject not willing. Yet, like the Ordinances it repealed, it set the powers it restored to the king in the framework of parliament, even though a parliament that could do nothing without him. And, unlike the Ordinances, it took cognisance of the Commons as part of that parliament. The long war with Scotland and the royal need for money had made the humble representatives of the shires and merchant towns increasingly necessary. In the twenty years of Edward II's reign they were summoned by writ to no less than twenty-five parliaments.

Edward II's triumph over his greater subjects was short-lived. Four years later, sickened by the autocratic rule of his new favourites, the Despensers, the country rose against him under his own queen. By making personal monarchy legally impregnable the framers of the Statute of York had left the nation's representatives only one remedy if the king infringed the liberties of the subject. That was to dethrone him. "He has stripped," it was said, "his realm and done all that he could to ruin his. . . . people, and, what is worse, by his cruelty and lack of character, he has shown himself incorrigible and without hope of amendment." [1]

Yet those set on changing their ruler—and at that moment they seemed to include almost the entire nation—wished to

[1] Twysden, *Historiae Anglicanae Scriptores Decem*, col. 2765; Rymer's *Foedera*, II, 650, transl. by Adams and Stephens, 99, cit., B. Wilkinson, *Constitutional History of Medieval England*, II, 170–1.

do so by legal means. Having resorted to force, they sought to cloak it under the forms of law. But the king could only legally be dethroned with his own assent. Intimidated by threats that if he did not comply the people would crown his wife's paramour instead of his son, the wretched man, weeping and groaning, gave way. The delegation returned to London with the royal insignia, and a new reign was proclaimed on January 25th, 1327.

When, "speaking in the name of all the earls and barons of the realm of England" as "procurator of all in the land and of the whole parliament," Sir William Trussell of Peatling renounced the nation's allegiance to Edward II, a new chapter in parliamentary history had begun. Though without the king's presence neither a court of law nor a legislative assembly, a parliament that had not even been constituted had virtually dethroned one king and set up another in his place. And, though the first had abdicated under duress and the other was in the lawful line of succession, the order assigned for the young king's crowning showed what had been done. "The earls, magnates and eminent citizens," it laid down, were to gather in the king's court to "treat about the election of the new prince and the confirmation of the laws and customs of the kingdom." When they had agreed to these they were to acclaim him with united voice and "exalt him with all gentleness and reverence as the custom of the kingdom" demanded. Then, having lifted him up and replaced him in his chair, still unrobed, unspurred and uncrowned, four of the earls were to inform the clergy of his election and demand that, "as he has been elected by the people, so he may be . . . consecrated to be king." [1] First introduced into the coronation of Edward II and now reinforced by the presence of representatives of the *plebs* at the meeting to choose his successor, the rite of Elevation, followed by that of Recognition, symbolised the dependence of the king on his people and the participation of the community in the "regnum" or rule of the State.

At that moment it must have seemed to the young king a mockery of all that kingship meant. In their triumph over his irresponsible and incompetent father the magnates appeared to have destroyed almost everything that the Norman and Plantagenet kings had done to unify and strengthen the realm.

[1] Maskell, *Monumenta Ritualia Ecclesiae Anglicanae*, III, 3–48 cit., Wilkinson, III, 97.

Rebellion in a medieval State could not take the place of stable government and justice. Great as had been parliament's part in preserving the national tradition of common counsel and consent at a time when, with its growing and increasingly efficient bureaucracy, the monarchy had threatened to become a despotism, an assembly of feudal nobles could not rule England. As the repository of executive power it was incapable of controlling its own members or of being anything but a discordant oligarchy. Like the nation whose divergent forces and estates it represented, to operate effectively it needed a king capable of ruling.

For all his youth Edward III was such a king. Like his grandfather he meant to rule. Since childhood he had seen the fatal consequences of a breach between a sovereign and the lords through whom so much of the administration of a feudal kingdom had to be exercised. He recognized that there could be no governing England without its greater nobles. With its mechanism of judges, Exchequer barons, Chancery and Wardrobe clerks, sheriffs, escheators, coroners, constables and militia a strong royal government could prevent baronial anarchy. Yet without the co-operation of the feudal magnates and their courts and retainers, the kingdom could never be at unity with itself. In an age when a journey from London to York took nearly a week, devolution of authority was essential.

After the struggles and tragedies of the past forty years what was needed was a compromise—a reconciliation between royal authority and the liberties of the subject. It was the supreme merit of this conciliatory yet shrewd young king to realise and achieve it. By doing so he saved for his country the strong, binding monarchy of his forebears. A few weeks after assuming control of the kingdom he proclaimed that his conception of rule was partnership. "Our affairs and the affairs of our realm," he wrote to the sheriffs, "have been managed in the past to our damage and dishonour and that of our kingdom and to the impoverishment of our people. We wish all men to know that in future we will govern according to right and reason as is fitting our royal dignity, and that the matters which touch us and the estate of our realm are to be disposed of by the common counsel of the magnates of our realm and in no other manner." [1]

---

[1] *Foedera*, II, 799, cit. Wilkinson, II, 173–4.

Yet even Edward III, the most popular of all England's Plantagenet rulers, had to learn the lesson that Englishmen could not be governed in defiance of what they regarded as their rights. Fourteen years after his accession, in grave financial difficulties as a result of a war with France, he laid charges of treason against his former chancellor, John Stratford, archbishop of Canterbury, and other officials whom he believed had wrecked his campaign by keeping him short of money. Taking his stand on the subject's right to appeal against arbitrary conviction and punishment and to demand trial by his peers, Stratford boldly reminded the king that "the most sovereign thing that holds kings and princes in due and fitting estate is good counsel." "Let it not displease you," he wrote, "to remember it in your time, for, by the evil counsel which our lord your father had, he caused to be taken, against the law of the land and the great charter, the peers and other people of the land and put some to shameful death, and of others he caused their goods to be seized. And what happened to him for that cause, sire, you well know." [1]

Having been an Oxford doctor of law and a Chancery clerk, the archbishop knew how to put the issue in its clearest and most compelling form. The principle at stake was whether a king of England could govern without resort to established law and to those who could speak for the nation. "By evil counsel," Stratford told the king, "you begin to seize divers clerks, peers and other folk of the land. You make suit, quite unfitting and against the law of the land, which you are bound by the oath taken at your coronation to keep and maintain, and contrary to the great Charter." The only place for judging such charges as Edward had brought against his chief subjects was parliament—the national assembly in which an English king could look into the hearts and minds of his people. "For the salvation of your enterprise," he urged, "be willing to take to you the great and the wise of your land . . . Be willing, sire, if it please you, therefore, to cause them . . . to assemble in a fitting place where we and others may securely come." The archbishop had been accused by his master, he was entitled to be judged by his peers in parliament.

It was a tremendous claim going to the root of the problem

---

[1] Robert of Avebury, *De gestis Mirabilibus Regis Edwardi Tertii, Rolls Series 1889,* 424.

men had been trying to solve since the days of Magna Carta; of how to allow a king the overriding executive power on which the peace and safety of the realm depended and at the same time to safeguard the rights and liberties of the subject. Once again magnates, knights of the shire and Londoners came together under the archbishop's lead to protest at a royal attempt to rule by personal will instead of by established law. Stratford's demand to be tried by his peers was a shrewd stroke, for it was a right that every magnate in the land wished to secure for himself.

Edward's need for supplies to meet his debts and maintain his war with France and Scotland forced him to yield. The national crisis set in motion by the king was resolved, as Stratford had proposed, "in a full parliament". And though the archbishop never received the trial *in pleno parliamento* which he had been demanding, since the king dropped his charges and, later, even had them annulled as contrary to truth and reason, the principle for which he had contended was triumphantly vindicated. It was Edward who, needing the support of his people, had had to submit to the judgment of parliament. Seeing that, if he was to have their support in his wars, he must conciliate them, he yielded with grace and good sense.

Edward made no further attempt to govern without consultation with the nation's traditional leaders and his customary constitutional advisers. In his triumphant heyday no king was more successful in making throne and nation one or in using the latter's representative institutions to serve his ends. By ruling with the advice and consent of the great officers of Church and State and the hereditary magnates, observing the forms of parliamentary consultation and utilising the representative taxing assembly that his grandfather had created out of the great council of the realm, the victor of Crecy was able to put into the field a professional army far better equipped and supported than anything feudal France possessed. A system of taxation by consent, administered by royal officers in whose appointment the taxpayers had confidence, gave to the English king financial resources unknown to his Valois rival, although the latter ruled a kingdom far richer and more populous.

As a result of his war with France, throughout Edward's fifty years' reign there was a steady increase in the influence and power of the non-hereditary and elected representatives of the lesser taxpayers. Summoned not by name like the lords but by general writs addressed to the sheriffs, the seventy-four knights of the shire and the two hundred or so burgesses who since the beginning of the reign had been called to almost every meeting of parliament, at first behaved as they had been treated, as very humble partners in the *universitas* of the realm. As late as 1348 they declined to advise the king on the conduct of the war as being "too ignorant and simple to counsel on such important matters." Their function, as defined in the traditional words of the royal summons, was "with full and sufficient power for themselves and their respective communities to do and to consent to those things which in our parliament shall be ordained"—in other words, to commit the taxpayers to such subsidies and taxes as the king should require.

Yet so stubbornly did they insist on their right to withhold consent to any new form of taxation—not only direct taxes on moveables but, after 1340, even custom duties in the royal demesnes [1]—that, with the Government's incessant need for additional sources of revenue for the war, they became an essential part of the national machinery of "counsel and consent." Without it being fully realised, their power to withhold supply made them indispensable to the management of the realm so long as the war continued and the costs of government continued to rise. The Crown's repeated demands for money for war caused the representatives of two very different social groups, the land-owning warrior knights and the trading burgesses, to draw together for consultations on finance. However hesitantly at first, they acquired the habit of meeting together to discuss matters that vitally affected both. In doing so they unconsciously and, as it were, accidentally, created a single assembly—called into being with each successive meeting of parliament—representing the communities of shire and borough. Unique among the rigidly divided class "estates" which made up the parliaments of other European

---

[1] In an oddly prophetic and pseudo-historical treatise on the powers and procedure of parliament called the *Modus Tenendi Parliamenti*, probably written in 1321 by a supporter of Thomas earl of Lancaster, the claim was made that the two knights who represented a shire in parliament had a greater voice in granting and withholding aid than the greatest earl. This, though untrue in Edward II's reign, had become partly true before the end of his son's. Wilkinson, III, 64, 323–31, 356.

kingdoms, they already formed by the end of Edward III's reign a continuing body which in the next century was to become known as the House of Commons. Sitting separately from the lords in a chamber of their own—at one time the Painted Chamber of the palace of Westminster, at another the chapter house of the Abbey—they came in the course of the fifty or so parliaments of the reign to develop a business and procedure of their own, distinct from the parliamentary procedure of earlier days which had been designed solely by and for the convenience of the king and council. This was largely due to the lawyers who were so often chosen by local communities to represent them because of their professional expertise, and who brought to the work of an evolving institution their habits of mental precision and insistence on procedure and precedent.[1]

Much of parliament's business centred round the petitions to the king for justice and reform of the law which poured in before the beginning of every session and which were increasingly referred by the king and his councillors to the Commons. Those that concerned public rather than private interests and seemed, after sifting and examination, to call for legislative action, the latter endorsed with a recommendation—usually the words, "whereof the commonalty prays remedy"—for presentation by the clerk of parliament to the king. If he approved them they then became the subject of either a royal ordinance or, in more important cases, of a statute formally assented to by both magnates and Commons and entered on the rolls of parliament as a permanent law enforceable in the royal courts. Sometimes such petitions were made the subject of a bargain between Crown and parliament, the Commons voting subsidies and taxes on condition that the king assented to such legislation as they required.

Above all, the members of the Commons acquired a corporate sense and habit of acting together. Their first elected spokesman or Speaker appeared by the end of the reign. Though with their superior social status the knights of the shire took the lead in their debates, they constituted a single estate—the commonalty or *populus* of the realm as distinct

---

[1] "It was the lawyers who so developed the procedure of parliament that it became a workable assembly and the only one of the medieval representative assemblies which survived and became an integral part of the machinery of government." W. Holdsworth, *Makers of Law*, 55.

from the lords and not, as in continental parliaments, separate estates of knights and burgesses. They represented, not classes or callings, but localities, and, by acting together for the "common good", made the needs and views of those localities known to the Crown and brought their influence to bear at the place where in England power resided—the royal council or, as it was tending to become in every major crisis of the nation's political life, the king in parliament. Their influence and prestige were the greater because, even when, as sometimes happened, they were cadets of baronial families, the knights sat with the burgesses as commoners. More perhaps than any other factor this created a sense of national identity and common interest. It made it easy for Lords and Commons to act together and hard for the monarch to encroach on the community's liberties by setting class against class. Without this, the tendency to absolutism inherent in the growing power of national monarchy might have become too strong to resist, as it did in almost every other European kingdom between the fourteenth and seventeenth centuries.

Between the accession of Edward I in 1272 and the deposition of Richard II in 1399, England became what, under changing forms, she has ever since remained, a parliamentary monarchy. By finding a constitutional means to reconcile a strong centralised authority with the liberty of the subject and his right to oppose and reform government, she made a contribution of supreme importance to mankind. In the creation of parliament, with its triple components of Crown, Lords and Commons, a land of obstinate men won rights by trial and error that were to become the basis of the laws and institutions by which free men still live. In the early part of that struggle the championship of private liberties and of the right to oppose arbitrary power rested with the greater lords and churchmen; later the knights of the shire and still humbler burgesses of the towns took their share in that process. Out of that conflict between the expanding power of central government and the medieval tradition of feudal and religious liberty was wrought the first great English reconciliation between order and freedom. When twice in three quarters of a century a successful revolution ended in the dethronement of a tyrannical king and the recognition by a parliament of his successor, the victors in both cases had the wisdom to preserve the continuity of strong royal government. For after Richard

II, claiming that the laws lay in his own breast, had roused his subjects to rebellion by depriving men of their property without process of law, the Commons, after his dethronement, declared that they wished his successor to be "in as great a royal liberty as all his noble progenitors were before him." It was this combination of respect for central national authority with insistence on individual rights and liberties that was to remain the continuing motive of English political history.

CHAPTER VII

THE MEDIEVAL VILLAGE

THE FOUNDATION of England's polity was the labour of some nine thousand scattered agricultural communities. Her government, law, landed wealth, merchandise, architecture and art rested on the native clearing in the wild and Piers Plowman in the "field full of folk" raising food for all. The owner of the soil, if not the Crown or an ecclesiastical institution, was usually—at least until the latter fourteenth century when English became the language of all classes—a French-speaking lord, resident or absentee, with his manor court to which every villager owed suit. Its pastor was the parish priest with his church, to which everyone repaired for communal worship on Sundays and feastdays and for all the important occasions of life. But its hard core and that of England's economy was the husbandman. In Kent and the Danelaw and the pastoral west and north he was as often as not a free man, owning the land he tilled and able to sell it. In the south and midlands the majority of cultivators were villeins: men tied to the soil.[1] They went with it and could not leave it without its lord's consent. They were not, legally speaking, slaves, for they could not be bought or sold as individuals but only with the land they cultivated. Nor, so long as they paid the feudal dues and services with which it was charged, could they be deprived of its fruits. At a time when there was more land in England than labour to work it they were indispensable. They held it by hereditary tenure of "fork and flail."

Yet, a villein, or serf as he was called, was far from free. If he or his children left the manor they could be brought back to it in chains on proof of villeinage. Their service was

[1] According to G. O. Sayles, in a proportion of about six to four. *Medieval Foundations of England*, 433.

"in the blood." The only legal escape was by public manumission, by entry into the church—for which the lord's agreement was necessary—or by residence for a year and a day in a chartered borough. There were many types of villein. They ranged from substantial farmers, employing other men's services and commuting for their own by money payments, to humble cottars and bordars holding only a few acres and supplementing their yield by working three or four days a week on their neighbours' land for wages. The average villein-holding was a yardland or virgate of thirty acres. For this a man had to till the lord's land with his own implements, personally or by deputy, for two or three days a week, perform cartage or carrying duties, give additional "boon" services at the spring and autumn sowing, harvest-times, hay-making and sheep-shearing, and render on special days a seasonal tribute of farm-produce, like the Easter eggs which still appear on our children's plates. Thus in the Black Book of Peterborough forty villeins at Kettering, each holding around thirty acres, are shown as having to plough with their own plough-teams 88 acres for the abbey. Every man owed three days' work a week on the abbey's land and contributed to it 50 hens, 640 eggs and 2s. 1½d. a year in cash—a sum worth perhaps a hundred times that amount in present-day values. As money became more generally used, services on the smaller estates—though seldom on the larger arable ones—were increasingly commuted for "fines" or cash payments. In a survey of Martham at the end of the thirteenth century Thomas Knight held twelve acres in villeinage, paid 16d. for it and 14d. in special aids. "He shall do," it was stated, "sixteen working days in August and for every day he shall have one repast—viz. bread and fish. He shall hoe ten days without the lord's food—price of a day ½d. He shall cart to Norwich six cartings or shall give 9d, and he shall have for every carting one leaf and one lagena—or gallon—of ale. Also for ditching 1d. He shall make for malt 3½ seams of barley or shall give 6d. Also he shall flail for twelve days or give 12d. He shall plough if he has his own plough, and for every ploughing he shall have three loaves and nine herrings . . . . For carting manure he shall give 2d." These arrangements, which varied from manor to manor, were supervised by the lord's bailiff and by an elected or nominated representative of the villeins called the reeve who directed the common husbandry. The larger the holding, the greater the services demanded. A poor cottar with four or five acres might owe only a single day's labour a week.

Though, like all holders of land, a villein had to pay tallages and aids to his lord, such as the merchet on his daughter's marriage, he enjoyed the usual hereditary rights of feudal tenure. On payment of a heriot of the best beast on his holding his heir was entitled to succeed to it. Nor were the "boons" he proffered to his lord wholly one-way. Attached to his services were certain customary privileges, like the hay-maker's right at Borley in Essex to receive for every load of hay three quarters of wheat, a pat of butter and a piece of cheese of the second sort from the lord's dairy, the morning milk from the cows, salt and oatmeal for a stew, and as much hay as each man could lift on the point of his scythe. A sower was usually entitled to a basketful of any seed he sowed, a cow-herd to the first seven days' milk of every cow after calving, a shepherd to twelve nights' dung from the folds at Christmas and a bowl of whey or buttermilk during the summer.

What distinguished villein service from the higher feudal tenures was that it was menial and "servile." To the extent of the time for which his service was due, the serf was at the disposal of the lord and his bailiff. He was not his own master and, as the great thirteenth century lawyer, Bracton, wrote, legally speaking did not know in the evening what he should do on the morrow. The stigma in his status was that he was not, in the old English phrase, "law-worthy." He could not defend his person or property in the royal courts or claim a freeman's right to be tried by his equals, though gradually, as the power of the Common Law grew, he received from it protection of life and limb and of the tools of his labour.

Yet the rule of the royal courts was comparatively new. They were not the only source of protection from violence and injustice. There were other and older courts to which a man could resort. The manor-court or moot belonged to the lord; its jurisdiction and fines were among the most valuable of feudal rights. It was presided over by his steward and met once a fortnight in his hall or outhouse, or in summer under the village oak-tree. But it was open to the whole village, and the assessors or jurymen who stated the local customs on which its judgments were based and which formed the law of the manor, were the tenants who owed it suit. Those customs were handed down from father to son and recorded on the court rolls. They expressed the common experience and conscience of the neighbourhood. Nor was it easy for even the most powerful lord to ignore the custom of those on whose labour and skill he depended. Like the great council of tenants-in-chief, who made the despotic King John promise to observe ancient law and govern with the consent of his chief men, the manor-court was the means by which, little by little, the English peasant community, often in the teeth of tyrannical encroachment, preserved and extended its rights.

In such courts, in thousands of villages up and down England, justice was done between man and man; offences against manorial custom were punished, and the services and rights of the villein-tenant enforced and recorded. On its rolls were entered the exact terms under which he held his land. In time, copies of these entries came to be regarded as title to his holding. It gradually became customary to claim possession of land by "copyhold", a form of tenure which was later recognised, as the villein acquired full legal rights, by the king's judges.

Service in the manor-courts helped to train Englishmen for a free system of society. It taught them to weigh evidence and distinguish between personal feelings and public needs. "Richard Smith" ran the entry of a court leet in 1311, "beat Alice Hannes twice—Mercy, Order, Poor." The village jury, that is, found him guilty and recommended him to the mercy of the court, which ordered a fine but remitted part of it because he could not afford it. In his everyday task of helping to administer a little corner of the realm of which he was part, the English peasant learnt to blend legal precision with human give-and-take. The village halimote, which dealt with cases of trespass, neglect of manorial duties and offences against the village peace, and which twice a year became a police-court to try crimes short of felony presented by a jury, had its formal pleadings like a royal court. A thirteenth century book, written to enable stewards and bailiffs to know their business, gives such examples as,

> "Alice, widow of. . . . . ., complaineth of . . . . ., her neighbour, that on such a day his pigs entered her garden and rooted up her beans and cabbages, so that she would not willingly have had that damage for 2s. nor that shame for 12d. and she demandeth that amends be made." [1]

[1] F. W. Maitland, *The Court Baron* (Selden Society), 75.

Keeping the king's peace in the village and enforcing his law and ordinance was a bucolic officer called the petty constable. Appointed by the high constable of the hundred from a rota of householders, he was usually unpaid and served, nominally at least, for a year. By traditional Anglo-Saxon law every able-bodied man between the ages of fifteen and sixty was obliged to take his share in the policing and defence of his native place, and it was the constable's business to see that he did so. An English village was responsible to the sheriff for public order within its boundaries and could be collectively fined for crimes committed in it. It had its stocks, ducking-stool—for scolding wives—and pillory. Its priest, reeve and four "lawful men" represented it at the sheriff's tourn and hundred court, at coroner's inquests and at the assizes where it had to answer for its corporate offences and present those suspected of felony. It had to keep a nightly "watch and ward" against suspicious travellers, and, when the constable raised the "hue and cry," to chase and apprehend them. "If any such passing strangers do not allow themselves to be arrested," ran an ordinance of Henry III, "then the watch shall raise the hue upon them on all sides and pursue them with the whole township and neighbouring township with hue and cry from township to township until they are taken!"

The petty constable was not only an amateur policeman but a soldier. In time of invasion, riot or rebellion he had to see that every man turned out at the sheriff's summons in the shire *fyrd*. England's Norman and Angevin kings used this rude national militia more than once against their turbulent French-speaking nobles. At first it was confined to free men— for to the continental feudal mind there was something shocking in the idea of a bondsman bearing arms—but it was later extended to all classes, including villeins. Edward I's great defining Statute of Winchester of 1285 placed it on a permanent basis. In every county, hundred and township, muster-rolls were prepared from which in time of war and emergency, Commissioners of Array selected and impressed men to serve as paid soldiers. Armed with daggers, spears, pikes and longbows, clad in quilted jerkins and iron headpieces, and exercised together once a year in the autumn array or muster, this reserve of amateur soldiers formed a second line of defence on which, in days before she had learnt to command the seas, England was able to draw in all her wars. Fyrd, *posse comitatus*, fencibles, militia, by whatever name it was called, it remained a homespun body, affording from the days of Shakespeare's Falstaff to those of Rowlandson much material for humourists. Of its services to the country perhaps the greatest was that, when royal despotism might otherwise have triumphed, it obviated the need for a standing army.

The Statute of Winchester also defined the subject's duties as a policeman and preserver of the peace. Instead of leaving the village cummunity answerable only for felonies committed within its borders, Edward made it jointly responsible with its neighbour townships for all felonies committed in the hundred. The unit of policing was made to conform to the needs, not merely of the village, but of the nation. As part of this policy the townships along the royal highways were also ordered, on pain of indictment before the justices on eyre, to cut back the brushwood on either side of the road to a distance of two hundred feet to reduce the risk of ambush from brigands and outlaws.

In the last resort such a system of delegated self-government depended on the readiness of the local community to identify itself with the assumptions and requirements of the remote royal authority in whose name the law was enforced. When, in the general breakdown of confidence and economic relationships that followed the Black Death and the failure of the French Wars, the peasants of south-eastern England rose against the attempt of their lay and ecclesiastical lords to impose new taxes and enforce antiquated feudal dues, the system failed completely to stem a revolutionary flood that all but destroyed the kingdom.[1] There must have been scores of Kent and Essex constables who marched under Wat Tyler and Jack Straw in their assault on the capital of 1381. Yet once the rebellion collapsed and the young king and his ministers had re-established their authority, the village resumed its traditional method of ruling itself under the supervision of the royal officers of the shire and hundred and the manorial courts.

The manorial system of cultivation was communal, though ownership was individual. In the Celtic and pastoral west scattered homesteads and hamlets, small unified holdings and little stone-walled fields were the rule. But in the flat, clayey

[1] For the causes of the Peasants' Revolt see the author's *Age of Chivalry*, 490–547.

midlands and the south, where corn-growing was the principal activity, the arable land around the village was grouped in two, or, in the better farmed manors, three fields, according as to whether a two or three year rotation of crops was followed. These open fields, fenced against the cattle in the summer, were usually several hundred acres in extent. They were divided, without hedges, into narrow, curving strips like elongated Ss, each a furlong or ox-plough-furrow's length. Between the strips were ridges made by the ploughs. As the course of husbandry was the same for all and enforced by the manor court, every villager had so many strips in each field, according to the size of his holding. In some villages the lord's land, called the demesne, and sometimes the parson's glebe land, were enclosed; in others they were scattered about the open fields, where their cultivation, like everyone else's, had to conform to the common rule. The crops were wheat, rye, barley, oats, vetches and peas. They were threshed on barn floors by flails cut from holly or thorn, and winnowed by hand. The wooden ploughs were usually drawn by teams of eight oxen. As few could afford a whole plough-team, they were shared. The normal arrangement was a team to every four yardlands, the hide—approximately 120 acres—being the measure, though it varied widely, of what an eight-ox team could plough in a year.

In addition to the arable there was the meadow lying beside stream or river and tended by the village hayward. Here, too, every peasant had his strip or strips. When the hay had been cut the village cattle were pastured on it, and, after the harvest—from Lammas to Candlemas—on the arable stubble, which they helped to dung. They were very small and scraggy, for, under a communal system of grazing, selective breeding was impossible. As there was little winter-feed—for root crops were unknown—they were mostly slaughtered and salted at Michaelmas. A few stalled cows and the breeding stock struggled through the winter till the spring.

Beyond the fields and meadow was the waste—forest, moorland, swamp and brackeny common—still covering more than half the country and surrounding the lonely villages like the sea. The lord of the manor might own the soil, but his tenants enjoyed the common use of its rough grasses and herbage for pasture and of its turf and brushwood for fuel. Every holding carried a right or "stint" to feed so many cattle, horses, geese and swine on the waste, and to take, "by hook or crook," sticks, fallen timber and loose bracken for litter, sand and clay for building, nuts, berries, rabbits and small birds for the pot. The adjoining woods were full of the villagers' thin, half-wild pigs feeding on beechmast and acorns. They also abounded in game and, in the wilder parts of the country, with robbers and outlaws, and occasionally wolves.

The life which such a system supported was very simple. There was little scope for initiative or progress, and the pace was that of the least enterprising. The cottages straggling along either side of the unpaved village street and flanked by heaps of manure—the peasant's principal wealth,—were mere rectangular-shaped shacks of timber-framing, filled in with wattle, turf and mud and thatched with straw or reeds. They contained usually a single unfloored, hearthless room in which the family slept in verminous squalor with the oxen stalled at the bed's foot, pigs roaming the floor and poultry perched on the beams. The only household goods would be a straw mattress or sack, a few cooking-pots, some homemade tools and, in the homes of the richer villeins, a rude oak chest and perhaps a stool or two. Behind the houses were little closes, growing cabbage, parsley, onions, leek, garlic, herbs, apples and quinces. Their owners' clothes were of coarse, greasy wool and leather, unwashed and unwashable, made from their own beasts. Their diet was cheese, bacon and, in the summer, milk; bean and vegetable broth; oaten cakes and rough, black wholemeal bread; herrings or other salt-fish, honey from their own hives, and small ale or cider. Its staple was cereal; a thirteenth century English agricultural writer reckoned the labourer's average allowance of corn at 36 bushels a year. Butcher's meat was a rare luxury. In Lent everyone fasted, not only because the Church enjoined it, but because, with the harvest so far away, there was no alternative. "Fridays and fast-days," wrote the fourteenth century poet, William Langland, "a penny's worth of mussels were a feast for such folks."

Though the village, especially on the large monastic and baronial estates, by now exported much of what it grew for cash-sales to the towns or to feed and finance some distant lord, it still supplied nearly all its own wants except for salt and iron brought by travelling chapmen. It spun and wove wool for clothes from its own sheep, and linen from its own flax. It made shoes from its own wood or skins. It had a miller —a tenant of the lord and usually the richest man in the place, for every villein had to have his corn ground by him—

a smith, a wheelwright and a millwright, a tiler and thatcher, a shoemaker and tanner, a carpenter wainwright and carter. Their callings, and those of the parish agricultural officers survive in our names: Shepherd and Foster, Carter and Baker, Parker, Fowler and Hunter; Wolf and Forester; Smith, Cooper and Carpenter. So do the country places, buildings and beasts among which they spent their skilful laborious lives: Field, Pitt, and Fox, Lane, Bridge and Ford, Stone and Burn, Church and Hill, Brook and Green, Lamb, Bull and Hogg, Sparrow, Crow and Swan. Other men were called after the masters they served—King, Bishop, Abbot, Dean, Prior, Knight, Squire—or after their own appearance—Black, Brown and White, Short, Round and Long.

Book education for the husbandman there was none. Few could read, nor was there opportunity for doing so. There were no printed books—only the priceless, laboriously-copied, jealously-hoarded manuscripts of the monastery libraries and of the very rich. The peasant's hours of labour were long, and when daylight failed wax candles were far beyond his reach: his sole illumination was a feeble rushlight dipped in fat. There was no travel for him, unless his cart was requisitioned for some baronial or royal service, for the vast majority of villagers never left home.

Yet he was not a wholly uncultivated man. From his father and the fields he learnt a knowledge of nature's laws. He learnt, too, from his earliest years to look after animals and to take pride in his hereditary work as husbandman or craftsman. Nor did he live by plough or adze alone; he was partaker in a Faith and a civilisation. If he could not read, he could see and he could hear. The brightly coloured and beautifully fashioned images and paintings that covered the walls and, later, windows of his parish church; the music and ritual which he enjoyed from childhood; the familiar legends and parables of the Christian legend linked him with the culture of Catholic Christendom. Its festivals, which were his days of rejoicing, gave him, it has been reckoned, something like six weeks' holiday in a year. Deeper than the servile divisions of class, the harsh bonds of status, the grinding poverty and squalor of the peasant's lot, the unity and consolation of the Christian faith sustained him and gave his life meaning.

The cold dark winters in the wild northern landscape must often have seemed very lonely and comfortless. It is no wonder that men suffered from superstitious fears and were haunted by ghosts, witches and demons. They must often, too, have been hungry. When the harvest failed, famine followed and, in its train, pestilence, haunting the noisome ditches and insanitary hovels. Yet at the darkest hour of the long northern night, rich and poor, old and young celebrated the beginning of things and the mystery of Christmas. The interminable procession of days in rain-sodden or frozen fields, with bare trees and grey, colourless skies, and the nights of shivering in draughty hovels, were broken by the sweet wintry festival of Christ's birth, with its bright fires, lighted windows and good fare. It came just when it was most needed and broke the winter into two halves, each bearable for the hope of the Christian feast that ended the one and the coming of spring that ended the other. Soon after it the first lambs were born and the earliest snowdrops appeared in fields made rigid by bitter winds. When everything was at its bleakest, a light was lit in darkness.

Every village possessed its priest or parson—the *persona* of the place—serving an ecclesiastical unit known as a parish, administering the Christian sacraments of baptism, confirmation, communion, marriage, penance and extreme unction, and entitled by law to an annual tenth or tithe of the produce of every parishioner. The system dated from pagan times when the lord's priest or magic man who served the former's temple had performed magic rites for his farming neighbours in return for a share in the common fields. The incumbent was usually a peasant's son, living the same rustic life as his flock. Taught, at best, in monastic or cathedral grammar school enough Latin to read the scriptures and declaim the services in a language his parishioners venerated but could not understand, and usually the only literate person in the parish, he lived by cultivating the glebe or "parson's close"— a holding usually of some fifty or sixty acres in the common fields. He also received dues and offerings from his parishioners for baptisms, weddings, churchings, death-bed visitations and burials. In many of the richer livings the right of presentation or advowson, as it was called, had been given by its patron—a descendant, perhaps, of the church's original donor—to some monastery, college, cathedral or other ecclesiastical foundation which, retaining the bulk of its revenues, paid a deputy to exercise the cure of souls. In other cases the owner of the advowson conferred the living on someone with family claims or on some promising youth marked out for preferment, who, by obtaining an episcopal dispensation to reside out of the parish, was allowed to employ a resident vicar or "perpetual curate" while he completed his education at the Church's universities of Oxford or Cambridge or performed some remunerative ecclesiastical function elsewhere. Usually the absentee rector kept the "great" tithe on crops, sheep and cattle while allocating to his vicar the farm of the glebe and the "lesser" tithes on pigs, geese, poultry, eggs, garden-produce, flax, honey and fish.

By the beginning of the fourteenth century nearly a fifth of the country's churches had been appropriated in this way. As only about a third of their income filtered through to the incumbents and, as the holder of a cure was supposed by canon law to devote two-thirds of the tithe to the upkeep of the chancel and relief of the parish poor, the latter and the church fabric tended to suffer. Deprived of the "great" tithes, a vicar was tempted to press his parishioners too strictly for the lesser ones—those that most affected the bondsman and small-holder—and to spend too much time cultivating his glebe and looking after his livestock. The pre-occupation of the humbler parish clergy with agricultural pursuits constantly figures in episcopal records. During an archdeacon's visitation the sidesman of one Devonshire church complained that the vicar, though in other ways a worthy man, stabled his beasts in the churchyard—"whereby it is evilly trodden down and foully defiled"—appropriated churchyard timber for his farm buildings and made his malt and stored his corn in the nave.[1]

Yet there was a compensation. To the average countryman the Church was represented by one of his own class, accustomed from childhood to the same agricultural pursuits and way of life as himself. Though he might not be able to construe the Latin prayers and services he chanted by rote at the altar, he understood the problems of those to whom he ministered. In the market towns and a few of the richer country parishes the incumbent might be a man of substance like the parson of Trumpington in Chaucer's tale who gave his daughter—he should not, by rights, have had one—a dowry when she married the miller. Usually he was a small freeholder's son or a manumitted villein—for a bondsman could not be

[1] G. G. Coulton, *Medieval Panorama*, 177–8.

admitted to holy orders until he had been freed by his lord—with an average income in the prosperous eastern counties of £10 or £11 a year. In some cases his emoluments amounted to only £3 or £4 a year, no more than the earnings of a peasant farming thirty acres of ploughland. His sympathies and interests were those of his parishioners even if his poverty sometimes led to disputes about his dues or involved them in that much-resented form of parochial excommunication, "a cursing for tithes."

To a university doctor such a poor rustic priest might seem little better than a "brute beast" who, immersed in mercenary calculations about crops and beasts, could scarcely expound an article of the Faith and was fit only to "patter up his Matins and Mass." To his parishioners he was invested with mysterious powers on which rested their hopes and fears of reward or punishment after their hard, brief lives on earth. When as the sanctus bell sounded he stood before the altar and officiated at the Mass, bringing about by his priestly office the miraculous transformation of the bread and wine into Christ's body and blood, he seemed a creature of another world. And when death struck and he hastened to the side of the dying, carrying lantern and bell, holy water for sprinkling, oil for anointing and the pyx containing the sacred elements, on him and his power to grant absolution and administer the sacrament of Extreme Unction depended the lonely, bewildered soul's readiness for its passage to salvation or eternal damnation.

The peasant's life was short and precarious and death a constant visitant. He knew how cruel nature and his fellow men could be; what destructive forces lurked in wait for him. For him the old heathen gods still lived on under new names. His mind was haunted by thoughts of demons that "fly above in the air as thick as motes in the sun," of diabolical tempters who might appear at any moment under any guise, animal or human, and beguile him into some fatal sin that could rob him of his hope of salvation. Such fears were strengthened by the pictures on the church walls: of the pit into which sinners were cast, with its "fire and brimstone," "venomous worms and nadders" and fiends with blazing eyes and mocking laughter, pitch-forking their victims into everlasting torture. "Some shall burn," ran the words of one medieval sermon, "in the great flaming of fire which is ten times hotter than any fire in this world; some shall draw their limbs

asunder and smite their bodies with fiery brands . . . There
shall be flies that bite their flesh and their clothing shall be
worms . . . There is no sound but horrible roaring of devils
and weeping and gnashing of teeth and wailing of damned
men, crying, 'Woe, woe, woe, how great is this darkness!' " [1]

All this enormously enhanced the priest's power over his
flock. Having learnt to understand a little Latin he was the
sole interpreter of the Bible story and of the Judaic and
Christian truths recorded in that work—one to which, in an
age when all books had to be copied by hand and were
fabulously expensive,[2] only the better educated clergy and a
tiny minority of rich laymen had access. It was the priest or
his clerk or acolyte who taught the village children the rudi-
ments of their faith, the creed, commandments, catechism
and Latin prayers of Pater Noster and Ave Maria in the loft
that often served for school above the church porch, who
joined husband and wife at the church door in view of the
community, who received once a year, usually at Easter, the
confession of every parishioner in the shriving-pew. There
were other times when, with the bell tolling in the tower
above, he stood before his congregation to read the dreaded
sentence of excommunication, casting out the accursed with
book and candle from the Church's communion as he blew
out the flickering taper and flung it, at the end of his
anathema, to the ground.

Every great event of a poor man's life, everything that
raised it above that of the beasts and invested it with beauty
or significance, centred round the parish church. Here every
Sunday and on the more important of the thirty or forty holy
days of the year which were his holidays and the occasion of
his feasts and fasts, he listened, in awe and with bowed head,
to the "blessed mutter of the Mass" and took part in the ritual
dramas and processions which told for an unlettered people
the Gospel story—the lighted candles carried round the
church by the congregation at Candlemas, the distribution
and blessing of the ashes on Ash Wednesday, the hanging of
the Lenten veil before the altar, the distribution of branches
on Palm Sunday, the dramatic creeping to the Cross in the
darkened church on Good Friday, the triumphant procession

[1] G. R. Owst, *Preaching in Medieval England*, 336–7.
[2] Before the invention of printing, a bible would have cost
roughly ten years of an average village priest's income. P. Hughes,
The Reformation, 9n.

with vestments and banners on Easter Sunday as the Host and Cross were borne, amid pealing bells and the chanting of the Resurrection anthem, from the Easter Sepulchre, where they had lain since Good Friday, to the High Altar. At Pentecost a dove was loosed from the rafters amid clouds of incense; at the feast of Corpus Christi the entire community knelt in church and village street while the Sacrament was borne in procession through their ranks. At Rogationtide the fields were blessed by the priest, at Lammas the loaf—firstfruit of the harvest—was presented by him at the altar, on New Year's Day he led his parishioners round the apple orchards to bless the fruit of the coming summer.

Many of these rites and the superstitions that attached to them had been adapted by the Church from the heathen worship of pre-Christian times. Others, like the exorcising of witches, ghosts and fairies and the lighting of fires on Midsummer eve, had never become part of the Church's doctrine and ritual but were tacitly accepted by a rustic clergy who had grown up with such beliefs and had to reconcile their parishioners' ineradicable loyalty to them with the Christian faith and discipline they were paid to teach. So incense had taken the place of pagan burnt offerings, holy water of haunted wells and streams, Christian incantations of sorcerer's spells.

Despite the manuals and instructions for parish priests issued by reforming bishops, the dividing line between religion and superstition was never clearly marked in medieval religion. The church bells were rung to still the approaching storm, "that the Devil hearing the trumpets of the Eternal king that be the bells may flee away through fear and cease from raising the tempest." When vermin infested a church or caterpillars the village orchards an anathema would be pronounced against them by the priest, while old women suspected of witchcraft were sometimes accused of stealing the consecrated elements to destroy the pests in their gardens or put spells on their neighbours. It was popularly believed that, when at the supreme moment of the Mass the Host was elevated, whoever gazed on it with a pure and penitent heart would be granted freedom for the rest of the day from the normal misfortunes and mischances of life.

Except in Lent the village parson seldom preached. Four times a year he was expected to expound in English the Creed, the Gospel precepts and Ten Commandments, and expatiate, like Chaucer's "poor parson of the town," on the seven deadly sins and their consequences, the seven virtues and the seven sacraments of grace. For the rest he relied, like every parish priest from Calabria to Scandinavia, on the dramatic ritual of the Catholic Church, the rites at the altar, the sonorous Latin prayers and incantations, the statues, images and pictorial representations of Christ crucified or risen in majesty, of saints and martyrs and angels, of the Last Judgment and Harrowing of Hell depicted in brilliant colours and terrifying detail over the chancel arch, of the stories from Bible and Apocalypse that covered wall, window and roof-space of even the humblest church.

In weaning pagan man from his primitive and bloodstained creeds of terror and human sacrifice the Church's supreme achievement was to domesticate and humanise the conception of Eternity. Everywhere he was confronted, in church and wayside shrine, with homely and familiar reminders of the Heaven he was enjoined to earn through the virtues of love, faith, compassion, humility, truthfulness, chastity, courtesy—virtues that came so hard and were so much needed by a hot-tempered, ignorant, primitive people. To help them on their way to Paradise and make them shun temptation were the likenesses of men and women, who, the Church told them, had struggled and overcome the infirmities of human nature and were now, like the Master whose example they had followed, blessed spirits enthroned in Heaven yet ready to intercede for struggling mortals who called on them for aid. So human were the saints, Christians were taught, that they would help them in their humblest concerns. So St. Christopher, who once carried Christ on his shoulders, was the patron and protector of porters; St. Bartholomew, who was flayed alive, of tanners; St. Apollonia, whose jaw was smashed by his torturers, of those with toothache; St. John, who had been plunged into a chaldron of burning oil, of candlemakers. St. Giles looked after cripples, St. Crispin cobblers, St. Katherine little girls, St. Eustace and St. Hubert huntsmen, St. Cecilia the makers of music, St. Blaise sufferers from sore throats. And because she had anointed Christ's feet with aromatic oils Mary Magdalene was the protectress of perfumers. If one's oxen were sick one called on St. Corneille, if one's pigs on St. Anthony, if one's chickens on St. Gall. There was even a patron saint, St. Osyth, for women who had lost their keys.

So, too, there were saints for countries and places—St. George for England, St. Denis for France, St. Andrew for Scotland, St. Patrick for Ireland; St. Hugh of Lincoln, St. Swithin of Winchester, St. Chad of Lichfield. It was the function of the saints to intercede with Christ for the forgiveness of mortals, to protect them from the demons who lay in wait for their souls, to assist them when they acted righteously and craved their succour in misfortune. One had to earn their protection by penitence and prayer as one knelt before their images and altars or called on them in toil or travail, but for those who sought it with humility their aid was always to be had.

Best loved of all who interceded for man was the Virgin. The Gabriel bell rang at evening to call Christians to recite Ave Maria, and the pilgrims flocked to see the replica of her house in the Augustinian priory at Walsingham, believing that the heavenly galaxy, the Milky Way, had been set to guide them there. The events of her life, the Annunciation, Purification, Visitation and Assumption, had taken their place among the great feasts of the Christian year; at the Purification in February, known as Candlemas, everyone walked through the streets carrying candles blessed at the altar in her honour. She was thought of as the embodiment of every womanly virtue; tender, pure and loving and so pitiful that even the most abandoned could hope for forgiveness through her aid.

In no land was Mary more honoured than in England. The number of churches and shrines dedicated to her was past counting; no other name figures so often in the lists of the royal oblations. When William of Wykeham founded his colleges at Winchester and Oxford he placed them under her protection, and at both the bishop still kneels in stone with outstretched hands before her to beg a blessing on his endowments. Nearly every church of importance possessed her image in silver, gold or alabaster given by some benefactor, and along the highroads and pilgrim ways were wayside chapels where travellers could tell their beads and say their prayers to the Queen of Heaven. The names on our parish maps, Ladygrove, Ladysmead, Mary's Well and Maryfield, and the flowers that country folk called after her, marigold and ladysmantle, bear witness after four centuries of Protestantism to the homage paid by our Catholic ancestors to Christ's mother.

It was this union of earth and heaven, matter and spirit, the assumption that the other world and this were in continual contact, that made medieval Christianity such a germinating and educative religion. For the ordinary man his parish church was the centre both of his spiritual and terrestrial life. It was the place where the whole community met. Its nave and aisles were the setting not only for prayer and liturgical processions but for proclamations and business transactions. Its porch was used for coroners' inquests and betrothals and for the payment of legacies; its oaken chest for depositing wills, charters and title-deeds. In the churchyard where the village children played and the dead, carried in the parish coffin, were laid in their shrouds to await the reunion of all Christians on Resurrection day, the parishioners met to beat the parish bounds, fairs were held, and miracle plays or "mysteries" were enacted by bucolic actors in which rustic exuberance and horse-play mingled, incongruously, with the piety of unquestioning faith. If by our standards such entertainments were crude and profane—if the shepherds at Bethlehem lauded the local ale or God appeared with a tiara, beard and gilded face—it was because the Christian faith was a part of the life of plain, unlettered men.

Medieval Christianity was an intensely human religion. It had place for comedy and farce. In the Palm Sunday procession a boy dressed as an angel standing above the west porch threw down cakes for which the congregation scrambled, while a wooden ass was drawn along behind the choir with a man belabouring it with a whip. Even in the deeply impressive Tenebrae services in Passion week when, one after another, the lights on the altar were darkened, the rustic singers in the loft were sustained during their long ordeal by wine and beer provided by the churchwardens, while the resurrection on Easter morning was hailed by the entire congregation banging on clappers.

All the community's corporate life that was not purely economic centred round the church—the May Day dances when the children went round the village collecting money, the bonfires lit on the vigils of saints' days when the houses were illuminated with candles and the wealthy spread tables of wine and sweet cakes before their doors for their poorer neighbours, the watches on Midsummer and St. Peter's eves when the parish was perambulated and, in the cities, men and apprentices marched through the streets in the liveries of their gilds. It was the churchwardens—elected annually by the parishioners at the Easter vestry—who organised, in church-yard or in church-house if the parish possessed one, church-ales to raise money for parish expenses, bride-ales to help young married couples set up house, bid-ales for those in need and distress. When a church was rebuilt or added to—and throughout the fourteenth and fifteenth centuries almost every town and village was refashioning and refurbishing its church—the churchwardens raised the money by arranging archery meetings and door-to-door collections. They appointed a village "Robin Hood" and "Little John" to lead the way to the butts after Mass on Sundays and holy days and collect the fees of the competitors, and organised the annual Hocktide collection when the young men and wives and maid-ens went in turn to one another's houses to rope in those of the other sex and make them pay forfeits for the church's benefit —"the devocyon of the people on Hoke Tuesday," as the churchwardens of St. Edmund's, Salisbury, called it. They held, too, the annual church audit when the parishioners, grouped under their respective trades and callings, came in turn to present their gifts and collections—"comyth in the yonglings and maidens," "comyth in the weavers," runs the account of the proceedings in one Somerset parish.[1] It was then that the churchwardens received any bequest left to the parish: the keep of a cow for the poor, a swarm of bees to provide wax for candles and honey, a woman's wedding ring, clothing for making into vestments and coverings. They were also responsible for the decoration of the church—with spring flowers on Palm Sunday and Easter, garlands of roses for Corpus Christi, and holly and ivy at Christmas.

At a time when most men lived in bare, almost unfurnished mud and wattle huts little bigger than those in which a small holder today keeps his farrowing sows, the wealth that was lavished on the church by even the poorest village seems little short of miraculous. As the church inventories of the fifteenth century show, small and remote churches, with no rich bene-factors to endow them, possessed chalices, patens, mazers, censers, candlesticks of silver and silver-gilt, panelled and gilded reredoses and altars, jewelled processional crosses and pyxes for the Host, embroidered vestments and altar-cloths of cloth of gold. They were furnished with carved rood-

---

[1] Bishop Hobhouse, *Churchwardens' Accounts* (Somerset Rec-ord's Society 1890), 13–18.

screens, misericords and benchends, stone and alabaster
statues, finely cast and engraved bells, and windows blazing
with glass bought from the *verreurs* of France and Germany.
All was paid for and accumulated from generation to generation by the village community, many of whose members—
carpenters, masons and smiths—helped to fashion it.[1]

Of what the service of the Church at its best could mean
to a country village we have the testimony of Chaucer. For
when, in his cavalcade of worldly pilgrims, lay and ecclesiastic, he reached the humble village priest, that cynical, tolerant
but scrupulously honest observer of the contemporary scene
paused in his amused catalogue of human frailty to draw the
portrait of one who came as near to fulfilling the precepts
of Christianity as a man can.

"A good man there was of religiön,
And was a poorë parson of a town;
But rich he was of holy thought and work,
He also was a learned man, a clerk,
That Christës gospel gladly would he preach;
His parishioners devoutly would he teach.
Benign he was and wondrous diligent,
And in adversity full patient,
And such he was i-provëd oft to be.
To cursen for his tithes full loath was he,
But rather would he given out of doubt
Unto his poor parishioners about. . . . . .
Wide was his parish and houses far asunder,
But yet he leftë not in rain or thunder,
In sickness and in mischief to visit
The furthest in his parish, small and great,
Upon his feet and in his hand a staff;
This noble example unto his sheep he gave,
That first he wrought and afterwards he taught . . .
He waited after no pomp nor reverence
Nor made himself spiced in conscience,
But Christës lore and his apostles twelve,
He taught, but first he followed it himself."

However unsatisfactory many parish priests may have been,
a good priest could make a Christian village.

[1] J. Maynard Smith, *Pre-Reformation England*, 121–3; J. Evans,
English Art, 1307–1461 (Oxford History of English Art).

Dreaming of his boyhood's home on the Malvern hills the poor London chantry clerk, William Langland, described in his great religious poem of the latter fourteenth century how

> "walking alone
> By a wild wilderness   and by a wood side,
> Bliss of the birds   made me abide,
> And under a linen in a glade   leaned I awhile
> To listen to the lays   the lovely fowls made . . .
> I saw the flowers in the wood   and their fair colours,
> And how among the green grass   grew so many hues."

That wild England of isolated villages must have been very beautiful with its clear rivers and great forests and the song of its innumerable birds. Its people were famed for their love of outdoor sports; the king and his lords were no more addicted to hunting, hawking and tournaments than the common folk to tilting, football, cock-fighting, quoits, hammer-throwing, baseball, cudgelling and quarterstaff. From their traditional dances, when the performers, joining hands, accompanied one another in interminable verses or "caroles", one can form some idea of their thoughts and dreams: of the rustic swains serenading the maidens in the Worcestershire churchyards with the refrain, "Sweetheart have pity"; of the transitoriness of earthly beauty—

> "Where is Paris and Heleyne
> That were so bright and fair of blee?"

of

> "Lenten is come with love to town
> With blossom and with briddes' round,"

of freedom and the spring and the green wood. One can see them with their gaunt frames and weatherbeaten faces: yeomen walking behind the plough or riding bareback to mill to grind their corn; shepherds on the hills at lambing and sheep-shearing, or driving their flocks at dusk into great stone sheepcotes; foresters in green jerkins with bows and arrows; "spinsters" turning their wheels at open doors on summer evenings; bellringers with the sweat gleaming on their foreheads, at their rhythmical, companionable art:

> "Bart the beadle   of Buckinghamshire,
> Reynold the reeve   of Rutland soke
> Mund the miller   and many more other."

CHAPTER VIII

TRAVELLERS AND TRADERS

BRIDGING THE uncultivated wild between England's villages and little towns ran the roads, trodden by growing numbers of men and horses. The metalled highways with which Rome had spanned the country had long become a ghostly network, their paved surfaces defaced, their causeways broken by quarrying and their course deflected to serve local needs. The medieval road did not run straight from city to city. It meandered round field, park and pale, respecting a thousand local "liberties" and quirks of history. It was not surfaced for wheeled traffic or swift travelling. It was merely a grassy trackway for horses, carts, cattle and sheep. It was not so much a road as a route over which travellers had a right to pass. Where there was a highway subject to the king's peace, the proprietors along its course were under an obligation to keep it open. No one might raise fences across it or dung-heaps or use it for quarrying stone or gravel. Towns and villages which permitted such encroachments were constantly being fined. In winter, in the clay lowlands, such soft roads became quagmires; in summer a maze of hard-baked hoof-holes and ruts. But so much of the countryside was still waste that it was easy to make a detour across adjoining land. This, however, created a multiplicity of tracks and made it equally easy to lose the way. There are records of medieval travellers on Watling Street finding themselves as far off as Buckingham to the west or Newport Pagnell to the east; those who could afford it often hired guides. Travel was so arduous and dangerous that the Church in its prayers grouped travellers with prisoners and captives, sick persons and women labouring with child. The repair of roads and bridges and the provision of hospitality for wayfarers were regarded as matters for Christian charity. Crosses were erected by the wayside in lonely places, lanterns kept burning in church-towers at night, and bells sounded to guide benighted wayfarers. Rich men left sums to provide rest-houses and *maisons dieu,* and monasteries and incumbents of rectories were enjoined to entertain and relieve travellers.

The lords of the highway, as of everywhere else in that aristocratic age, were the earls, barons and prelates, with their trains of followers, their armour, ceremonial furs and emblazoned mantles and banners, making their way to council or parliament or travelling from one estate to another. The greatest of all were the king and his Court. In a single half year Edward I moved his residence seventy-five times. In days when there were no regular posts or means of transmitting news, it was the only way in which a ruler could know and control what was happening in his kingdom. The grander members of the Court travelled on horseback, the vast army of menials, scullions and poor suitors on foot. Its treasure, plate, pavilions, hangings, beds, cooking-utensils, wine, legal and financial rolls were borne in panniers on pack-horses or in rough, box-like, two-wheeled carts, drawn by oxen, donkeys or dogs and requisitioned from the countryside. A few great ladies—a queen or some royal invalid—might ride in a litter borne between horses or in a gilded wagon with an arched roof hung with tapestry and suspended on carved, unsprung beams and huge nailed wheels. But the normal mode of transport was the cavalcade: the long procession of jingling, brightly-accoutred, splendidly-caparisoned horses, with riders chattering or singing as they wound their way across the fields. To journey in company and make music as one went was the mode of the time. Only the king's messengers, forerunners of the post, travelled alone, and lepers with their bells and clappers, sores and pallid, hooded faces, and adjured felons making their way from sanctuary to the nearest port with bare feet and loose white tunics and wooden crosses as signs of the Church's protection.

The chief interest of the age being religion, there were many clerical travellers: monastic officers visiting their estates and bishop's commissaries perambulating the diocese, pardoners selling indulgences, summoners with writs for breaches of ecclesiastical law, papal agents collecting money, grey and black-gowned friars, and poor clerks on their way to the universities. These were the religious professionals; others were amateurs. Every spring men and women would set out in company, with wallet, staff and scallop shell, broad-brimmed hat and jingling Canterbury bell, to visit some distant or local shrine and return with relics—for the rich a splinter from a saint's staff or a flask of holy-water, and, for ordinary folk, a pewter-badge to be worn on cap or breast as a souvenir. Pilgrimage was one of the penances set by the Church for winning remission of time in purgatory—the place of punishment to which it was believed those not immediately translated to Heaven or Hell were consigned after death until they had expiated their sins. Pilgrimage could sometimes be a penance of the most onerous kind, one in which a man left home and family for years, braving immense hardships and perils to visit the Holy Land or Rome or some remote shrine like St. James's of Compostella in Spain. But for most people, though seen as a means of acquiring grace, a pilgrimage was an excuse for a holiday, to be taken preferably

> "When that Aprillë with his showers sweet
> The drought of March hath piercëd to the root."

As soon as the roads dried out after the winter they were thronged with parties making their way to some favourite shrine and beguiling the journey with tales, singing, and the playing of bagpipes. The most popular places of pilgrimage were St. Thomas's shrine at Canterbury—the word "canter" entered the language through it—and Our Lady's statue at Walsingham in Norfolk, with its famous phial of the Virgin's milk, "the most holy name in England." Both were visited every summer by huge crowds. So were Joseph of Arimathaea's winter-blossoming thorn at Glastonbury, the philtre of Christ's blood at Richard of Cornwall's abbey of Hayles in Gloucestershire, the rood of Bromholm, and the Confessor's glittering shrine at Westminster, where the hollows worn by the feet of kneeling pilgrims can still be seen.

The innkeepers along the pilgrim-ways did a roaring-trade. There were chapels, stables for hiring horses, cells, where hermits received alms, and hostels like the gild-house at Coventry where a poor woman was kept to wash the pilgrims' feet. The "Bell" at Tewkesbury, the "New Inn" at Gloucester, the "George" at Glastonbury all began as houses maintained by charitable gilds for the relief of pilgrims. By the fourteenth century catering for them had become an immense industry. At Christ Church, Canterbury, they were met by a monk at a special door and, after being sprinkled with holy water,

were led into the north transept to an altar marking the spot
where St. Thomas was killed. Then, after inspecting the relics
of his martyrdom in the crypt and kissing the rusty blade of
his murderer's sword, they ascended the stairs to the shrine
on their knees and made their oblations to the custodians of
that marvel of jewels and gold, receiving in return tiny *am-
pullae* of Canterbury water—coloured it was supposed, by a
miraculously inexhaustible drop of Becket's blood—while
those suffering from rheumatism rubbed their limbs against
the surrounding stones.[1]

Hundreds of lesser places of pilgrimage were scattered
about the island. Such was the holy well at North Marston in
Buckinghamshire of Master John Schorne, a poor country
parson who, being visited by the Devil, cunningly lured him
beyond the altar-rails and conjured him into a boot. A mechanical replica of the miracle re-enacted it before the eyes of
pilgrims, and small wooden reproductions said to be good for
gout, were sold by the shrine's custodians, becoming forerunners of the child's toy, the Jack-in-the-Box. It was symptomatic both of the simple credulity of the age and the isolation
of one part of England from another that villages in Norfolk, Suffolk, Devonshire and even Northumberland all
claimed and commemorated the same saint and incident.

The most cautious road-users were those who travelled
with merchandise or money, for the woods and thickets were
full of thieves. In the early Middle Ages the main roads,
especially those to the southern and eastern ports, were much
used by foreigners—Flemings and Italians buying Cotswold
or Yorkshire wool, Spaniards with steel blades from Toledo,
Lombards with silks and spices, Easterlings with furs and tar
from the Baltic. But by the end of the thirteenth century
such trade was beginning to pass to Englishmen. As there
were no posts and few facilities for transferring money from
one country to another, a merchant had constantly to be on
the road attending his business. Like the poor man in
Chaucer's tale who was deceived by his wife and the young
monk, he was always off to Bruges or Bordeaux at break of
day.

Humbler traders like pedlars, chapmen and charcoal-sellers
went on foot, with their wares on a pack-horse or in a box

[1] G. C. Carpenter, *The Church in England,* 181; Cook, *The English Cathedral,* 34–5.

or sack on their backs. So did a host of poor itinerants, travelling from one village to another: minstrels, buffoons and balladsingers, some aiming high at the castles and others at gaping rustics on the village greens; bears and bearwards; men with performing monkeys; clowns, jugglers, girls who danced on their hands with swords in their mouths, and herbalists selling panaceas for every disease. There is a picture of one in a thirteenth century herbal-book, spreading his wares on his carpet or drugget and haranguing the villagers.

At certain times of the year the roads became crowded with travellers converging on a single spot. Fairs were occasions when a rural neighbourhood did its shopping and caught a glimpse of the outer world. The greatest fair in England was Stourbridge near Cambridge—the property of Barnwell priory. Here for three weeks every September a town of wooden booths offered for sale everything a rustic community needed. There were streets that sold soap, streets that sold garlic, streets that sold coal. Others vended fish, nails, grindstones, Sussex iron and Worcestershire salt, shovels, brushes and pails, oil and honey, pots and pans, horses and packsaddles. The most important place in the fair was the duddery, where the "duds" or cloths of East Anglia were displayed. Among those who brought their wares were Spaniards and Moors with Damascus blades and armour, Venetians with gems and velvets, Flemings with linen, Dutchmen with cheeses, Greeks with almonds and spices and Germans or Easterlings with tallow, fur, and pitch. A special court of *Pied Poudré* or "dusty foot"—called by the English "Pie Powder"—was held to preserve order and enforce the regulations of the fair's owners about weights and measures and the quality of foodstuffs. In the jovial mode of England the fair also provided horse-races, wrestling-matches, tippling, gambling and music booths, rope-dancers and a maypole.

Other famous fairs were St. Bartholomew's in Smithfield and St. Giles' on the hillside at Winchester, St. Frideswide's at Oxford and St. Audrey's at Ely, whose tinselly wares gave the word tawdry to the language. They were a great source of revenue to their ecclesiastical proprietors. St. Botolph's at Boston, and St. Ives in Huntingdonshire, St. George's at Modbury, the Barnet horse and the Abingdon cattle fair were all famous far beyond their locality. So was Woodbury hill in Dorset, with its five days—Wholesale, Gentlefolks', Allfolks',

Sheep Fair and Pack-and-Penny. But the number of fairs was legion; in Somerset alone there were nearly a hundred.

What fairs were temporarily, towns were permanently. But they were much more exclusively regulated. At first the Conquest had checked the growth of town-life. In York and Lincoln, the two chief cities of the north, as well as in lesser boroughs like Cambridge, houses had been demolished to make room for castles: others had been burnt by plundering soldiery or deliberately destroyed as a punishment for rebellion. But during the reigns of the first three Henrys there had been a steady growth in the size and number of towns. The Crown and the great secular and ecclesiastical lords found the sale of free burgess-tenures and the tolls of markets and fairs a valuable supplement to their agricultural revenues. They encouraged commerce by letting the citizens and gild-merchants of favoured towns buy charters of freedom from the tolls and custom-dues which impeded the flow of goods at city gate, port, and river crossing. Control of the hours of dealing, of prices, weights and measures, and of the quality of goods sold, was delegated by royal or baronial charter to their corporations and, often, to associations of their traders. These merchant-gilds were empowered to fix wages and prices fair to both buyer and seller, to exclude nonmembers from trading in the town and to fine and punish for breaches of their rules. They appointed hours, announced by bell, for the opening and closing of markets and levied tolls on goods brought for sale. They also made treaties, interchanging commercial privileges, with the traders of other towns. And in the larger cities, craftsmen and traders associated themselves in livery companies or fraternities, partly commercial and partly religious and social, to regulate the conditions of their trade and afford one another mutual protection.

Like the juries of the villages, these self-governing corporations helped to train Englishmen for political responsibility. They were administered by voluntary officers elected annually, whose duties were borne by the members in turn, and governed by rules reached after mutual and open discussion. Members were punished for selling inferior goods, for sharp or shoddy practice that lowered the name of their craft, for brawling and eavesdropping and breaches of social and professional etiquette. A trader who sold food made from diseased carcasses, who put sand in his bread or water in his wine or otherwise tricked the public, was sentenced by his fellow craftsmen to be drawn through the streets on a hurdle or to sit in penance in the pillory with the offending goods hung round his neck and his crime published on a placard. "The said John Penrose," ran the order of one London court, "shall drink a draught of the same wine which he sold to the common people, and the remainder of such wine shall then be poured on the head of the same John, and he shall forswear the calling of a vintner in the city of London for ever."

Every English town with the possible exception of London —whose link with Roman days may well have been unbroken —had originally grown out of a village. Its institutions had a rustic origin: the borough and ward officers with agricultural names, like the poundkeeper at Canterbury, the moot that had begun as a manorial jurisdiction, and the burghmote horn that summoned the burghers to its meetings; the annual perambulation of the bounds when the city fathers, like their village forebears, solemnly beat the young fry over the boundary-stones to make them remember where they stood. The sanitary arrangements of the borough also derived from the village. Such drains as it had, ran down the unpaved or, at best, cobbled roadway. The household refuse and ordure, thrown out of the windows at nightfall, were scavenged by pigs, dogs and kites. Even in London, where the poorer dwellings were totally without privies, for long there was only one public latrine for every ward and a dozen dung-carts for the whole city. The larger the towns grew, the more unwholesome they became, though, after a time their corporations, alarmed at the rising death-rate, began to issue regulations about street-cleansing and water-supply.

Yet, though the towns were dirty, they were also beautiful, with their church towers and spires, their stately gateways and half-timbered houses, and the trees and blossom of their gardens. Their encircling walls were designed more for preventing robberies and controlling suspicious travellers at night than for war. Except on the Welsh and Scottish borders they were seldom the elaborate affairs of the continent, where even the smallest town was heavily fortified. Some of the later boroughs, like Cambridge, never even had walls, but only palisades and ditches crossed by gated bridges. Being in little danger of attack, they were free from the military restrictions that cramped life for European burghers. They did not need governors and garrisons.

For this reason, too, they spread outwards rather than upwards, running to leafy suburbs that, secure in England's immunity from invasion, nestled outside instead of inside the walls. Yet, as no town save London had more than 10,000 inhabitants and few a third of this number, the fields were never far away. Most of the richer merchants had farms or orchards in the surrounding countryside, as well as gardens, stables and cowstalls round their houses. English urban economy was as much rural as urban. Even the city of Norwich, capital of the clothmaking industry of East Anglia and the third largest town in England, suspended trade during the harvest and sent its weavers into the fields.

The first sight the traveller had of a medieval town was of its towers and spires on the horizon, with, perhaps, a castle on higher ground. Boundary stones beside the highroad marked the beginning of its land—the arable strips of the "town field" with hired labourers working on them, and the great meadow along the river where the cattle grazed under the municipal cowherds. Entry was through a stone archway and a vast wooden gate, closed from sundown to sunrise by a porter who collected the corporation's tolls. The streets were narrow and winding, with upper stories overhanging the cobbled roadways till they almost touched. Gilded signs swung and creaked in the wind, while apprentices bawled out the wares set out on the benches before open doors. Through these could be seen journeymen working at their trade. The shouting was terrific, the hoofs and ironrimmed wheels on the cobblestones made a perpetual hammering, and the bells of the churches and monasteries kept pealing and chiming. The stink, too, was overwhelming, especially in the streets occupied by tanners and butchers. For mutual protection and cooperation all the bakers and cook-shops tended to be in one street, the mercers in another, the goldsmiths, shoemakers or saddlers in another. Leading out of them were narrow alleys giving on to stables and laystalls and the foetid, tumbledown hovels of the poorer artisans and labourers.

In the centre of the town were the fine stone houses of the richer citizens, the gildhall with its belfry-tower and the marketplace—a square or broad street, like Oxford's Cornmarket, with a cross where the town-crier made public announcements with bell or horn. Here, too, were the stocks, where offenders were pelted with filth and rotten fruit, and the duckingstool for scandal-mongers. On market days the surrounding countryside poured in to sell its produce, doubling the population for a few noisy hours and filling the cook-houses and taverns.

One town in England stood alone. With the royal courts of law sitting permanently in the king's palace and hall of Westminster, London had long taken the place of the old Anglo-Saxon capital, Winchester, as the seat of government. One of Henry II's subjects, William FitzStephen, wrote an account of it as it was a century after the Conquest: its clear river bordering it on the south, the royal palatine castle in the east whose keep was set with a mortar tempered with the blood of animals, the high and massive walls with their seven double-gates and towers, the thirteen conventual and hundred and twenty-six parish churches. Most of the houses were still flimsy single or two-storied wooden structures; one winter gale flattened more than six hundred, and fires often swept away whole wards. But the richer merchants' and knights' houses were already being built of stone, and red-brick tiles were gradually replacing thatch. Two years before Henry's death the Londoners began their first stone bridge; a monument of faith in the country's stability, which took thirty years to complete and lasted for six centuries.

FitzStephen described the merchandise that flowed up the river to the Pool beside the Tower and the little hithes and quays along the north bank—gold and spices from the East, arms from Scythia and purple silk from China; the wine and cook-shops where travellers could buy hot dishes at any hour of the day or night; the market outside the walls in the meadow called Smithfield, where high-stepping palfreys with gleaming coats were put through their paces and country folk brought their goods and livestock for sale. He drew a picture, the first in our history, of the Londoners at play; their summer evening walks among the suburban wells—St. Clement's, Holywell, Clerkenwell—and the sparkling streams whose mill-wheels made so cheerful a sound; the hunts in the great Middlesex and Essex forests after stag, fallow deer and wild boar; the apprentices and schoolboys playing football in the fields while "the fathers and wealthy magnates came on horseback to watch the contests and recover their lost youth"; the archery, running, jumping, wrestling, dancing and stone slinging, rowing and skating, with which the youths and maidens regaled themselves on holy days.

By the fourteenth century, the population of London had risen to about 50,000. Though still much smaller than the great continental cities of Paris, Milan and Florence, with its "square mile" along the Thames between the Tower and Ludgate it was by far the country's largest town—four or five times the size of York, Bristol, Plymouth, Coventry and Norwich and probably ten times that of Gloucester, Newcastle, Salisbury, Exeter and Winchester. Newcomers were all the time being drawn into it by the commerce of its tidal river and the business of the royal Chancery and the courts of law at Westminster two miles to the west. Already the Strand—the highway between the two places—was lined with nobles' and prelates' palaces whose gardens sloped down to the unembanked Thames. The king himself, unlike his cousin of France, had no palace in his capital—only the Tower on its eastern wall, with its little garrison of knights and men-at-arms, and the Wardrobe or Household clothing store at Baynard's Castle.

For the City was a law to itself. "Come what may," ran an old saying, "the Londoners should have no king but their mayor." This functionary—though only a merchant, had taken his place at Runnymede among the great magnates of the realm who imposed Magna Carta. He ruled the capital with the help of two sheriffs, elected annually like himself, and a court of aldermen representing its twenty-five wards. Behind this court's weekly hustings in the Guildhall lay the general body of the corporation—the old folkmoot of the citizens assembled three times a year by bell in the open air outside St. Paul's. With the population growing fast, there was a constant tendency on the part of the less privileged to try to gain control of the city's government and oust the older merchant families who monopolised it—a struggle which resulted in frequent faction-fights and rioting. During Edward I's reign the antiquated and unmanageable public assembly was abandoned in favour of an elected Common Council. Through its officers the corporation collected the royal customs on foreign merchandise and levied its own tolls on all goods coming in from the country. It made bye-laws on such matters as building, public order, the use of fountains and precautions against fire. It decided who should have the right to trade in particular districts, where swine should be allowed to wander, when taverns should close and slops and refuse be emptied from the windows. It also fixed the hour of curfew, after which none with swords were allowed in the streets, "unless some great lord or other substantial person of good reputation."

London could be a very turbulent city. Behind its bridge and seven portcullised gateways crowded the warlike rabble of apprentices and journeymen who, when roused, became a terrible raging beast. Any infringement of its rights brought it swarming through the narrow streets like a torrent. Once, when some Hoxton residents enclosed a meadow where the Londoners had long taken their Sunday walks, a turner in a fool's coat ran through the streets crying, "Shovels and spades!", upon which the whole town turned out to level the hedges and ditches. The German merchants of the Cologne Steelyard in Thames Street and the rich Italians of Galley Quay and Mincing Lane barricaded their houses against their English neighbours like fortresses.

Yet the beauty of medieval London impressed travellers even more than its turbulence. It was bordered on the south by a wide, clear river, teeming with fish and with swans on its waters. Beyond it, save for the disorderly little suburb of Southwark, lay unsullied meadows and the wooded Surrey hills. To the north of the walls cornfields and pastures, diversified with streams and water-mills, stretched to the heights of Hampstead and Highgate. To the east lay the great hunting forests of Epping and Hainault. All round were thriving villages supplying the city's needs—Stepney, Bethnal Green, Islington, Hoxton, Holborn, Marylebone, and, farther afield, Bow and Bromley, Hackney, Highbury and Stoke Newington, Kilburn, Paddington and Knightsbridge. Though, save for its immense cathedral on the hill and its famous twenty-arch bridge crowned with houses, London lacked imposing buildings, the towers and spires of its churches and monasteries made a wonderful show as they crowded above the walls and river. The sound of their bells was almost continuous. And between the brightly painted wooden houses and red-tiled roofs were countless little gardens or "herbers" and orchards of waving fruit-trees—mulberry, apple, plum, peach and cherry.

By the time of the Black Death, though only about a third of that of France and Italy, the population of England and

Wales had risen to somewhere between three and four millions. Most of it was concentrated in the south-east, notably in the wheat-growing and sheep-raising districts of East Anglia and the southern midlands. The taxation yield of Norfolk was almost twice that of the next highest yielding county, Kent; after which followed, in order, Gloucestershire, Wiltshire, Lindsey in south Lincolnshire, Suffolk, Oxfordshire, Somerset and Essex. Hampshire, Northamptonshire, Sussex, the East Riding of Yorkshire, Berkshire and Cambridgeshire came next. The yield of the three northern counties of Lancashire, Cumberland and Northumberland together was less than a tenth that of Norfolk.

The country was still predominantly agricultural; a rich primary-producing land, exporting vast quantities of fine wool and, in good years, grain and dairy-produce. It also exported hides, leather-goods, dried and salted fish, embroideries, metalware, tin, coal and lead, mostly to the overpopulated Low Countries in exchange for wool and, later, manufactured cloth, to Gascony and the Rhineland for wine, and to the Baltic for timber and shipbuilding stores. Wool was its main source of wealth. The finest—the short wool of the Ryelands sheep and the long of the Lincolns, Leicesters and golden Lion breed of the Cotswolds—came from the Severn valley and the limestone belt between Somerset and Lincolnshire. But almost every part of the country, except the far north and extreme south-west, exported wool of some kind. It was reckoned that on an average 30,000 sacks or eight million fleeces went abroad every year, mostly to northern Italy and the cloth-manufacturing towns of Flanders, Artois, Brabant and Hainault.

Though for most of the Middle Ages England was primarily a supplier of raw wool to others, cloth was always manufactured on a small scale for home consumption in most of the larger towns. Edward III's marriage to a Hainault princess brought a new stimulus to native manufacturers; one of his earliest acts was to grant letters of protection to a Flemish weaver named Kempe. Other colonies of Flemish weavers, attracted by the cheap and abundant supplies of the raw material of their trade and the social stability of England, established themselves during his reign at Norwich, York and Cranbrook in Kent. Queen Philippa herself made a practice of visiting one of these settlements in Norwich whenever her husband went on progress in East Anglia.

Export of wool and the increased imports which it paid for of spices, wine, silks, furs, timber, pitch, tar, oil, salt, alum, rice and fruits were a great stimulus to native shipping and shipbuilding. Southampton, Bristol, Plymouth and Falmouth were the chief ports of the west, Lynn, Boston, Newcastle-on-Tyne, Kingston-on-Hull and the Cinque Ports of the east. After London the most important was Southampton, whose deep tidal water, protected by the Isle of Wight from Breton, Gascon and Flemish pirates, rivalled the Thames estuary as the starting-point for the convoys of little sailingships, mostly of less than a hundred tons, which carried England's wool to the continent. It was a terminus port, too, for the wine fleets from Bordeaux, Bayonne and La Rochelle, and for the Genoese and Pisan carracks which during the early years of the fourteenth century started to export wool-fells from the Solent and Thames to the mills of the Arte della Lana of Florence in return for luxuries from Italy and the Orient. To Southampton came by barge down the Itchen—then navigable as far as Winchester—the wool of the Wiltshire, Berkshire and Gloucestershire downs, while coastwise vessels from Poole, Melcombe Regis, Bridport, Lyme and Exeter brought that of Dorset, Somerset and Devon. Other wool travelled down the Severn and Warwickshire Avon for shipment at Bristol. Carts and pack-horses took the canvas-wrapped bales and fells on their journey from the upland pastures to the nearest river.

In days when water provided by far the cheapest form of transport, England's commerce gained from two circumstances. Though her rivers were small compared with those of the continent, the sea was never far away and her coast abounded in estuaries where goods could be shipped either abroad or to her own ports. And at a time when every ruler was trying to fill his coffers by levying tolls on merchandise, England with her strong, unified royal government was the largest free-trading area in Europe. Almost her only internal transportation-tolls were petty portages and viages levied to recoup expenditure where a bridge or road had been provided by private enterprise. Only at the courts of Brabant and Hainault and in the Italian and Flemish cities was the movement of trade as free.

With a coastline longer for her size than that of any western kingdom, England possessed a substantial maritime population living by fishing, coastal trade and voyages to the

Baltic, Low Countries, France and Biscay. Though most of her ocean carrying-trade was still in the hands of foreigners and her ships were of much smaller tonnage than those of the Mediterranean trading states—Genoa, Pisa, Venice and Aragon—her seamen, accustomed to the Channel and North Sea tides and storms, were tough, skilful and notorious for their pugnacity. Constantly involved in harbour broils with their Norman, Breton, Flemish and Basque rivals, they fought as often among themselves. Whenever the seamen of the Cinque Ports met the fishermen of Yarmouth, whom they viewed as interlopers, they engaged them in pitched battle "on lond and strond." With their seven chartered ports—Winchelsea, Romney, Hythe, Dover, Sandwich, Hastings and Rye, and their outlying "limbs"—the portmen of the Sussex and Kent lagoons and inlets had long been the aristocrats of the narrow seas, producing their feudal quota of ships for the king in time of war and living in peacetime by a well-tried blend of fishing, piracy and trade with northern France and the Low Countries. But, with the gradual silting up of their harbours and the development of sail, their ascendancy was already beginning to be challenged by the west country seamen. With the richest fishing grounds in the world at their gates and a Catholic country to feed that lived on fish all Lent and Fridays, coastal Englishmen were learning the business of mastering the watery wastes in which their island was set. Though they seldom yet ventured further than Spain or Norway—Chaucer's shipman knew the coasts from Jutland to Finisterre—the stormy and changeable seas they sailed were well adapted for teaching the finer points of seamanship. A breed apart, transmitting their sea-lore from father to son, they introduced into the make-up of a rustic people an adventurous, carefree strain which was to have far-reaching consequences in the sixteenth century after the discovery of America and the ocean trade-routes round the Cape.

The merchant town, with its life of freedom and opportunity, was little by little transforming the racially divided society that England had become after the Norman conquest into a fluid one in which every social grade shaded imperceptibly into the next. Many of the leading merchant families, especially in London and the larger ports, traced their descent from foreign traders who had settled in England, like the Bocointes and Buckerells who had come from Italy and the Arraxes who took their name from Arras. Far more were enterprising English countrymen, often of villein blood, who had fled from bondage on their paternal acres to seek their fortunes behind the walls of the self-governing chartered boroughs. Many who did so perished of poverty or disease in their overcrowded slums, defeated by the monopolistic restrictions with which the established burgesses protected themselves and their crafts and trades. Others passed, sometimes in less than a generation, from the harsh, unchanging life of the manor to affluence, the dignity of aldermanic or mayoral status, and even office under the Crown—always in England quick to avail itself of the services of men of business and financial experience. Merchants unknown to the hereditary feudal hierarchy with rustic names like Dunstable, Haverill and Piggsflesh served as royal chamberlains, butlers and purveyors, loaned money to the Crown or some great magnate, arranged for the transfer of funds from one part of the Plantagenet empire to another and offered mortgages to supply their social superiors, lay and ecclesiastic, with the ready cash to cater for their increasingly luxurious tastes. In doing so, though many fell by the way, they made fortunes for themselves, investing their gains in land and founding landed and knightly families.

Exchange of goods and merchandise—immensely stimulated by the crusades and the spread among the rich of eastern tastes and habits—was throwing the careers open to the talents. In every city a race of men had arisen who pursued money-making as an end in itself and who bought and sold not primarily to supply the consumer with goods but to increase their stock of money and use it for making more. Usury, forestalling, regrating, making a corner in commodities and artificially lowering market-prices in order to buy and raising them in order to sell—all the practices which the Church had taught were unchristian and unneighbourly—were pursued as a profession by men who made fortunes by doing so and put ordinary folk out of countenance by extravagant living and the grandeur of their ways. Merchants whose grandfathers or even fathers had been simple craftsmen or serfs were addressed by their fellow townsmen as worshipful or sire, wore scarlet robes and costly furs as masters and liverymen of monopolistic merchant companies, founded originally to protect and foster honest craftsmanship but since grown into exclusive chartered societies of wealthy entrepreneurs—Mercers, Drapers and Goldsmiths, Grocers, Fishmongers and Vintners, Skinners, Salters, Leathersellers and Ironmongers—famed for their lavish hospitality and elaborate ritual and pageantry.

Once they had attained burgess status such men could not be touched by their former lords and enjoyed the protection, not only of the borough, with its jealously guarded rights, but of the royal courts. How quickly the transformation could be affected is shown by an action for assault and imprisonment during Edward II's reign by a London mercer and alderman, one Simon de Paris, against Walter Page, bailiff of Sir Robert Tony, lord of the Norfolk manor of Necton, the place from which the plaintiff had originally come and to which he and his forebears had belonged. While paying a visit to his former home this rich, proud man had been seized and detained by the manorial authorities, presumably in the hope of black-mail. Their defence was that, though he might now be a burgess, he had been born a villein and, being found at Necton "in his villein nest," was bound to perform the servile services of his hereditary status. When the lord's bailiff tend-ered to him the office of village reeve he had refused it and so had been arrested under the law of the manor and detained "in custody from the hour of terce until vespers," when the uproar he made seems to have secured his release. The alder-man's case was that he was a free citizen of London, had been so for the past ten years, acting as the king's sheriff in the city and "rendering account at the Exchequer," and "to this very day" was an alderman against whose person no man could allege villeinage. To which counsel for the defence replied that

> "with what they say about his being a citizen of London we have nothing to do; but we tell you that from granddam and granddam's granddam he is the villein of Robert, and he and all his ancestors, grandsire and grandsire's grandsire and all those who held his lands in the manor of Necton; and Robert's ancestors were seized of the villein services of Simon's ancestors, such as ran-som of flesh and blood, marriage of their daughters, tallaging them high and low, and Robert is still seized of Simon's brothers by the same father and same mother ... Where as he says that we were not seized of him as

our villein, he was born in our villeinage and their our
seizen began, and we found him in our nest."

Upon which the presiding judge, observed:

"I have heard tell that a man was taken in a brothel and
hanged, and if he had stayed at home no ill would have
befallen him. So here. If he was a free citizen, why did
he not remain in the city?"

It took four years before, after repeated adjournments, the
case was finally decided in the alderman's favor and judgment
for £100—an enormous sum in those days—was given
against the lord and his bailiff.

The prolonged conflicts with Scotland and France of the
three Edwards provided an enormous stimulus to the development of the merchant class. Though no English trader could
at first offer the Crown the credit-facilities of the great bank-
ing and cloth-manufacturing houses of Florence and Lom-
bardy, by the end of the thirteenth century there were already
native financiers rich enough to play a leading part in equipping the royal armies. It was to those who dealt in wool, "the
sovereign merchandise and jewel of this realm of England",
as parliament put it, that the Crown turned. For alone of
England's commodities wool could always be converted into
cash; Flanders and Italy could never have enough of it. It
was with the help of the great Shropshire woolmonger, Lau-
rence of Ludlow, the builder of Stokesay castle—"*mercator
notissimus*", as the royal lawyers described him—that Edward
I equipped his expedition to Flanders in 1297. When Laur-
ence was drowned in an overloaded ship taking the wool to
Holland, the monastic chroniclers saw in it the hand of God
avenging the lowered prices to the home—and ecclesiastical
—producer with which the financier and his fellow monopo-
lists passed on their losses.

The bargaining power which the collection and export of
wool gave to the rich subject in his dealings with the Crown
played a major part in the development of national taxation
and of parliament. There were three ways in which the Government could raise money from the trade. The first was to
requisition part of the season's crop and, treating it as a
forced loan from its owners, sell it abroad. The second was
to borrow from foreign or English capitalists in return for a

temporary monopoly of the wool export. The third—the method finally adopted after much trial and error—was to procure from parliament a tax on exports and set up a customs-staple in some town or towns, either at home or abroad, through which all exported wool had to pass. The right to levy customs had always been a royal prerogative but, in an age of primitive economy, if the Crown wished to raise money quickly it could do so only with the co-operation of those who dealt in the goods it wished to tax. Sometimes, instead of summoning a parliament and asking for a subsidy from the entire merchant class as represented by the elected burgesses, the king convened an assembly of leading wool-merchants and negotiated with them a levy on exported wool. But as soon as it became realized that the wool-mongers invariably passed on the tax by lowering the prices paid to wool-producers, the latter's representatives in parliament began to demand that the Crown should negotiate with them instead of with those who paid the tax only in name. In doing so they put forward as a *quid pro quo*, however at first humbly and tentatively, demands not only for redress of grievances but for control over the expenditure of the money raised and of the royal officers who administered it.

The means by which the wool tax was collected was the staple. It was first set up in London and thirteen other English ports at the beginning of Edward I's reign to collect the "ancient or great custom" of half a mark—6s. 8d.—a sack granted to him by parliament. When in 1297 he forcibly borrowed all the available stocks of English wool to finance his expedition to the Low Countries, a foreign staple had had to be set up, first at Dordrecht and later at Antwerp, to weigh and price the commandeered wool and levy the hated *maltote*, as it was called, on that of the merchants. Here, and in the domestic staple towns in England, the royal officials—collectors, controllers, searchers, surveyors, clerks, weighers and crane-keepers—adminstered both the ancient and great custom and the so-called petty custom which Edward at the end of his reign imposed on foreign exporters. For though freedom in trade increased both the export of wool and the prices paid to the producer, the Crown could no longer subsist without the revenue of the customs and the credit that could be raised from it. Early in Edward III's reign to finance his wars with France the foreign staple was revived to become a permanent feature of the wool-trade and the national system of taxation. It enabled the king to borrow money on the security of the customs and direct the export of wool to whatever city in the Low Countries suited his foreign policy of the moment. After the capture of Calais in 1347, that town became England's chief staple port and, later, when the export of cloth began to supersede that of wool, the spearhead for its sale to Europe.

The raising of wool was the concern of almost the entire rural community. Not only were the owners of the great feudal and ecclesiastical estates dependent for ready money on their fleeces, but so were knights of the shire, rich franklins and even humble villeins whose communal village flocks helped to swell the flow of wool from the manorial demesnes to the quays and warehouses of the collecting merchants. Travelling with their packhorses to grange, village and monastery and buying up the year's produce to sell to the exporters who shipped it to Flanders or Italy, the "woolmen", by offering credit in exchange for low prices, earned a high rate of concealed interest without infringing the Christian rules against usury. Many of the larger landowners, as well as keeping flocks, engaged in this collecting trade, buying the wool of their smaller neighbours who lacked the capital and know-how to dispose of their own produce. The Cistercian abbeys of the northern and western dales were particularly active in such business, drawing from it and their flocks the revenues that enabled them to replace the autere habitations of pioneer days with the magnificent buildings that still, after centuries of desolation and decay, make the ruins of Fountains and Tintern, Rievaulx and Byland places of aesthetic pilgrimage.

Picturing Plantagenet England, one sees the traces of this rural industry everywhere—the open downlands nibbled close by immense flocks of tiny sheep with their shepherds, tinkling bells, sheepcotes and dewponds; the fells and fleeces stacked in great barns of stone and timber; the up-country towns and the marketplaces of York and Lincoln, Grantham, Louth, Ludlow and Shrewsbury, Winchester and Andover crowded with dealers and factors; the trains of pack-horses and barges moving towards the sea; the London merchants in their furred robes doing business with the king's officers; the English cogs and tall Italian carracks beating out from the Thames estuary and southern ports towards the hungry mills of Flanders and distant Tuscany.

"The sward the black-face browses,
    The stapler and the bale,
    The grey Cistercian houses
    That pack the wool for sale."

The pastoral economy of shepherding and tending "the silly sheep," of sheep-shearing and dispatching the wool-fells to their remote destinations made a lasting impression on the nation's character. It embraced both the solitude and meditation of the shepherd's life, and the journeyings and bargainings involved in selling the wool that the mills of Ghent and Arno transformed into raiment for Europe's rich. The lonely sheepcotes and farms of western and northern England, the epitaph in the downland church,

"Faithful lived and Faithful died
    Faithful shepherd on the hillside,
    The hill so high, the field so round,
    In the day of judgment he'll be found"

is one side of the medal; Chaucer's merchant off to Bruges at break of day and the bustling wife of Bath at her clothier's trade the other. Wool-growing, wool-carrying and wool-mongering all tended to make men more thoughtful and resourceful than the uneventful life of communal arable agriculture by which peasant Christendom lived.

They made, too, for a sense of freedom. The man who owned or tended sheep on the uplands felt himself more his own master than the husbandman of the three-field village closely bound by manorial custom and watched by prying neighbours. "Because," ran the report of a case in the King's Bench,

"it was testified before the sheriff of Nottingham and Derby . . . that Sir Thomas Folejambe was accustomed to make rescue and offer resistance to the king's ministers and bailiffs who wished to distrain him for debts and other things due to the king, the aforesaid sheriff with our lord king's bailiff of the Peak . . . came to Tideswell to make distraint. . . . And because he did not find any distress save sheep, he caused his sheep which he found there to be taken. And while he was elsewhere, there came people, who are still unknown, and rescued the said sheep and drove them away no one knew where. The sheriff, when he heard this, caused the hue and cry to be raised up to the vill and through the vill of Tideswell, but the people would not come at the hue and cry as they ought to do. The sheriff was then told that the forenamed Sir Thomas had other sheep in a sheepfold outside the vill. The sheriff went there and found some of Sir Thomas's sheep, but his men went into the sheepfold and would not allow the sheriff to have the sheep as a distress but held the sheepfold against him and against the king's peace by force and arms.

"Wherefore the sheriff, in order to assemble more people to witness his action and to fulfil the king's command and preserve his estate and peace, raised the hue and cry by horn again from the said sheepfold up to the vill of Tideswell . . . And whilst the sheriff was doing this, Sir Thomas came to the said sheepfold and harshly abused those of the sheriff's men whom he found . . . And Sir Thomas demanded of the sheriff by what warrant he had done this, and the sheriff showed him the king's writ under his privy seal. And Sir Thomas, biting his nails on his palfrey, read the writ and looked at the seal and said that he knew it well, and further said, 'A fig for that! Produce another warrant.' "

Subsequently, after the sheriff had caused the hue and cry by horn and mouth to be raised a third time, Sir Thomas, taking counsel with his friends, surrendered himself with his three shepherds and sheep. Yet he came to no ultimate harm by doing so, for after two years a jury found him and his collaborators not guilty.

During the last half of the fourteenth century the domestic cloth trade started to expand so rapidly that by the middle of the following century—the last of the Middle Ages—it was already absorbing most of the native wool crop. In 1353, two thousand cloths were exported; forty years later, during Richard II's reign, twenty times as many. In 1420 the export of cloth for the first time exceeded that of raw wool, and by the end of the fifteenth century, despite a halt during the Wars of the Roses, was twice as much. The introduction from the East of the fulling-mill and its exploitation by English capitalists had created a new industry wherever flowing water was plentiful and good sheep pasture near. It brought an enormous accession of wealth to these localities. In the valleys of the Stroud and the Wiltshire Avon, in the upper reaches of the Aire and the Pennine streams, where the mechanisation of the fulling process laid the foundations of the prosperity of the West Riding towns; and in Suffolk along the Stour and its tributaries there occurred a rural industrial revolution. West Country, broadcloths—"Stroudwaters," "Cotswolds" and "Castlecombes"—and the serges and worsteds of East Anglia became as famous on the continent as the products of Ghent and Ypres. In the fifteenth century it was reckoned that nearly 25,000 workers were engaged in the trade. It was an industry based, not on cities but on villages and small towns where, free from the restrictive labour and price regulations of municipality and guild, enterprising clothiers supplied the raw material to cottage weavers from whom they later collected the spun wool, distributing it to the shearers, fullers and dyers before their pack-horses carried the finished product to London or the ports for shipment overseas. Pioneers of what was long to be the country's greatest industry, these rustic capitalists left their mark in the tall-towered churches and stone manor houses—witnesses to their faith, wealth and enterprise—which they raised among the limestone hills that spanned England from Somerset to Lincolnshire. There, too, can be seen the brasses that preserve their likenesses—the forked beards, hawks and horses, the hallmarks of quality and honest dealing that they stamped on their bales, the fine Flemish beaver hats in which they rode out to bargain for the midsummer clip or autumn fell with Gloucestershire squires and Yorkshire abbots. Such were William Grevil, ancestor of the earls of Warwick, who was buried in 1401 in the beautiful church he built at Chipping Campden—"late citizen of London and flower of the wool merchants of all England"—Thomas Paycocke of Coggeshall, and John Barton of Holme who had engraved on the windows of his house:

> "I thank God and ever shall,
> It is the sheep hath paid for all." [1]

The success of the cloth trade and the fierce and often armed resistance it provoked from foreign competitors—especially the German Hanse in the Baltic—favoured the growth of London. Except for Bristol, with its merchant

[1] Eileen Power, *The Wool Trade in English Medieval History*, 17.

princes and shipowners like the Canynges—builders of the great Perpendicular church of St. Mary Redcliffe, "the fairest, goodliest and most famous parish church in England"—the burghers of the older provincial towns lacked the capital to finance so costly and speculative a business. The monopoly of the trade with the Low Countries, by far England's most lucrative market, was in the hands of the London Society of Merchant Adventurers. Like the older Merchants of the Staple, they formed the nucleus of a new aristocracy, marrying into the gentry, founding landed estates and playing a part in the luxurious court of Edward IV—a great patron of London merchants and their wives. It was through them and the Mercers' Company that the wealth of the cloth trade flowed into the capital, drawing with it growing numbers of tradesmen, craftsmen and artificers. By the end of the fifteenth century the city's population was nearly 75,000; during the sixteenth century it more than doubled. Even before Henry VII's death in 1509 its suburbs almost joined the outlying villages of Hoxton, Clerkenwell and Shoreditch whose fields—once the Londoner's playground—were giving way to houses. Its riches were beginning to compare with those of the Lombard and Flemish cities; an Italian traveller counted more than fifty goldsmiths' shops in Cheapside; "so rich and full of silver vessels is it," he wrote, "that in all the shops of Milan, Rome, Venice and Florence put together there would not be found so many of the magnificence that is to be seen in London". This was an exaggeration, but the Scottish poet, William Dunbar, received much the same impression when he visited it in 1501 with the mission sent to negotiate the marriage of James IV with Margaret Tudor:

> "Upon thy lusty bridge of pillars white
> Be merchantïs full royal to behold;
> Upon thy streets goeth many a seemly knight
> In velvet gownës and in chains of gold. . . .
> Rich be thy merchantïs in substance that excellïs;
> Fair be thy wives, right lovesome, white and small.
> Clear be thy virgins, lusty under kellis:
> London, thou art the flower of cities all!"

CHAPTER IX

GOTHIC GLORY

WHEREVER MAN in the Middle Ages turned his eyes he was confronted by the majesty of the Church. A traveller could not approach a town in any part of Christendom without seeing the familiar sight of its towers and spires rising above its walls and houses. For the Church did not depend for its teaching on books and sermons or even on the candlelit mystery and drama of its Latin liturgy. In an age when not one man in a thousand could read it drove its lessons home in sculptured stone and vaulted space, and in the carvings and paintings of artists who employed their genius to make the Christian story familiar to everyone. The supreme expression of medieval man's faith was the work of the "engineers" or architects who, at abbot's or bishop's command, sketched on deal boards the designs of their vast buildings, and of the master-masons who carried out their conceptions with teams of travelling craftsmen. There were hewers trimming the stone with axes and dressing it with chisels, setters laying the walls and making mortar-matrixes, turners with stone-lathes shaping column and shaft; carvers and glaziers, slatters, smiths and plumbers, wrights and joiners. They fashioned the timber supports from the heart of the tree, graved statues, made ironwork fittings for doors, raised with primitive cranes and pulley-wheels the baskets of stone and rolls of lead to the soaring walls and roofs, and filled the windows with geometrically patterned and brilliantly coloured glass. During the twelfth and thirteenth centuries nearly every great cathedral and abbey church in the French-speaking lands on either side of the Channel was partly rebuilt or enlarged in the style which later became known as Gothic. The plain rounded vaulting, small windows and heavy columns of the Romanesque and Norman past were superseded by delicately pointed arches, clusters of slender pillars and tiers of long lancet-windows that flooded the vast buildings with light —the crying need of the cloudy north—and lit the jewelled shrines, painted walls and stained glass within in radiant hues. The transformation was the result, partly of revolutionary advances in engineering technique—which rendered unnecessary the unbroken masses of wall space needed to support roof and tower—and partly of new ideas introduced into northern Europe during the Crusades from the Saracen and Byzantine East. The overwhelming impression was one of height, light and energy. With their soaring pinnacles and flying buttresses—built to take the outward thrust of the immense arches and fenestrated walls—these great new buildings, glittering in white stone, looked from a distance like giants on the march.

Inside they were filled with delicate carving, with sculptured shrines, tombs and statues, and with colour and ornamentation that humanised their immense size and made them resemble gigantic jewelled boxes. In England this tendency to find internal decoration was carried farther than in almost any other western land. Forests of airy shafts of Purbeck marble, exquisitely moulded trefoil arches, flowing leaves and flowers naturalistically carved in stone on capital and arch, elaborate and deeply carved roof-bosses were distinguishing marks of the English school. So were the compound piers that the Anglian masons, stubbornly persisting in an ancient native tradition, evolved to carry the intricate ribbed vaulting—itself partly an English invention—and which reached perfection in the nave of Wells, where dynamics and pure poetry blend and become indistinguishable. So, too were the vast traceried windows and the immense timber trusses and posts of native oak—the hardest in Europe—which, bearing the laminated stone roofs gave a sense of illimitable height and mystery to the worshippers in choir and aisle below.

The first English essays in Gothic were made towards the end of the twelfth century. Their starting-point was the fire which, four years after Archbishop Becket's martyrdom, destroyed the choir of Christ's Church, Canterbury, England's metropolitan church. Rebuilding was begun in 1175 under a French mason, William of Sens, who, though starting in the familiar Norman idiom, imported many revolutionary features from the great new cathedrals of northern France. Three years later, following his fall from a scaffold, the work was taken over by "William the Englishman," a man small in body but in all kinds of workmanship most acute and honest. It was possibly he who adopted the use of Purbeck marble, brought by sea from the cliff quarries of Dorset, and he who made the beautiful crypt of the Trinity chapel to house St. Thomas's bones.

Canterbury illustrates the transitional stage from Norman to Gothic. The first example in both England and Europe of pure Gothic, without any Romanesque intermixture whatever, was the choir of Lincoln cathedral, raised for its Burgundian bishop Hugh of Avalon, during Coeur de Lion's reign. The good bishop, who once refused to pay an unjust tax and bearded the furious king in his own camp, carried, we are told, the hods of stone and building-lime with his own hands. With its vaulting like some great bird's wings, its trefoil arches, carved foliage and lancet-shaped windows, St. Hugh's choir was the signal for an outburst of English Gothic. It was closely followed by the galilees or porches at Durham and Ely—the former a chapel built to enable women to hear the services without breaking the monastic rule—the retro-choir and lay chapel at Winchester, the choirs of Wells, Rochester, Lichfield, Worcester, Fountains and Southwell, the greater part of St. David's cathedral and St. Saviour's, Southwark, the west front of Peterborough and the transepts, nave and chapterhouse of Lincoln. And in the heart of London, towering above its two-storied houses, arose the immense cathedral—first begun after the fire of 1135—that for five hundred years dominated the city until its destruction in a still greater fire.

These tremendous buildings, so far transcending the apparent economic and technical resources of the time, were not raised like the architectural monuments of the East by slave-labour. They were made by craftsmen able to bargain and of the same faith as those who orderd their making. In addition to wages they occasionally received—as a special reward or spur—the much sought-after ecclesiastical indulgences or remission of penance for sins, which the Church at a price conferred on the rich and powerful. Though behind them lay the quarrymen and burners of the limestone-hills, the seamen and drovers who brought the materials to the building-sites, and the labour-services and carrying-dues of the local manorial tenants, the main work of building was done by bands of travelling masons who, under their contracting-masters, moved from one great church to another. The name of the lean-to "lodges" which they erected against the rising walls for shelter still survive in the nomenclature of modern freemasons and trade unions.

Their services were eagerly competed for by prelates whose desire to outbuild one another was as much a stimulus to the craft of building as the later rivalry of eighteenth century country gentlemen. So were the new fashions of Christian worship that necessitated the erection at the eastern end of great churches—sometimes, as at Canterbury and Lincoln, round a semicircular walk or ambulatory, more often in England in rectangular transepts—of chapels to house the shrines of saints, the tombs of benefactors and the relics which the greater religious houses accumulated to attract the offerings of pilgrims. Particularly popular were the Lady chapels, where men and, still more, women, prayed to the Virgin Mother, whose worship afforded an outlet at this time for a kind of sublimated chivalry and adoration of the womanly virtues of pity, tenderness and compassion.

More utilitarian were the chapter-houses which provided meeting-places for the monks or prebendaries who controlled these great churches. In England, following the example of Worcester, built in the Norman style in the twelfth century, these were often polygonal in shape, the lofty vault of the roof being supported by a single, delicately-moulded central-column and the windowed walls cut with niches to accommodate the brethren. All this brought about during the first half of the thirteenth century an enlargment of the eastern ends of presbyteries of cathedrals and abbeys, which was later balanced by the addition of preaching-naves. This made English churches—generally inferior to those of France in height —exceptionally long.

The most complete example extant of thirteenth century English architecture is the church which rose in the Avon water-meadows at Salisbury. Here, following quarrels between the cathedral clergy and the garrison of Old Sarum castle, Bishop Richard Poore—formerly dean—embarked in 1220 on the prodigious task of rebuilding the cathedral on a new site. Its designer was one of the canons, Elias of Dereham—a distinguished connoisseur who, as Archbishop Stephen Langton's steward, had been the joint creator of Becket's shrine at Canterbury. He was assisted by a master-mason named Nicholas of Ely. Built of freestone from the Chilmark quarries twelve miles away and taking half a century to complete, Salisbury cathedral still stands as its builders designed it—save for its spire and upper tower added a century later—the only medieval cathedral in England which is all of a piece. Inside, it was brilliantly coloured, with scarlet and black scrollwork walls, white-painted vaulting and gilded capitals, across which jewels of ruby and blue in the windows cast glittering reflections with every change of sun and shadow. But, outside, in the close, and in the cloisters—the largest in England with their arches looking on to the quiet garth—one can still feel the faith that prompted men to raise such monuments to their belief in the unity of earth and heaven.

Among those who watched its rising walls was the young king Henry III from his hunting palace of Clarendon a few miles away. The Cistercian abbeys of Yorkshire, and south Wales, the re-building of Malmesbury and Glastonbury, the presbytery at Ely, the transepts at York and Beverley, the choirs of Christ Church, Oxford and Carlisle, the great abbey of Hayles—built by the king's brother, Richard, earl of Cornwall, to house a phial of the Precious Blood—all date from his germinative reign. So do the wonderful chapel of the Nine Altars at Durham and the great west front of Wells, begun in 1239, with its hundreds of life-size statues of saints and missionaries, bishops and kings, telling the story of Christian England from the earliest times and rivalling the finest contemporary sculpture in Europe.

One national possession above all others England owes to Henry. From his earliest days he had been brought up to venerate the Anglo-Saxon saints. In 1244, four years after the consecration of St. Paul's, he started to rebuild the abbey church of Westminster in honour of its founder, Edward the Confessor, in whose name he had christened his eldest son. In doing so he drew his inspiration from the new cathedrals which, under his brother-in-law, Louis IX of France, were being raised on the other side of the Channel. From Amiens and Rheims—the crowning-place of the French kings—and, above all, from the exquisite Sainte Chapelle in Paris, he borrowed the lofty eastern chevet and the mosaic-paved ambulatory with its semicircle of radiating chapels, and, to the west of them and St. Edward's shrine, made a raised theatre where the coronation of England's kings could be solemnised. Yet though the abbey's eastern outline was taken from Rheims and the soaring pointed arches, flying buttresses and great circular rose-windows from Amiens, its general plan, with its bold transepts and the exquisite craftsmanship of its interior, was English. The master mason who supervised its building was an Englishman, Henry of Reyns, and so were his successors—for the work took a quarter of a century—John of Gloucester and Robert of Beverley. At one time eight hundred workmen were employed on it. From the Abbey muniments we know the names of many of these craftsmen, who were settled by the chapter in houses in Westminster: Alexander the carpenter, Odo the goldsmith and Edward his son, Henry the glazier, John of St. Albans, the great master-sculptor whose twin angels, once brilliantly coloured, still swing their censers under the vast rose-window of the south transept. The work of another English artist—Walter of Durham, the king's painter—is represented by the huge figures of St. Christopher and St. Thomas touching the side of the risen Christ, which were discovered a few years ago, hidden by monuments and buried in dirt, on the wall of the south transept. The rest of his painting, like the original coloured glass of which only a few panels now remain, and the marble and mosaic-work of the Confessor's jewelled shrine, were destroyed by the iconoclasts of later ages. The shrine—after that of St. Thomas the most famous in England—was made of mosaics of marble and gold, with delicate twisted columns, and, set with emeralds, rubies and precious stones, "placed high like a candle upon a candlestick so that all who enter into the house of the Lord may behold its light." Above it hung a vast corona with innumerable candles burning continuously, while on the shrine itself stood silver basins containing lamps. Such shrines and their chapels, fitted with apertures for the crippled limbs of pilgrims, were usually sited in an ambulatory behind the sanctuary so that worshippers could approach without disturbing the liturgical services in the choir.

By the end of the thirteenth century the lead in ecclesiastical building had passed from the monks to the canons of the "secular" cathedrals and the "courtier" bishops, enriched by their ministerial services to the Crown. Edward I's reign had seen the culmination of the rebuilding of Lincoln's glorious cathedral—its towers crowned with three immense spires in an extension of the presbytery to house the shrine of St. Hugh. The king himself had been present at the translation of the saint's bones to their new resting place. With its huge traceried east window and double-banked lights extending the full width of every bay, the new choir was more brilliantly lit than any building yet erected. Beneath the windows of the clerestory, filling the spandrels of the triforium arches, thirty smiling stone angels looked down, some like those carved a generation earlier in Westminster Abbey with musical instruments, others holding crowns, scrolls and censers. Some had their feet on monsters, others presented souls at the Judgment seat, one with stern face expelled a crestfallen Adam and disdainful Eve from Paradise. These exquisite figures, saved by their great height from the Protestant iconoclasts of a later age, were painted in vivid colours and patterned with stars.

It was light above everything else that the new architecture sought—the crying need of the sunless north. One after another the great churches of northern England followed the lead of the Angel choir. At Ripon, where every canon contributed a tenth of his prebendary income until the work was done, the east end of the choir was rebuilt during the closing decade of the thirteenth century with a huge window; at York a few years later, a new nave was begun in which, in the search for greater light and space, the upper windows of the clerestory were extended downwards to incorporate the triforium, so that the two stories, though divided by the concealed roof of the aisle, presented a continuous double bank of light along the church's entire reach. The work took more than half a century to complete, and during that time, like almost every major church in the land, the minster must have been full of scaffolding and of the sound of hammer and chisel. Yet this great revolution supplemented rather than superseded the country's older ecclesiastical architecture, so that everywhere, in the English mode, new Gothic mingled with old Norman and even, in places, Saxon. At Malmesbury, where the nave of the abbey church was rebuilt in the thirteenth century, the Norman doorway was preserved inside a new porch; at Ely, Norwich and Peterborough Romanesque pillars blended with Gothic vaulting.

In the south the most important additions to English architecture in Edward I's reign were the commencement of St. Stephen's chapel in the palace of Westminster—the English counterpart to the Sainte Chapelle at Paris—and the completion of the Gothic work at St. Paul's. The cathedral's new choir, added to the Norman nave and the vast double-aisled transept, made it the largest church in Europe. At its eastern end, towering above the roofs of the city, was the biggest single group of lights in the country—an enormous rose window filling a space equal to the height of the combined clerestory and triforium, and, below, seven conjoined lancets separated only by thin mullians linked by trefoiled heads. Above the cathedral rose a five-hundred foot tower and spire, crowned by a ball and cross filled with sacred relics.

As remarkable, on a smaller scale, were the beautiful polygonal chapter-houses of Salisbury and Wells, completed at the end of the thirteenth and beginning of the fourteenth century. Here, debating the business of the chapter, the canons sat in a circle, enthroned on stone niches under traceried windows, every one an equal, facing the graceful multi-shafted central pillar which bore the vaulted roof. In the north the new chapter-houses at York and Southwell were vaulted without a central pillar, the former having a free-standing span of nearly sixty feet. At Southwell the naturalistic carving, which had recently taken the place of the more formal stiff-leaf, reached its zenith in the wonderful variegated leaves and flowers carved on the capitals during the years when Edward I was trying to subdue Scotland. Like Pygmalion's Galatea they possess all the qualities of life except movement, though made of stone.

Carved figures as beautiful, wrought in metal and stone, rose at Edward's behest in his father's rebuilt abbey at Westminster. Soon after his return from his Welsh wars he had commissioned William Torel, the London goldsmith, to make a bronze effigy of his father to lie on his tomb at Westminster above a stone base engraved with royal leopards. Beside it a decade later he placed the effigy of his wife, Eleanor of Castile, recumbent with sceptre in hand and jewelled robe and crown under a canopy of Purbeck marble. Two other noble examples of the sculptor's art were added to the abbey's treasures in his reign—those of his brother, Edmund Crouchback earl of Lancaster, under an elaborately carved canopy guarded by painted and gilded regal mourners and angels holding candlesticks, and of his uncle, William de Valence. With his copperplate armour coloured with rich enamels, his mailed hands crossed in prayer and his expression of serene confidence that the aristocratic society he had adorned on earth must be mirrored in Heaven, William's effigy was the forerunner of a whole army of recumbent knights in stone, metal or brass. During the fourteenth century there everywhere appeared in the parish or collegiate church enriched by his benefaction or bequest the likeness of some local worthy, clad in the armour and heraldic trappings of his warrior craft, with his lady in long trailing mantle, kerchief and wimple at side and his hound or supporting heraldic beast at his feet. Though those that survive constitute only a small fraction of the splendid knightly company that once glittered under the painted roofs and windows of England's churches, owing to Edward I's law of entail they proved more enduring than the statues of saints and holy personages that shared their resting places. For when the latter were smashed as idols in later centuries these memorials to bygone benefactors received the protection of those who had inherited their blood or lands.

The brightness of a Gothic cathedral, with its painted walls and jewelled shrines—the gleaming or *nitens* of the monkish chroniclers' phrase—is hard to visualise from the bare, grey stone interiors of today. We see the noble skeleton but not the flesh and blood with which our forefathers clothed it. The walls were frescoed with paintings, telling the Christian story by masters whose names, like their works, have been obliterated by time, though from the few that remain, faint and resuscitated from agelong layers of neglect and defacement, we can dimly comprehend their glory. The paintings on the sedilia in the sanctuary of Westminster Abbey—of the Virgin's blue robe and pink mantle and of Gabriel in mauve and green of a lovely limpidity—executed when the first masterpieces of the Italian artistic renaissance were beginning to appear at Siena, Pisa and Florence; the scenes from the life and Passion of Christ in the little Northamptonshire church of Croughton; the East Anglian figures of saints on the vaulting of the north ambulatory of Norwich cathedral and others recently discovered at Little Missenden in Buckinghamshire and in the beautiful circular room at Longthorpe Tower— once the home of the stewards of Peterborough Abbey—are among the survivors of thousands of pictures that told the Bible story to a people unable to read but able to behold and adore. Among the most beautiful is the thirteenth century roundel in the bishop's palace at Chichester at the Madonna in robe of rose and jewelled crown holding her infant son against a background of blue, powdered with golden fleur-de-lys.

As rare today is the coloured glass that filled the windows. These, too, like the frescoes, told in picture the story of Christ and His saints and martyrs. Divided by uprights of stone or lead, each pane—medallion, lozenge, circle or square —formed part of a continuous pattern of colour and light. Most of the glass was imported, either through the Channel ports from Normandy and the Ile de France, where the French *verrours* had given mankind the splendours of Chartres, Bourges and Rouen, or from Hesse and Lorraine by way of the Rhine and Meuse to England's eastern rivers. Owing to the very richness of this early glass, with its deep reds, blues, greens and golden yellows, some of the quality of light sought by the Gothic windowbuilders was lost, and towards the end of the thirteenth century a whitish grey or grisaille glass began to be used. One of the few examples that survives is the Five Sisters window in the north transept of York, whose huge lancets are paned with plain glass framed in thin strips of red and blue, patterned with a delicate and scarcely perceptible scroll and leaf design.

In all this there was a growing elaboration unknown in western Europe since the days of imperial Rome. As the thirteenth century merged into the fourteenth a richer architectural sumptuousness began to succeed the simplicity of "Early English," pointed arch and geometrically traceried window giving place to flowing curvilinear lines, fantastic pinnacles, crockets and finials decorated with carved globular buds known as ballflower. Pierced balustrades, wave parapets and foliate stone tracery radiated from the mullions of windowheads like the branches of a tree. And everywhere were niches filled with statues of the heavenly family, angels, saints and martyrs, Christian princes and prelates, brilliantly gilded and painted. Such was the passion for carving and ornamentation that the masons, working high above column and clerestory among the roof trusses and rafters, fashioned whole legions of tiny figures on the bosses—foliage masks of men and monsters, fauns, satyrs and beasts, and the leaves and flowers of their native woods and fields—here the Lamb of God, here St. George wrestling with the dragon, here a peasant with toothache or two lovers kissing, here the face of a king or bishop or of a fellow workman, here David with his harp or the Virgin crowned—all carved with a care that must have been born of creation for its own sake, since, once the carver's work was done and the platform of scaffolding removed, no eye but that of some unborn craftsman repairing the roof in similar solitude would ever see them again. In Exeter alone, rebuilt between 1301 and 1338, there are more than five hundred carved bosses; in the vast late fourteenth century Bristol church of St. Mary Redcliffe over eleven hundred. When the might of the medieval Church was broken and fanatics swept through every place of worship with axe and hammer, smashing and defacing the sculptured masterpieces that to them seemed only painted idols, this invisible host of carved roof-bosses remained, unknown for nearly four hundred years until the telescopic lens of the modern camera revealed their testimony to the genius of English medieval craftsmanship.

The first great cathedral to be rebuilt wholly in the decorated style was Exeter. Between Edward I's accession and that of the early years of his grandson's reign, through the zeal of five great building bishops, the old dark Norman structure was transformed into the broad graceful edifice of today with its multiple-shafted marble pillars, the flowing tracery of its windows, its pinnacled sedilia and bishop's throne, statued screen and reredos and carved roof-bosses representing every kind of man and animal, angel and demon known to the medieval imagination. Another West Country cathedral, Bristol, was rebuilt about the same time, with a feature, unique among English cathedrals, of three aisles of equal height and a vault of lierne ribs of a completely novel pattern.

During the early decades of the fourteenth century almost every great church in England was added to or partly rebuilt is this richly ornamented style. There was Selby with its crocketed gables and parapet adorned with wave mouldings and little figures, Carlisle whose flamboyant east window was made during the sieges and raids of the long Scottish war of independence, the south aisle of Gloucester with ball-flower blossom climbing like roses all over it, and the prior's door at Norwich with saints and angels grouped round the seated Christ against a background of intricate lace-like arcading. During the same period many of the larger parish churches were rebuilt with arcades and windows of curvilinear tracery, elaborate ball-flower ornamentation and decorated parapets and towers. To these years belong the towers of Wells and Hereford and the West Country abbeys, Leominster, Ledbury and Ludlow, rising above apple orchards and sheep pastures; the traceried windows of St. Wulfram's, Grantham, modelled on the Angel choir of Lincoln; the spire of the university church of St. Mary's, Oxford, and the Tree of Jesse window at Dorchester-on-Thames. Most of the ports and upland towns that were growing rich from the export of wool built or refashioned their churches in the new style: Newark, Donington and Sleaford, Beverley and Hull, Boston, Holbeach and Great Yarmouth, Deal, Rye and Winchelsea, of which last only the choir remains with its canopied statue of Stephen Alard, admiral of the Cinque Ports. All were decorated with the same profuse wealth of carving; at Heckington in Lincolnshire the exterior sculpture alone included thirty-one statues in ogival niches, eighty carved corbels and a hundred and ninety-eight gargoyles.

Though the greater Benedictine houses were comparatively little affected by the new style—only Milton Abbas, destroyed by lightning in 1309, was completely rebuilt in it—the Cistercians, with their wealth from wool had by now abandoned their former austerity and started to build in the grand manner on the sites of their primitive encampments in the wilderness. Fountains had already been rebuilt in Henry III's reign; Tintern, Rievaulx and Byland were refashioned in the enriched architecture of the Edwardian age. Even the friars had left their squalid abodes in the city slums and were raising great churches out of the benefactions of merchants who recalled with gratitude the days when they or their fathers had fled from villeinage to the hovels of the nearest town and were there befriended by the mendicants. As with their evangelical mission the Franciscan and Dominican friars had no need to provide for the elaborate liturgical and processional services of the monastic Orders, their churches were usually built without aisles and with naves larger than the choirs to accommodate the middle-class congregations who flocked to hear their sermons. The most celebrated of all was the vast Greyfriars church in London founded in 1306 by Edward I's second queen, who was buried in it. Almost as large were the Whitefriars churches which the Carmelites built at Gloucester and Plymouth and the one at Blakeney on the lonely Norfolk coast, with its groined roof, clustered shafts crowned by carved bosses, and glorious east window. Another was built by Edward II for the Dominican friars at King's Langley in Hertfordshire in memory of, and to house the dust of his murdered favourite, Gaveston.

In 1321 the monks of the Benedictine abbey at Ely began

to build a Lady chapel with the largest span of vaulting yet seen in England and, under its traceried roof and wide decorated windows, arcaded niches filled with hundreds of gilded and painted statues, today mutilated and headless, telling the story of the Virgin in sculptured stone. Scarcely had the work begun when the central tower of the abbey church fell, crashing into the choir below and destroying three of its bays. Faced by the problem of revaulting so large a space, the sacristan, Alan of Walsingham, who later became prior, employed a London mason referred to in the abbey accounts as Master John, who, it is conjectured, may have been John of Ramsey, member of a famous family of Norwich masons. He and one "Peter Quadraterius" built, instead of a new tower, an octagonal lantern of revolutionary design with four traceried windows to flood the centre of the Norman church with light. And, as the seventy-foot span proved too wide to bridge with stone, the monks called in William of Hurley, the king's master-carpenter, at a fee of £8 a year to vault it in timber with eight gigantic hammer-posts and hammer-beam trusses. The work took twenty years to complete and, when finished, constituted, as it still does, the only Gothic dome in Europe.

Though the new style was decorative rather than structural, in its seeking for ever greater illumination it continued the trend which had begun with the evolution of the Gothic arch. Even before Edward III's accession in 1327, there were signs that English masons were beginning to feel their way towards a further architectural revolution. There was a sense of ever-growing light and unity in the many-ribbed vaults that broke through the older vaulting system of each separate bay and in the marriage between piers, vaulting and roof. The pillars of the new nave of York were like the trunks and branches of a beech wood, and the lierne vault of the choir at Ely like the stars on a winter's night.

It was the reign of this famous warrior king that saw the first flowering of the Perpendicular style, England's supreme contribution to the art of architecture. Hitherto, with their broad bases and close relationship to the earth, her cathedrals had not sought to emulate the perilous height of the Gothic churches of the Ile de France. But now, under the lead of William Ramsey, the king's chief mason, English architects began to evolve a technique which produced the effect of height without sacrificing structural proportion or safety. It was an art not of mass but of line, in which the vertical mullions of vast rectangular windows extended upwards and downwards to form, with the horizontal lines they crossed, continuous rectilinear panels of wall and glass. First essayed by the London masons in the new chapter house and cloisters of St. Paul's and the royal chapel of St. Stephen's, Westminster, its end—a reaction against the excessive ornamentation of the Decorated style—was an all-embracing unity in which the separate parts, arch, pier, vault, window and wall, were subordinated to a single whole.

It is in the west country abbey which sheltered the murdered body of Edward's father, the hapless Edward II, that the earliest surviving example of the new style can be seen. Aided by the gifts of pilgrims to the king's shrine, the monks of Gloucester began in the fourteen-thirties to transform the dark Norman south transept by substituting for the end wall an enormous eight-light window crowned with a lierne vault. During the next decade they rebuilt the choir, marrying the massive Norman pillars to delicate vaulting shafts and encasing the walls in a framework designed to flood the interior with light. And at its east end, in place of the Norman apse, they made the largest window in Europe, canting the walls of the last bay outwards to increase its size. This great wall of glass, seventy feet high and nearly forty wide, with over a hundred lights, was glazed, through the munificence of a local lord, with the shields and likenesses of his fellow commanders at Crecy—Edward III and the Black Prince in their midst— and, above them, Christ surrounded by apostles, seraphim, saints and martyrs singing the *gloria in excelsis* for the crowning of the Virgin. In the foreground, high above the choir, the masons carved on the bosses of the vault fifteen angels, each with a different musical instrument, to accompany that chant of praise sung by figures poised in painted glass between the glittering interior and the grey Gloucestershire skies.

During the years that saw England's martial triumphs in France one magnificent ecclesiastical building after another was raised by the genius of her craftsmen. The Lady chapel at Lichfield, the cloisters at Norwich, the retrochoir and St. Andrew's arches at Wells, the choir of Bristol, the exquisite decorated nave of Exeter were all completed or partly completed in the same decade as Crecy. So, in the north, was the lovely Percy tomb at Beverley and the west front and nave—

finished in the year of Edward's victory—of York Minster. And at Salisbury Richard of Farleigh crowned the thirteenth century cathedral with a decorated tower and spire whose proportions have never been surpassed.

Even the Black Death of 1348/9, carrying off probably a third of the country's craftsmen, only temporarily halted the rebuilding of its churches. Almost before the pestilence had ceased, the master-mason of Christ Church, Canterbury, was summoned to Windsor to succeed the dead William Ramsey in his task of raising a chapel and college dedicated to St. George to accommodate the King's new Order of chivalry, the Garter, while five hundred masons, carpenters, glass-makers and jewellers were requisitioned by the sheriffs of the southern counties and issued with scarlet caps and liveries to prevent their absconding to rival employment. In the same year, under the supervision of Hugh of St. Albans—a contemporary of Giotto—the walls of the royal chapel of St. Stephen's, Westminster, were painted with a frieze of angels with peacock wings and pictures of Job and Tobias and the adoration of the Magi on a background of gilt gesso. Round its walls were arcades with silver-gilt statues, the chapel's crowning glory being a golden image of the Virgin and a painting by Hugh of St. Albans of the victorious Edward III and his sons being presented to the heavenly throne by St. George. In the following year Abbot Horton of Gloucester began to rebuild the cloisters of the abbey, roofing them with a fan-vault of novel design. About the same time building was resumed at Exeter, Ely and Winchester.

It was at Winchester that, in the reign of Edward's grandson, Richard II, the master-mason, William Wynford—designer of the western towers of Wells—started to rebuild the Norman nave of the cathedral, making it after St. Paul's the longest in England. In the same city he built for his bishop, William of Wykeham, a college for boys and another for the bishop's other scholastic foundation, New College, Oxford, equipping both with Perpendicular chapels dedicated to the Virgin. In the same reign a still greater architect, Henry Yvele —for forty years the king's master mason—rebuilt the nave of Canterbury and, supervised by the Clerk of the Works, the poet Geoffrey Chaucer, reconstructed William Rufus's hall at Westminster, calling in the royal carpenter, Hugh Herland, to span its 240 foot length and 70 foot width with a hammer-beam roof of Sussex oak—the first of the great hammer-beam roofs which, with the fan-vault and the Perpendicular style, were England's most original and enduring architectural achievements.

In the century that followed Richard II's dethronement, when, after their victories at Agincourt and Verneuil, the English were trying to hold down the French provinces Henry V had conquered, and during the bitter years when the dynastic quarrels of York and Lancaster escalated into civil war and near-anarchy, the work of church building still went on. It was now the turn of the parish churches to be refashioned, many through the munificence of the merchant capitalists, woolmen and clothiers who continued to grow rich while the feudal princes and nobles were destroying one another in their sterile faction fights. It was an age of towers which arose everywhere above the western end of rustic churches to become the crowning glory of the English landscape. One of the loveliest was the four-staged tower of St. Michael's, Coventry, begun in the reign of Edward III and completed with a soaring three-tiered steeple in that of his great-great grandson, Henry VI. Yet it was only *primus inter pares*. The towers of Lavenham, Boston and Halifax, of Oxford Magdalen and Merton, of All Saints' Derby, and Cotswold Cirencester, Chipping Campden and Northleach, and a score of great Norfolk and Somerset churches, have equal claims to perfection of beauty and proportion. Some of the finest were raised by a few hundred parishioners, like the 300 feet steeple of Louth, begun in 1501 and finished in 1515, less than a generation before the English Reformation, "there being", the churchwardens' book records, "William Ayleby, parish priest, with many of his brother-priests there present, hallowing the weathercock and the stone that it stands upon; and . . . . singing *Te Deum Laudamus* with organs; and then the churchwardens made ring all the bells and caused all the people there to have bread and ale, and all to the loving of God, Our Lady and All Saints." [1]

One tower of the time stands in a class by itself, the great "Bell Harry" of Canterbury, raised during Henry VII's reign by Archbishop Morton's master-mason, John Wastell, and completed in 1497—the year that the Portuguese rounded the Cape of Good Hope. It was the same artist who vaulted and

[1] *The First Churchwardens' Book of Louth* ed. R. C. Dudding, 181. cit. A. G. Dickens, *The English Reformation*, 10.

roofed the wonderful chapel of King's College, Cambridge, begun by Henry VI as the companion foundation to his school at Eton. By a strange irony the culmination of English Gothic was reached a generation later, in the very year of Luther's challenge to the Roman Church, when William Vertue completed the building of Henry VII's Chapel at Westminster, crowning it with the canopy which, in John Harvey's words, is "one of the wonders of the world."

CHAPTER X

TWILIGHT OF HOLY CHURCH

WHEN THE KING sailed to France before Crecy the most famous preacher in England—the great theologian Richard FitzRalph, dean of Lichfield and archbishop elect of Armagh —bade the people pray, not that he should overcome his enemies, since that might be contrary to Christ's laws and offend God, but that he should "be directed with prudent and sane counsel to obtain a just and happy issue and a just peace" so that his subjects might live "a quiet and tranquil life . . . piously and chastely." Above his allegiance to king or lord the medieval Christian had one loyalty transcending all others. It was to the Christian faith and the Church that was its repository.

Within the Church, set to guide both rulers and subjects in their spiritual duties, was a vast hierarchy—cardinals, archbishops and bishops, abbots and priors, deans and archdeacons, monks vowed to perpetual prayer and contemplation, parish and chantry priests, confessors and chaplains, learned doctors expounding the lore of the universe of which the Church was the sole interpreter, wandering friars and solitary hermits. In England, with a population of not more than four million before the Black Death and perhaps two and a half million after it, there were between eight and nine thousand parishes, each with at least one priest or deacon and many with an unbeneficed chaplain as well; some seventeen or eighteen thousand regulars living under corporate vows and rule; [1] and a large, though uncertain, number of unbeneficed priests and chantry chaplains. York, with at the outside 10,000 inhabitants, had forty-one parish churches and over five hun-

[1] M. D. Knowles, *The Religious Orders in Medieval England*, II, 256.

dred clergy; Norwich, twenty churches and forty-three chapels. Even in the overcrowded capital there was a church for
every five hundred people.

In addition to priests and deacons in holy orders who were
forbidden to marry and who alone, with their attendant acolytes, officiated in the presbytery or eastern portion of the
church shut off from the congregation by the rood-screen,
there was a huge army of clerks in minor orders. These had
received the Church's initial tonsure—the small round patch
cut in the centre of the head by the officiating bishop as a
reminder of Christ's crown of thorns and which, by bringing
its wearer under the Church's protection, secured him "benefit of clergy". Among them were the acolytes who tended the
church-lights and helped the priest at the altar, parish-clerks,
readers who read and sang the lessons, exorcists who laid
evil spirits, door-keepers who looked after the church and its
bells. They included, too, the students of the universities who
numbered at least another two thousand. Probably one in
every fifty of the population was a cleric. The Poll tax returns
of 1381 listed more than 29,000 inferior clergy in England,
exclusive of friars.[1]

The English Church or *Ecclesia Anglicana* was part of the
universal Church of western Christendom. Yet it was also
part of the English State. Its bishops and abbots were not only
fathers in God but feudal magnates, leaders of the local community and royal advisers. A bishop was a great territorial
magnate, enjoying the revenues of numerous manors and
knights' fees, who wore princely attire and lived in state. His
income of two or three thousand pounds a year was fabulous
compared with the yearly wage of forty or fifty shillings earned
by a shepherd or ploughman. The bishop of Durham's castle
above the Wear was the greatest fortress in the north; the
bishop of Exeter had nine residences in Devon alone. The
archiepiscopal palace of Bishopthorpe was only one of a score
of similar homes owned by the northern metropolitan; the
bishop of Lincoln had ten palaces and forty manor-houses including, like every other prelate, a mansion in London from
which to perform his duties as a peer of the realm and attend meetings of parliament and the royal council. When a
bishop travelled it was on horseback or in a litter with a

[1] Maynard Smith, 38; V. H. H. Green, *The Later Plantagenets*,
40.

retinue of thirty or forty mounted clerics and attendants, including knights and men-at-arms drawn from his tenantry to guard him.

For the Church was not, as the saints had sought to make it, above the world; it was part of it. Everywhere was a tacit collusion between Church and State, in which loyalties did not so much clash as merge. Both supported one another; every re-enactment of the great Charter began by guaranteeing the freedom and rights of Holy Church, while anyone who infringed Magna Carta incurred the penalties of excommunication. Clerics adminstered the Chancery and Exchequer, sat on the judicial bench and headed diplomatic missions and fiscal enquiries. King and community had showered wealth on the Church yet, by doing so, they had made churchmen servants as well as spiritual leaders of the realm, subject, as owners of national land and property, to the same common law as everyone else. England was a country in which the sanctity of canonical doctrine and law was scrupulously respected so long as it did not override the legal rights of Crown and subject. Its very churches were proprietary ones, whose lay owners, having given and endowed them, retained the right to confer their emoluments on any qualified priest who conformed to the spiritual requirements demanded by the Church.

Since every worldly activity was conducted in the Church's name and with the Church's blessing, it followed that official Christianity had grown into a very worldly religion. It was one that had made existence richer and fuller, had fostered artistic and intellectual achievement and, at a time when life was harsh and precarious and death a constant visitant, had given millions a sense of hope and security. Yet many if not most of those who served the Church were very ordinary men who, without any particular sense of calling, had entered it as the only profession offering advancement for anyone who was not a warrior, land-owner or merchant. It was the avenue to wealth, power and dignity and to every learned and intellectual pursuit.

For cleric and layman alike the drama of Christ's life, death and resurrection was seen as a wonderful success-story in whose honour the whole glittering edifice of medieval religion had been raised. The splendid churches and their treasures, the processions, pageants and thrilling rites, the familiar company of tutelary angels and saints ready to help all who propitiated them, and Holy Church itself, watching over man's spiritual fortunes like a wise and far-sighted banker over his client's securities, were all there for his enrichment. And on the principle that to those that have shall more be given, it was the "possessioners", as the richer clergy were called, to whom the Church offered most.

For though entry to the Church was open to all, and even a bondsman's son, if his lord would free him, could rise, with the necessary parts and patronage, to the glittering top of the profession, there was an unbridgeable gulf between those selected for preferment and the common ruck of poor clerks. Whether the successful aspirant owed his fortune to birth and aristocratic connections, or whether he was a youth of humble antecedents whose talents had brought him to the notice of authority, the pick of the Church's benefices were available to enable him to pay for his education and to support him for the rest of his life in comfort and even affluence. So far as it gave financial independence to men of ability the system had much to commend it and brought outstanding talents to the service of Church and State. But it was subject to grave abuses. Lords and rich landowners with younger sons unfitted for arms or with a taste for clerkhood would present them to livings before they were in their teens; a brother of the earl of Gloucester in Edward I's reign accumulated in the course of his far from edifying career no less than twenty-four benefices, in addition to two canonries and three other collegiate and cathedral appointments.

Nor was there any point of contact between the untutored peasant priesthood and the university-trained ecclesiastics who by the end of the fourteenth century all but monopolised the higher ranks of the Church. In their subtle labours of theological and philosophical analysis and classification, expressed in language only intelligible to those trained in dialectic, the regent masters of Oxford and Cambridge were too busy disputing with one another to have time to popularise their learning for the rustic clergy from whom nine Englishmen out of ten derived their religion. The amorphous image conjured up for superstitious parishioners by the Mass magic of bucolic priests bore little resmblance to the highly intellectualised God of the great doctors. Nor did the Church seem concerned by this double standard in its teaching. With reckless disregard of its own canon law it continued to dispose of parochial endowments as though the training and competence of the parish clergy were a matter of minor importance. Of the 376 rectors whom one bishop instituted to benefices in lay patronage only 135 were in holy orders; in another diocese, of 193 parishes visited more than a third were held *in absentia*.[1]

This separation of the clerical sheep from the goats was aggravated by the Crown's demand for clerks of parts for the kingdom's growing administrative machine. It was accepted as a necessity of state that the Church should train and support in a condition of dignity its ablest sons to serve the king; one of Edward I's clerks of the Exchequer held twenty-one livings. For such pluralism seemed almost a civic virtue; "clerks in the king's service," it was laid down by statute, "shall be discharged of their residence." From time immemorial it had been the Church's task to guide and counsel the State and its rulers, and it seemed natural that part of its wealth should be used to maintain those who performed such duty and that the descendants of the princes and lords who had endowed it should be able to call on churchmen for those administrative services which only churchmen were trained to give. During the fourteenth century more than half the English bishops were employed in offices of state. Many were chosen from the clerical administrators of the royal household. In 1300 there had been only two civil servants on the episcopal bench; a quarter of a century later there were twelve, most of them Wardrobe or ex-Wardrobe officials. Under Edward III it was the keepers of the Privy Seal who were most favoured; in 1350 six out of the seventeen bishops had held this office. Though there was never in England an aristocratic monopoly of high ecclesiastical office as in some continental countries, about a fifth of the bishops came from the landowning and warrior families who surrounded the throne—Beaumont, Cobham, Berkeley, Burghersh, Arundel, Courtenay.[2]

Great nobles too, needed clerical servants, not only for spiritual, but worldly purposes. A fifteenth century earl of Northumberland had ten priests in his service as well as a clerk of the signet, a clerk of the works and a surveyor, a private secretary and a secretary of his privy council. Thanks

[1] *History*, N.S. xxxiv, V. F. M. Garlick, "The Provision of Vicars in the Early Fourteenth Century."

[2] W. A. Pantin, *The English Church in the Fourteenth Century*, 12; R. Highfield," The English Hierarchy in the Reign of Edward III" (*R.H.S.T.*) 5th series, vi, 133.

to the pious bequests of their forefathers such territorial magnates seldom lacked advowsons to provide for them. For centuries the rich and powerful had showered wealth on the Church; and if a rich man, eager for salvation, offered to endow a chantry, a college, a hospital, a perpetual mass for the souls of himself and his relations, to give a stained-glass window, rebuild a church or provide a wayside altar or rest-house for pilgrims, the Church could not do other than accept it. Provided the rich made a show of conforming to its observances and dogma, it reserved for such benefactors a place in the heavenly as in the earthly kingdom, negotiating, as it were, a special relationship between them and the Almighty. With their endowments for obits, masses and private chantries, their benefactions to parish and collegiate churches, their gifts of gems and relics, altar-cloths, statues and painted windows, they were permitted, and encouraged, to buy themselves into Heaven. A rhyme of the time depicts them doing so:

> "Thou shall'st kneel before Christ
> In compass of gold,
> In the wide window westward
> Well nigh in the middle;
> And Saint Francis himself
> Shall folden thee in his cope
> And present thee to the Trinity
> And pray for thy sins."

So the friar in Langland's *Piers Plowman* held out an inducement to the wicked Lady Meed:

> "We have a window a working,   will stand us full high;
> Would ye glaze the gable   and grave there your name,
> In Mass and in Matins   for Meed we should sing
> Suddenly and soothly   as for a sister of our Order."

In the Norfolk church of Burnham Norton the local donors of the pulpit can still be seen, sharing its panels with the four great doctors of medieval Christendom, St. Augustine, St. Gregory, St. Jerome and St. Thomas Aquinas.

Pride and privilege not only helped to raise and sustain the Church's fabric; they penetrated the very sanctuary. Instead of having to confess to low-born parish priests, nobles were allocated confessors of rank, and the lord of the manor and his lady worshipped with the clergy in the chancel instead of with the congregation in the nave. Even at the moment when all Christians, living and dead, were supposed to be united in the sacrament of Christ's sacrifice and when, before Holy Communion, the paxbrede or picture of the crucified Saviour was passed round to be kissed in token of brotherly love, there was jostling and shoving for precedence. Such pomp and vain glory—the sin of *superbia* as theologians called it— was most frequently to be met in the fine new town churches raised by the merchant community and nobility. One indignant preacher spoke of "great lords and ladies that cometh to holy church in rich and noble apparel of gold and silver, pearls and precious stones and other worldly, worshipful attire before our Lord God Almighty," each fine lady "stirring up the dust with her train, making the good laymen, the clerks and the priests all drink of it and making it fall upon the altar of the Lord."

This growing identification of the Church with wealth and power resulted in a grave loss of spiritual influence. Since it had inherited, and insisted on retaining, so large a share of Caesar's goods, it was forced to render unto Caesar the things that were God's. Because its prelates were great landowners and magnates, it had had to concede to the Crown the right of appointed them. They were seen by the laity as servants of the State rather than of the Church and therefore as agents of the State's oppression and injustice. Whatever their gain in worldly dignity, their possession of excessive wealth and the luxurious display that accompanied it lost them the respect of many true Christians. For the values that attached to the pursuit of wealth were not Christian values; by the Church's own tenets they were sometimes diabolical ones. The bishop of Winchester was joint owner of the Southwark stews; even the wonderful new nave of Winchester cathedral and William of Wykeham's scholastic foundations of Winchester and New College, Oxford, were partly and indirectly raised on the profits of prostitution. Such confusion of worldly and spiritual values ran through the Church's structure like an ugly flaw.

The Church's obsession with its wealth—with "Christ's land," "Christ's goods," "Christ's property"—had other consequences. It made it seem obese and conservative. It was no longer, as in the days of St. Bernard and St. Francis, on the march; it was resting on its endowments. The "possessioners" who enjoyed its wealth would admit of no change. Religion in their hands had become materialistic and mechanical; it was the quantitative in worship that mattered, not the spirit of the worshipper. Salvation was measured by the number of prayers and masses said—so many *Pater Nosters* an hour, so many *Ave Marias*, so many candles lit, so many benefactions to Holy Church. Great men would hurry into church before the elevation of the Host and then hurry out again, conscience and public opinion satisfied that they had rendered homage for the day. Outward and visible signs seemed everything, inward and spiritual grace tended to be forgotten. Among those to be met on the highways in the latter Middle Ages was the pardoner, a sanctified huckster licensed by papal or episcopal letter to sell indulgences at every price-range to anyone prepared to buy. These pardoners, with their wallets "brimful of pardons come from Rome all hot," not only sold their wares but, though not themselves in holy orders, preached sermons advertising them. Sometimes they sold them on behalf of some chantry or work of piety such as a hospital, the repair of a church or a new painted glass window; sometimes they were complete charlatans, pretending they had the power to absolve from any sin and travelling with a string of forged indulgences round their necks, like the one who was sentenced to ride through Cheapside with his face to his horse's tail and a penitent's paper hat on his head.[1] As a sideline they also peddled faked relics which were supposed to secure for their purchasers remission from punishment or protection from accident. Chaucer's pardoner had a pillow

> "which he asserted was our Lady's veil.
> He said he had a goblet of the sail
> St. Peter had, . . .
> a cross of brassë full of stones
> and in a glass he hadde piggës' bones."

The Church did not approve such abuses, but by its practice, it condoned them. In its need for ever more money to support its huge bureaucracy and magnificent court, the papacy countenanced ways of raising money which amounted to a wholesale sale of indulgences. The ecclesiastical authorities in every country did the same. The theory of an indulgence was that punishment for any venial sin could be partly remitted, with the aid of the Church's intercession, for any genuine penitent who received absolution and did pen-

[1] G. R. Owst, *Preaching in Medieval England*, 109.

ance. With the advance of civilisation the Church had tended to substitute for physical penances, like flogging and fasting, such useful acts of public service and charity as the building and repair of churches, the endowment of almhouses, schools and hospitals and the provision of bridges and wayside chapels. Penance could also take the form of money payments to provide priests to say prayers and masses for an offender, securing for him, provided he had confessed his sins and shown true contrition, remission of so many days in purgatory. Such vicarious intercession by the Church could, it was held, secure earlier release from untold suffering. In practice, it proved a step to the tacit assumption by the unrighteous that anyone with a long enough purse to purchase the Church's indulgence could commit sin with impunity.

The sale of indulgences was not the only way of raising money for the Church that aroused criticism. Its finances, the taxation of its vast wealth, the enforcement of its rights and its relations with the temporal power and laity were all regulated by canon or ecclesiastical law. And canon law was binding, not only on every officer and servant of the Church, but on all Christians. Growing in complexity with the advance of civilisation and the multiplication of bureaucratic functions, it operated through an ascending hierarchy of courts that stretched from the humblest rural deanery to the papal *curia* at Rome or Avignon and with rights of appeal at every level up to the Holy Father himself. It sought to adjudicate between nation and nation—for the Church was traditionally the peace and truce maker of Christendom. It investigated and suppressed heresy; it dealt with the moral problems, offences and rights of princes and rulers. It tried—though, as capitalist enterprise grew, with diminishing success—to enforce good faith and equitable dealing in economic matters and to impose the ideal of the just price and wage. Its officers had jurisdiction over every matter that concerned the salvation of souls.

In many respects the canon law affected the lives of ordinary men and women far more closely than that of the king's courts which normally touched only criminals and men of property. The ecclesiastical courts had cognisance of marriage, bigamy and divorce, intestacy, wills and probate, provision for dower and orphans, libel, perjury and breaches of good faith, as well as sexual offences, including adultery, fornication and brothelkeeping. They dealt with sacrilege, blasphemy, failure to pay tithes and church dues or to attend

Mass, and the crime of simony or trading in ecclesiastical preferments. Offences on consecrated ground also came within their jurisdiction. These ranged from poaching and cutting down trees to infringements of the right of sanctuary, for which tremendous penalties could be inflicted. In such cases the Church was both party and judge.

Since the ecclesiastical courts also possessed wide, and in some cases overriding, powers in matters affecting the individual rights of clerics, and since the term cleric included, not only those who had been ordained, but anyone who could claim "benefit of clergy"—by the simple device of translating a verse of a Latin psalm known as the "neck verse"—laymen often suffered what they regarded as gross injustice through the one-sided leniency of the ecclesiastical courts. Among those whom canon law protected were university students—a particularly unruly type—schoolmasters, professional men like doctors, and nearly all schoolboys. Nor was it only clerks in minor orders who were a menace to society. A canon of Walsingham was found guilty of stealing, breaking into the sacristan's box in a neighbouring church and committing a rape.

Though in some ways the canon law was more merciful than the law of the king's courts, it was in others less just. Under the latter a man was assumed to be innocent unless he could be proved by the testimony of others to be guilty. In the courts Christian he could be forced to take an oath of purgation and so either condemn himself or commit perjury. To fall foul of the Church and its legal officers was no light matter. Its courts could fine, imprison for life, sentence to whipping and scourging, excommunicate—a terrifying penalty involving exclusion from the sacraments and all contact with other Christians under pain of like penalty for them, and, in cases of persistent obduracy, eternal damnation. They could also impose a whole range of penances. The only thing they could not do was to inflict the death penalty, for canon law forbade the taking of blood by churchmen. But in cases where death seemed the appropriate punishment, they could turn the criminal over to the secular arm and ask the Crown to deal with him.

It was the inquisitorial methods of the courts Christian and their petty interference in men's daily lives that aroused resentment. Laymen could be convicted for brawling in the churchyard, for failing to attend Mass, for irreverent be-

haviour in church and disrespect to the clergy, for working on
Sundays and holy days. And many of the penances to which
they could be subjected were of the most humiliating kind.
A man might be sentenced to be whipped at the church door,
to appear on consecutive Sundays barefoot in shameful garments, to stand before the high altar holding a candle whilst
his crime was proclaimed to the congregation. Thus for mow-
ing a meadow on the feast of St. Oswald two labourers were
sentenced to four whippings and to perambulate the village
on the next saint's day bearing bundles of hay, while two
women who had washed linen on St. Mary Magdalene's day
were given "two fustigations with a hank of linen yarn." For
the more serious offence of attacking a priest with a spade a
Taunton man in the fifteenth century was excommunicated
and, when he submitted himself for correction, was con-
demned

> "to walk in procession with bare head and feet and
> clothed only in a shirt and breeches, and holding in his
> hand the spade, round St. Mary Magdalene on two Sun-
> days, and on one Sunday to walk round the chapel of
> James and also to walk once round the market-place and,
> when he comes to the middle of it, to stand still for a
> time at the discretion of the chaplain with a whip in his
> hand who follows him." [1]

The court which most affected the ordinary man was that
of the archdeacon. Nobody much liked archdeacons—"the
bishop's eyes", as they were called—not even their fellow
churchmen; it was an old ecclesiastical jest to speculate
whether an archdeacon could get to Heaven. He was employed
by the bishop to investigate and punish cases of embezzle-
ment and misapplication of church funds, unchastity both
of churchmen and laymen, and breaches of the Christian
code. The agent, and often instigator, of such petty persecution was the archdeacon's summoner. He was the most hated
of all the Church's officials. Usually a clerk in minor orders,
he seems all too often to have been a man of the lowest
character who kept *agents provocateurs*, including loose
women, and made his living by spying and blackmail. The
specimen in Chaucer's *Canterbury Tales*, with his drunken
bullying ways and fiery face, carbuncles, whelks and pimples,
knew the secrets of the entire neighbourhood and would

[1] P. Kendall, *The Yorkist Age*, 244–5.

V

"allow just for a quart of wine
Any good lad to keep a concubine
A twelvemonth and dispense it altogether,"

yet would strip anyone of his possessions who was not prepared to bribe him. "Purse," he used to say, was "the good archdeacon's hell," by which he meant that any offender could escape penance and punishment provided he paid enough. The customary rate of what was known as "sin-rent" was £2 p.a.

Medieval man believed that divine justice ruled the universe and that sooner or later every breach of it would be punished. To define justice—*justicia* or righteousness—he looked to the Church. Yet, though the Church existed to teach men how to live righteously, it was all too apparent that this was what so many of its ministers failed to do themselves. Having, like all institutions with a monopoly of power, created an overstaffed profession, it was forced to sacrifice its standards to maintain it. While it admonished men to be virtuous, it virtually allowed them to buy absolution and spare themselves the trouble of trying. Official Christianity had become a gigantic vested interest, living on pardons, indulgences, relics, miracles, shrines, masses for the dead and almost every conceivable device for extracting money out of the faith it taught.

The growing sense of disillusion with the clergy had been intensified by a terrible calamity—the Black Death—which in the middle of the fourteenth century swept across Europe from the East, reducing the population of England in a few months by a third. Recurring three times in epidemic form in the next thirty years, by the end of the century it had halved it. The medieval Church, like the medieval agrarian system, never wholly recovered. For too often it was those who remained at their posts who died and those who fled and betrayed their faith who lived. That a priest out of fear for his life could deprive the dying of the last rites and rob them of their hope of salvation was a thing so shattering to the medieval mind that it struck at the roots of belief. Those who suffered most in repute were the friars. A parish priest could only escape the pestilence by openly running away, and most of them, for all their natural fears, probably died at their posts. For a friar, with his vagrant commission, it was easy to evade his Christian duty; those who performed it were the bravest of all, going out of their way to succour the sick and dying but almost inevitably succumbing. This survival of the worst did the mendicants untold harm. Their very eloquence made their hypocrisy seem the more glaring.

Nor did the damage done to the Church by the Black Death stop there. By demoralising weak natures it drove men, including many of the clergy, to a hectic pursuit of pleasure. "Where," asked a preacher, "will you find the priests of to-day? . . . Not mourning between the porch and the altar but playing lasciviously around the prostitute and the brothel; not praying in the choir but wandering about the market place; not in the sanctuary but in the tavern and alehouse where sometimes they imbibe so much that they can say neither vespers nor matins properly." A popular rhyme of the time put it still more forcibly:

> "At the wrestling and at the wake,
> And chiefë chanters at the ale;
> Market-beaters, and meddling-make,
> Hopping and hooting with heave and hale.
> At fairë fresh, and at wine stale;
> Dine and drink, and make debate;
> The seven sacraments set a' sale;
> How keep such the keys of heaven's gate?" [1]

Thus in the half century that followed the Black Death there grew up a widespread feeling that the Church was failing Christ's people. Bishops too often seemed proud luxurious lords, archdeacons and proctors blackmailers, monks gluttons, friars scroungers and liars. There was no lack of devout Christians in England, a country famed for its orthodoxy. It was the age of the mystic recluse, both clerical and lay—but particularly the latter—who, withdrawing from the world to a life of religious contemplation, found in the inner experience of the heart a new revelation. Some of these wrote treatises and books enshrining their experience for the benefit of their fellow Christians, to teach, as one of them put it, "simple men and women of goodwill the right way to heaven." It was among such men and women that dissatisfaction with the Church was strongest. The contrast between Christ's life of poverty and the wealth and self-indulgence of so many of its leaders was too great to overlook. The better among the clergy

[1] G. R. Owst, *Preaching*, 258; G. C. Coulton, *Chaucer and his England*, 28.

repeatedly drew attention to it. William of Rymynton, prior of the Cistercian abbey of Sawley and at one time chancellor of Oxford university, asked how a priest could correct layfolk if he was "the slave of gluttony and lechery, given over to filthy lucre . . . and engrossed in vain or illicit pursuits?" [1] In the manuscript sermons that have come down to us from this time of disillusion one can feel the intensity of resentment aroused by the scramble for pluralities and the debasement of those engaged in it—the young scholars of promise, "poor and often innocent in everything at first, who before they grow rich are devout in their attendance at the churches, in their prayers and the many things they promise to God, but who, as soon as they have increased and waxed fat and wealthy, repudiate God their maker." [2]

As for the papacy, it was even more fatally damned by its wealth and the shameless rapacity with which its officials and agents pursued it. Its bankers and lawyers, levying toll on every country's ecclesiastical revenues, had become the chief tax-collectors of Europe. To provide for its luxurious court and ever-growing bureaucracy it employed, in Christ's name, the techniques of the lawyer, tax-collector and money-lender. In place of the theological and philosophical ferments of the twelfth and thirteenth centuries the chief canonical controversies of the late Middle Ages centred round papal taxes, fees and subsidies, procurations to meet the expenses of legates and papal emissaries, the sale of pardons and indulgences, fines or *spolia* on the property of dead prelates, and—most resented of all—the annates or first-fruits demanded of all new incumbents for provision to benefices by the Holy Father, the cash to pay being advanced by the papal bankers at crippling interest-rates which were subsequently enforced in disregard of the Christian prohibition against usury by threats of excommunication.

The English were devout Catholics and, like all western Christians, believed in the unity of Christendom. But they were growing increasingly insular and did not like to see native benefices and endowments diverted to provide for foreign papal nominees and benefice-hunters. They liked it still less when, during Edward III's wars with France, pope after pope was a Frenchman and the papacy itself resided in

---

[1] Owst, *Literature and Pulpit*, 274–5.
[2] *Idem*, 255–6.

a French enclave at Avignon. The Holy See seemed to have become the preserve of their enemies, its occupant "the French king's tame cat." In 1376 the knights and burgesses of parliament went so far as to present a petition to the king and council complaining that "the court of Rome, which ought to be the fountain, root and source of holiness and destruction of covetousness, simony and other sins," had attracted to itself the collation of so many "bishoprics, dignities, prebendaries and other benefices of Holy Church in England" that it was drawing from the country more than five times as much as the total royal revenue from taxation. This was a gross exaggeration, but it showed how far popular feeling had been exacerbated by papal practices. Other items in the Commons' complaint were that bishops were so heavily indebted to the *curia* for the fees and first-fruits of their benefices that they were forced to cut down their woods, borrow from their friends and demand crushing aids and subsidies from their tenants and diocesan clergy; that, as a result of simony by "brokers of benefices who dwell in the sinful city of Avignon," "a miserable fellow who knows nothing and is worth nothing" would be advanced to an incumbency worth a thousand marks, while an English doctor or a master of divinity had to content himself with a fiftieth of that amount, "so that clerks lose hope of preferment by their orders and talent for learning, . . . and people are ceasing to send their children to school, and the clergy, who are the substance of Holy Church and our holy faith fall into decline and annihilation." It was even alleged that the papal tax-collectors were French spies who sent out of the country "secrets to the great prejudice of the realm" and that, whenever the pope wished to ransom one of his French friends who had been taken prisoner, he demanded a subsidy from the English clergy! "Let it be considered," the petitioners concluded, "that God has committed his sheep to our holy father the pope to be fed and not to be fleeced." [1]

So unpopular was the papacy with the English at this time that when, in the last year of Edward III's reign, the city of London put on a pageant "with great noise of minstrelsy, trumpets, cornets and shawms and many wax torches," the highlight in the procession was a mock pope accompanied by twenty-four cardinals and "eight or ten arrayed with black

[1] *Rot. Parl.* II, 338.

masks like devils, not at all amiable, seeming like legates." [1]
When, following an attempt to re-establish the papacy at
Rome, the French cardinals in 1378 challenged the election
of a fantastically irascible and autocratic Italian pope and set
up a rival one at Avignon, Christendom was confronted for
forty years with the shocking spectacle of two popes. At one
time there were three. Each pope demanded payment of ecclesiastical taxes, excommunicated the other's supporters and
hired "crusaders" to harry the other's lands.

The "great schism," as it was called, was the culmination
of the scandals that shook men's faith in the Church at the
end of the fourteenth century. It was against a background
of popular indignation at simony, papal provisions, pluralism,
non-residence and the sale of indulgences that the Oxford
theologian and philosopher, John Wycliffe, raised his voice of
protest. This radical-minded Yorkshireman—at one time Master of the little Oxford college of Balliol and "holden of many
to be the greatest clerk then living"—began by opposing papal
claims on native benefices on behalf of parliament, went on
to denounce ecclesiastical wealth, and ended by attacking
nearly all the institutional assumptions of the Church. He
based his stand on the life and teaching of Christ as revealed
by the scriptures, which he maintained were alone necessary
for salvation and capable of interpretation by the humblest.
"No man," he declared, "was so rude a scholar but that he
might learn from the words of the gospel according to his
simplicity." All that was necessary was that they should be
made available in his native tongue. "To be ignorant of the
Bible," he wrote, "is to be ignorant of Christ."

Wycliffe spoke with contempt of the "possessioners": of
monks with "red and fat cheeks and great bellies" and gowns
of superfine cloth big enough to clothe four or five needy
men; of the blasphemous sale of papal indulgences, of the
worship of relics and images, of excommunication for political
and financial ends. The "dowering of the Church with lordship of the world" had been a heresy, for "Christ came of
poor folk." Its wealth and power were millstones round its
neck, its over-elaborate conventual services "the religion of
fat cows." Even the pope himself was only "a naked servant
of God."

[1] *Harleian* MS, 247, f. 172 v. cit. Rickert, *Chaucer's England*,
233.

Wycliffe's revolutionary indictment traversed the Church's whole position: that it had been exclusively entrusted with the salvationary powers won for mankind on the Cross. Against its claim that God's will could only be known through its sacraments and ordinances, this gaunt, uncompromising North Country puritan set up, not only the right of every man to judge the scriptures for himself, but the direct responsibility of the individual conscience to God. The ministry was requisite for the well-being of the Church but not for its existence; its business, and sole business, was to teach the gospel. Everything that came between the individual and Christ was evil, and that included most of the ecclesiastical establishment of the day, including episcopacy. Far in advance of his time Wycliffe foreshadowed an age when family and congregational worship would take the place of the ritual and mystery of the candle-lit altar and what he indignantly called "the drawing of the people by curiosity of gay windows, . . . paintings and babwynerie."

For a short time Wycliffe was the most popular man in the country. He was supported against the papal charges of heresy by the masters and students of Oxford—at that time, after Paris, the most important university in northern Europe—by the royal Duke of Lancaster and the Princess of Wales, by an anti-clerical parliament and the London mob. The rising middle-class delighted in his defence of national rights and his opposition to foreign ecclesiastical taxation, while many applauded his proposal to confiscate the surplus wealth of the Church and distribute it among deserving noblemen and knights "that wolden justly govern the people and maintain the land against enemies." But when he extended his theological arguments and attacks on the institutional side of religion to its central mysteries, repudiating transubstantiation and insisting that the Host remained bread and wine and that it was blasphemy to pretend that Christ's body and blood could be made by the incantations of an ignorant and possibly sinful priest, he lost the support of his patrons. The ordinary Englishman was ready to support an attack on excessive clerical wealth, papal interference and Caesarian bishops but took fright at the idea of challenging hallowed beliefs that were the sacred preserve of the Church. He could see no sense in incurring the risk of excommunication and eternal damnation by abstract speculations that affected neither his personal life nor his purse.

Nor, however much he wanted to see it purged of corruption, did he wish to destroy what was still the most valued and venerable thing in the kingdom's polity—Holy Church. Though riddled with imperfections, its beliefs and practices, including its very superstitions and abuses, were part of the community's continuing life. It had created the society and civilisation to which medieval man belonged, and, without it life would have seemed bleak and unthinkable for him. Owning as it did something like a third of the nation's wealth there can have been few, even of moderate means, who did not have some interest in its survival. This was true even of the monasteries whose widespread financial ramifications, fame and hospitality made them centres of regional social life. Ecclesiastical and lay society were intimately interwoven; many a local knight was proud to act as steward to some neighbouring religious house, and the humble ancestors of Samuel Pepys, by serving the great abbey of Crowland for two and a half centuries as reeves, rent-collectors and granators, raised themselves from servile beginnings to respectability, yeomanry and even gentry.

During the fourteenth and fifteenth centuries the part of the laity in religious activities was steadily growing. In earlier times the Church had borne the sole responsibility for almost every charitable activity—hospitals, education, the care of the aged and indigent, alms at the convent gate, even bridges and causeways for travellers. Now, though such work was still done in its name, laymen were taking an increasing share in it. The most popular form of religious endowment in the late Middle Ages was the chantry—a small chapel, either inside an existing church or, more occasionally, one built for the purpose, in which masses, prayers and chants were offered in perpetuity for the donor's soul in return for his provision of some continuing work of charity—an almshouse, a school, an annual distribution of food and largesse to the aged and crippled poor, the provision of marriage dowries for destitute girls or apprenticeship-fees for orphans, a bridge or a resthouse for pilgrims. Often such endowments were made by some self-renewing gild or fraternity of pious laymen who, having bought a licence from the Crown to transfer land to mortmain, vested it in their corporate heirs for the use of charitable and religious objects. They were particularly popular among the town merchants who, having grown rich, were as eager as lords and landowners to use their wealth to ensure the future welfare of their souls. Such was the fraternity which John Enfield and other London citizens founded in 1343 to restore the roof and steeple of All Hallows, London Wall, and that established in the same year by a group of wealthy fishmongers to provide a chaplain to sing the anthem, *Salve Regina*, every evening in the church of St. Magnus, London Bridge, "to the honour of God and his glorious Mother our Lady Mary the Virgin, . . . for inciting the people to devotion at such an hour, the more to merit their souls." [1]

Most cities and country towns possessed such gilds by the end of the fourteenth century. At Ludlow—centre of the Shropshire wool trade—a brotherhood founded in honour of St. John the Evangelist maintained a hospital for thirty poor folk and a house for its chaplains, while another provided a free school and schoolmaster. The grammar-school at which Shakespeare was to be educated was founded by the gild of the Holy Rood of Stratford-on-Avon. Sometimes gilds were even founded by working folk, like the one dedicated to Our Lady at Ellesmere in which every married man paid fourpence a year and every servant earning more than five shillings p.a. twopence, or that of St. Helen and St. Mary Beverley, in which the members marched in procession to the church on St. Helen's Day headed by an old man with a cross, another with a spade and a youth dressed as Queen Helen, and where, after hearing a solemn mass, each man contributed a penny.[2]

For this, as well as for other reasons, Wycliffe's attack on clerical abuses failed to make any impression on the Church establishment of his day. It was too sweeping, too academic and too colourless for the ordinary unthinking man. It not only challenged vested interests, it proposed to abolish them altogether. Papacy, episcopacy, endowments, monasteries, friars, images, pilgrimages, masses for the dead, even tithes and the sacrament of the altar, all were to go and, with them, the outward grace and beauty of religious observance. In stripping Holy Church of its corrupting wealth, Wycliffe and his followers sought to strip it also of its charm. Had they

---

[1] D. Rock, *The Church of our Fathers*, II, 442–3.

[2] A. Hamilton Thompson, *The English Clergy and their Organisation in the Later Medieval Ages*, 140; E. Rickert, *Chaucer's England*, 235.

had their way nothing would have remained but the authority of the Bible as interpreted by the individual worshipper, a parish priesthood supported by voluntary offerings, and a presbyterian system of church government under the ultimate authority of the Crown.

Forbidden to lecture in the university and banished to his rustic living at Lutterworth, where he spent his last years supervising the translation of the scriptures, Wycliffe and his heresy passed—for a time—out of the main stream of English life. Though for a generation after his death in 1384, preached on village green and highway by the russet-clad evangelists he had trained, his doctrines received the support of many younger churchmen and knights of the shire and even as late as 1414 precipitated, on the eve of Agincourt, a rising against the government of Henry V, the ecclesiastical authorities re-acted against the "mutterers" or Lollards, as they were called, with ruthless repression. In this they were zealously backed by the new Lancastrian dynasty which, seeking to buttress its dubious right to the throne by its orthodoxy, procured from parliament a statute—*De Haeretico Comburendo*—which not only forbade unlicensed preaching and the holding of views "contrary to the faith and blessed determination of Holy Church", but empowered the civil arm to burn, "in some prominent place", any persistent or relapsed heretic con-demned by a spiritual court. In March 1401, rejecting all his persecutors' attempts to make him recant, a London chaplain, William Sawtrey, was burnt at Smithfield, the first martyr of the coming Protestant Reformation. It was still more than a century distant, awaiting the day when the introduction of printing and the growth of a literate laity could bring the forbidden vernacular scriptures to a wider public than existed in Plantagenet and Lancastrian England. Yet, though driven underground by Caesarian bishops, Wycliffe's heretic creed survived, smouldering in secret conventicles and hearthside readings in the little towns of the Chilterns, east midlands and home counties and in the capital until, fanned by fresh persecutions, it broke into renewed flame under the early Tudors. Nor did it survive only in England. Carried by the courtiers of Richard II's Bohemian queen to Prague, it lit in the pyres of the Hussite martyrs a still more prophetic con-flagration on the banks of the Elbe, where, a hundred years later, the Saxon monk Luther challenged the Roman Church at Wittenberg.

INDEX

INDEX OF NAMES AND PLACES

\